REFUGEES ARE HERE TO STAY

TO STAY

GET USED TO IT

By Seye Onabolu

SCL Press

COPYRIGHT

REFUGEES ARE HERE TO STAY: GET USED TO IT.

Copyright © 2022 SCL Press

Cover Design by Augment Design
Cover Photo/Illustration Copyright ©
921353784/istockphoto.com

ISBN: 978-1-7397263-2-4

Printed in the United Kingdom

DISCLAIMER

Dedicated to displaced people everywhere.

CONTENTS

Acknowledgments 1

Introduction 2
1 Who are Refugees? 8
2 What Causes Refugees? 25
3 The Crisis 51
4 The Journey 60
5 Arrival 71
6 It's Not My Fault 92
7 Refugee Stories 117
8 Will It Benefit Us Economically? 128
9 Who Has Culture? 151
10 Social and Scientific Impact 173
11 What Can We Do as Individuals? 200
12 What Can Be Done Politically? 221
Conclusion 247
Appendix 264
About The Author 282
References 284

ACKNOWLEDGMENTS

This book wouldn't have been possible without the months of research and invaluable contributions of four key people; Felix Ford, Gabriel Salter, George Maskell and Shere Hussain. Thank you for taking on the challenge and turning what initially started as a series of blogs, into something far more compelling.

My special thanks to Esther Hamilton-Ivory, Khadija Hussain and Mahira Khanom for adopting the book as their own and putting extraordinary hours and matchless care into their editorial support and guidance.

I owe an enormous debt of gratitude to those who contributed to the blog posts, long before the idea of a book was ever conceived, including Zoe Allen, Katy Cottrell, Aanya Bhandari, Katie McAdam, Atisha Mahajan, David Cregan, and Agnese Pierobon.

I want to acknowledge the brilliant Sona Circle team, both past and present, who have made my professional life such a pleasure: Archibald Troko, Riah Uddin, Pollie Sortain, Omar Zahri, Tahir Alam, Ajmain Sahidi, Deesha Relwani, Judith Nanyonga, Lloyd Henry, Anthony Simpson, Linda Arowolo, Abdur Rob, Vanessa Ammah, Frederick Bale, Mahdia Syeda, Ayse Huggett, Rumana Begum, Andrew Doran, Michael McKay, and Kirit Vaidya.

I've greatly appreciated the counsel of Christiana Orton, Lara Olafisoye, Chris Chancey and Bola Sokunbi who gave freely of their time to offer advice, discuss nuances of the text and push me to clarify concepts and explore particular facets of insight work.

Finally, thank you to my friends, family and loved ones, those that I see every day, and those that I see less often. I'm grateful for your unconditional support, encouragement, and love.

INTRODUCTION

Author: Hello there!

Reader: Hello...Wait, I'm confused? Who on earth are you? What am I doing here?

Author: This book tells the stories and experiences of refugees. I'm the author. You're here to listen to these stories.

Reader: I'm not in the mood right now, I'm having a tough time at the moment, I'm locked out of my house because I've lost my keys!

Author: You've been having a tough time?! Not trying to invalidate your feelings right now but wait til' you hear about the tough time that refugees are currently facing.

Reader: Seriously, now is not a good time! And what have the problems of refugees got to do with me?

Author: Just hear me out...

More than half of the world's refugees are children.[1]

One person is involuntarily exiled from their home approximately every two seconds.[2]

There are 79.5 million people around the world who have been forcibly displaced.[3]

Since 2014 almost 23,000 people have died trying to cross the Mediterranean.[4]

---

[1] (Knudson 2021)

[2] Ibid

[3] Ibid

[4] (Missing Migrants Project 2021)

INTRODUCTION

Thousands are forced to sleep in improvised shelters or out in the open in sub-zero temperatures.[5]

Families are resorting to burning rubbish to try and keep warm and shield their children from hypothermia.[6]

86% of the world's refugees are hosted by developing countries whose citizens are themselves struggling.[7]

And whilst you can relax in a bookshop and wait for a couple hours until you can return to the comfort of your home, refugees all suffer unspeakable horrors that they may never recover from, and they may never be able to return home.

Millions of these people, like you and me, just want happiness, safety, and prosperity for themselves, their families, and friends.

Here we look at the lives of many whom we often ignore, despise, misunderstand, or misrepresent.

Akoi Bazzie fled horrific violence and Civil War in Liberia to seek safety in Sheffield. There are people like Imad who came to London looking for a better life and set up a successful food business.

By presenting the stories and experiences of those millions of people, we hope to change stereotypes and popular opinions and finally make people aware of the difficulties they face.

This book will not only tell tales of love, success and triumph over adversity, but will also tell tales of war, pain and hardship.

---

[5] (UNHCR 2021)
[6] (UNHCR 2016)
[7] (Knudson 2021)

Migrants and refugees are not just people to be pitied. They bring skills, culture, and benefits to whichever society they settle in. Countries that host refugees reap enormous economic benefits. New technologies are invented, new discoveries are made, and new businesses are started.

Many economists also believe that refugees provide a vital solution to one of the worst economic crises of our time - the crisis of demographic ageing.

Refugees also provide huge cultural benefits that are often overlooked. Without refugees, you wouldn't be able to enjoy a salt beef bagel on the weekend or fish and chips by the seaside.

Additionally, there are numerous sporting stars from refugee backgrounds that entertain fans worldwide, such as Alphonso Davies of Bayern Munich and Francis Ngannou of the UFC.

Freddie Mercury is another example of a talented refugee who went on to be a global phenomenon. The above are just few examples of the cultural influences' refugees have on Western society.

In developed nations, the media has not always been known for portraying refugees accurately. It has often distorted the realities of refugees and migrants in order to demonise them and promote hatred, rather than highlighting the suffering they experience and the benefits they bring to nations.

Rather than acknowledge their responsibility for the refugee crisis, Western governments often portray refugees as cheats, liars, and thieves, blaming them for their own suffering.

Because of this animosity towards refugees, a hostile environment has been created in the West that has led to untold suffering for refugees. Refugees do not have easy access to our borders. They drown or suffocate on their journey to safety, and should they make it to one of our countries, they receive little to no support upon their arrival.

It is imperative that we counteract this narrative. This book's purpose is to dispel myths about refugees and migrants and, crucially, to encourage Western countries to change how they treat refugees.

Western nations should take care of refugees and help them thrive, so that we can all flourish.

However, we shouldn't just pay attention to refugees because of what they bring to the table. We should pay attention to them because, as the title of this book states, refugees are here to stay.

What do we mean by this?

Refugees are not going anywhere. There will be a growing number of refugee crises in the future. Climate change is predicted to displace around 1 billion people by 2050, a staggering number. More people will be displaced by war, famine, and poverty. At this very moment, the Taliban are flooding across Afghanistan, displacing thousands. This refugee 'problem' (whether you like it or not), is not going away anytime soon... So, refugees are here to stay.

GET USED TO IT!

The goal of this book is to help you discover why it is in your interest to "get used to it". The book has no political motivations, and it only acts as a platform to entertain and inform, so it is not to be misconstrued as a political agenda.

This book contains a wide range of lessons, ranging from the heart-breaking stories of refugee children to the insightful examination of world economies. Each chapter starts off with an entertaining dialogue between the 'Author' and the 'Reader', and there are helpful tips on how you can get more involved at the end of the book.

Throughout the book, you will find various sections, some of which will be enjoyable for you, some of which may annoy you, and possibly some of which will give you an insight into anguish or guilt. All the emotions you may experience during the book have a purpose, and that is to give you a more comprehensive picture of refugees and immigrants.

So, what is the purpose of writing this book? It's for those who want to see a different perspective on stories they've read before. This book provides insight into such topics that are often overlooked when discussing historical events.

There is so much more to learn about refugees and immigrants. We are familiar with their different languages and enjoy their cuisine, but most of us have not seen what lies beneath that.

As we live in multicultural societies, the best way to appreciate everyone's differences is to learn a little more about them, and that's what I have tried to do with this book.

The book is organized chronologically in an effort to explain the refugee crisis and how it impacts society. There are three parts, each with subsections that provide more detail.

Part One: The Nature of the Refugee Crisis. This section examines the causes and experiences of refugees - both within their countries and upon arrival in a new country. The section begins with a discussion of who refugees are, defining refugees and migrants and how they are grouped, the terminology used to describe them, stating where they are from, what cultural aspects they leave behind, and where they go.

It then discusses the causes that lead people to become refugees, including war, persecution, climate, economics/politics, religion, internal displacement, civil strife, and wider immigration. As the book continues, it examines the domestic conditions that cause refugees to become displaced, as well as how they travel to reach the country in which they seek refuge and what they encounter when they arrive.

In the final segment of part one, the West is scrutinised, focusing on why the West is partly responsible for some of these crises and why it is best equipped to deal with refugee issues.

Part Two: What Do Refugees Contribute? Here we investigate the contributions of refugees to western society by examining economic growth, demographic ageing, and various industries such as the tech and food industries. Next, we examine how refugees' cultures are introduced to other countries, for example, through food, entertainment, art, sport, and social and scientific impact.

Part Three: What Can We Do To Help? This section focuses on individual and political actions that can be taken to help. It looks at ways that individuals can personally help refugees by donating to charities, non-profits, political parties, and taking direct action. We then explore how Western governments can, and should, help the refugee crisis.

1

WHO ARE REFUGEES?

Author: So, who do you think refugees are?

Reader: Don't they sing that song, er 'Ready or Not'?

Author: Not Fugees, refugees

Reader: Oh yeah, you're right, it's 'Stayin Alive' they sing, isn't it?

Author: Unbelievable. I'm talking about refugees. As in the group of millions of people. Who are they?

Reader: Oh right, err...Muslims?

Author: No

Reader: Job stealers?

Author: No

Reader: Migrants?

Author: No

Reader: Err...Syrians?

Author: I'm gonna stop you there. Wow, we've got a lot of work to do. Why don't I give you some insight into who refugees actually are?

Refugees are talked about everywhere in our media and culture. And yet, often people are not certain what the term 'Refugee' really means.

Frequently, people in newspapers, in politics, on TV and in day-to-day life will (like you just did) use words like refugee, migrant and asylum seeker as if they all mean exactly the same thing.

They are all lumped together as one menacing group, who chose, out of great malice of forethought and hatred for you personally - yes, you (!), to come to your country, steal your job, destroy your marriage and eat the last Mars bar in the corner shop.

You must have really wanted that bar of chocolate to lift your mood and fill that hole left inside your heart. Of course, we're both aware you're having a tough time at home, all alone since your wife left you...you get the picture.

As a result, many people have no idea that there is a difference between these terms.

So, before we talk about refugees, migrants and asylum seekers, their experiences, where they come from and how we treat them, we should clarify exactly what all these terms mean so we can accurately distinguish between them.

Yeah, ok I can hear you groaning. No one likes reading about definitions, but just trust me, this is important.

The term 'Refugee' actually has a very precise legal definition. According to the 1951 Refugee Convention of the UN, a refugee is "someone who is unable or unwilling to return to their country of origin owing to a well-founded fear of being persecuted for reasons of race, religion, nationality, membership of a particular social group, or political opinion."[8]

This charter, which most Western countries have signed, entitles refugees to protection and sanctuary in their place of

---

[8] (UNHCR 2017)

settlement.[9] So, someone can only be a refugee, legally, if they are fleeing a country for those very specific reasons. This is what we mean when we say 'Refugee' throughout the book. So, note it down!

The term 'asylum seeker' is also very precise. This refers specifically to an individual who has already left their homeland, arrived in a new country, and has made an application for refugee status there. Asylum seekers may then become refugees if the government of the state to which they apply accepts that they meet the definition of the 1951 convention. However, they also may have their applications rejected.

By contrast, 'migrant' has a fairly vague meaning. 'Migrant' is an umbrella term used to encompass all those who, like refugees, leave their homeland for another country but, unlike refugees, don't do so because they are persecuted politically.

A migrant may leave their country for a variety of factors. These include poverty and economic difficulty (usually termed 'economic migrants') floods, droughts, hurricanes and typhoons ('climate migrants') or because their family and community have moved, and they want to be with them.[10] Usually, these factors interlink. For example, climate events often have economic impacts and family movements are often triggered by economic difficulty. As such, most migrants move for some combination of all these factors.

There is one final group of people who it is also important to distinguish, the 'internally displaced.' These are people who are forced to flee their homes for all the reasons above: from political persecution and war to climate/environmental events and

---

[9] (UNHCR 2011)
[10] (European Parliament 2020)

economic reasons. However, unlike refugees and migrants, the internally displaced do not leave their country of origin, even if they do travel significant distances within it.[11]

So put simply: refugees and migrants cross borders, whereas internally displaced people do not.

And these are all the definitions you need.

So, I bet you're feeling happy now, right? Breathing a big sigh of relief?

Now you know the difference between all these terms. You've read through all these boring definitions, and you've come out the other side with genuinely useful and important information. You're an educated, informed citizen. Just wait till you get to impress your friends with all that knowledge. Look at you, feeling all chuffed with yourself.

Well, get ready to stop.

Because in a way I was lying when I said that this information was important. In many ways, it doesn't matter at all.

Or more accurately, it *shouldn't* matter.

Of course, those who are legally designated refugees are, in theory anyway, treated differently from those who are migrants or asylum seekers. Refugees have inalienable rights internationally (again in theory) to seek protection in all the countries who have signed the 1951 charter. Migrants, by contrast, are allowed into countries

---

[11] (UNHCR 2020)

only at the discretion of the policy of any nation's government of the day.

However, these distinctions, which are used to classify and justify the treatment of an entire group of people, should constantly be questioned.

Why should someone forced to flee their homeland by a hurricane, a flood or a drought be treated completely differently to one who happens to have been forced to flee due to political persecution? Why is it completely reasonable to bar the former but illegal to bar the latter?

Who is to say that those who are forced to migrate because of the experience of horrendous poverty, or an economic crisis are less deserving of access to protection and opportunities than those who meet the precise, but ultimately fairly arbitrary, definition of 'Refugee'? Shouldn't both be protected?

Why should only the state in which you arrive decide whether you are a successful asylum seeker deserving of protection, or an illegal immigrant deserving expulsion and scorn? Having travelled thousands of miles in the most horrific and dangerous conditions, does that not acutely show their desperation and make them deserving of support and protection even if they don't meet the legal definition of 'Refugee'?

Moreover, why would countries even want to distinguish and keep some groups out when (as we will see later in the book) people can bring along with them many benefits to the countries in which they settle.

Therefore, the terms refugee and migrant *are* in a sense interchangeable. Not because they are all an evil menace, but because they are all people who have been compelled by circumstance to seek a better, more safe and prosperous life in a different country and because all have the potential to be incredible assets to their country of settlement, if given the opportunity.

Fundamentally, as human beings, we all deserve to be treated with dignity and respect.

So, the definitions have been outlined, the laws have been spouted and everyone is wiser to the rules and regulations surrounding refugees. But there is more to unpack.

In the 21st century there is usually a stereotype of who a refugee is and where they come from. The word refugee seems to paint a picture of someone struggling to flee Syria, or the fighting in the Middle East, but this is simply because that's a more shocking and headline-grabbing atrocity than mentioning the millions who are displaced because of 'water'.

It's important to know that refugees come in all different shapes and sizes, skin-tones and religions, and all have varied reasons as to why they have been given the title of 'Refugee'.

Let's see what history has to offer and look at how long refugees have existed and which parts of the globe they come from.

We can go as far back as Jiahu settlements (modern day China) in 5,700 BCE that were wiped out by overflowing rivers and flooding, causing the Jiahu people to leave and resettle elsewhere in strange new lands. That unsuspecting thing called H2O managed to expel whole communities even in the form of a small river.[12]

---

[12] (Whelan 2020)

13

740 BCE saw the banishment of the famous 'Lost Ten Tribes' from ancient Israel by the Assyrians, who were simply out to conquer Mesopotamia (present day Syria, Iraq, Iran, Turkey and Kuwait). The whereabouts of the tribes remains a subject of religious and historical debate and emulates the struggles for land in the same regions today.[13]

The Mayan communities who lived in Central America during their Late Classical Era (600-900 CE) were often at war. Based on ancient evidence these wars were over things such as land, natural resources and even human sacrifice captives. This eventually led to smaller states falling victim to larger cities, and ultimately being forced to abandon their land and disappear from the area entirely.[14]

Refugees also existed in Europe in the Middle Ages, particularly between France and England. England, who had been engaged in wars for over 600 years with the French, took in 50,000 French refugees around 1685-1705. The Huguenots (a group of French protestants) were fleeing the Catholic persecutions that were taking place in France. Those that remained in France faced continued injustice. They had their churches burnt down, their marriages and ultimately their children delegitimised by the state. Those that left made new lives for themselves abroad, many arriving penniless but with profitable business skills. Of the thousands that fled to England, many were skilled craftsmen, watchmakers, silversmiths, doctors and teachers. It is thought that the word rés or refugee was first coined during this period of mass migration.[15]

---

[13] (Chalabi 2013)
[14] (Salem Media n.d.)
[15] (Gwynn 1985)

If we look at more recent history, there are a number of atrocities that have led to people being displaced worldwide. The Russian Pogroms (violent riots) of the late 19th and early 20th century, as well as WWI and WWII, saw huge numbers of European Jews seeking refuge worldwide. Meanwhile Africa saw civil wars throughout the continent during the 20th century.

The civil war that broke out in Nigeria during the mid-1960s saw over 4 million people displaced, with anywhere between 1-3 million being officially declared as refugees.[16]

The 4 million people displaced during the Nigerian Civil War was then matched during the 26 year-long Angolan Civil War that started in 1975.[17]

The first Sudanese Civil War that lasted 16 years, saw up to a million people killed and further hundreds of thousands abandoning their homes and towns.[18]

The Guinea-Bissau Civil War from 1989-1999 involved 250-350 thousand nationals being forced to leave their towns and cities.[19] This figure may seem relatively small compared to other conflicts but considering the population at the time was just over a million people means that around 30% of the country had to seek refuge elsewhere.

The Rwandan genocide in 1994, much like the Nazi regime in WWII, saw a Hutu-controlled government set out to massacre the minority Tutsi population in the country. There were media campaigns and radio broadcasts that fuelled the violence, encouraging Hutu civilians to kill their Tutsi wives and other Tutsi

---

[16] (Norwich University Online 2017)

[17] Ibid

[18] Ibid

[19] (Pictures 1999)

neighbours. The carnage spanned just over 100 days but ended the lives of more than 800,000 people, the majority of which were from the Tutsi communities. Over 2 million people (equating to a third of the population) abandoned the country, most of whom were Hutu civilians.[20]

It is important to note that refugees can come from any part of the world and that this is not something that is based on one specific action. The term refugee seems to refer to people who have been relocated to another country, but millions are never documented because they have only been displaced and forced to resettle in other parts of their country. This is a form of refugee, but it is 'unofficial' and is therefore overlooked by the media and the general public.

Colombia is a great example of a country that has seen millions of its citizens suffer from relocation due to violence and corruption, but most do not have to travel across an international boundary to seek refuge and, therefore, are unable to seek reparations and the attention they desperately need. Colombia's conflict started in the 60s and over the decades, the UN estimates that there are 5.8 million displaced people in the country.[21] This migration crisis which is still ongoing today has not attracted the attention of the international community that many argue it warrants.

After looking at so many different situations and historical accounts of refugees, hopefully, it's a little more obvious to see that there is not one place of origin. There are many more thousands of stories involving displaced people and chances are, you are the descendant of somebody who once found themselves in that situation.

---

[20] (Encyclopedia Britannica 2016)
[21] (International Organisation for Migration 2020)

The term refugee could be placed above the head of anyone at any given time. The country you live in could be hit by a natural disaster, a global pandemic or even fall victim to war, and at that point there is every chance that you could be displaced from your homes and be in search of a new place to live.

Whether we realise it or not, culture is an essential part of all of our lives. We quickly take culture for granted throughout our daily routines, but culture allows people to identify and bond with one another and offers a sense of belonging.

In the UK, so many people spend their Sundays with close family and friends, tucking into a succulent roast dinner, a very staple part of British culture and society. Imagine if you had to flee your home and found yourself living in a completely different part of the world. It could be quite hard to try and uphold these traditional cultural norms in a place that doesn't necessarily recognise them.

Migration can be credited for the widespread diversity of cultures across the world.

Later, we will look at the new cultural aspects migrants and refugees bring to the Western world from their home nations. First, however, it is essential to acknowledge the heritage that many of them leave behind when their lives become uprooted.

When refugees are forced to flee their countries for their safety, they are also left with no choice but to abandon their homes, friends, jobs, and many of their personal possessions. But what is sometimes overlooked, and deserves more consideration, is the loss of the unique culture and heritage of their home country. Sometimes this can lead to cultural bereavement, where in addition to other traumas that refugees face, they must grieve the loss of their native culture.

Unsurprisingly, this can have a severe impact on the mental well-being of the individuals that have migrated. On top of losing material objects and no longer seeing those closest to them, refugees also become deprived of the social systems they are used to, such as their religious and cultural norms.

Researchers from Georgetown University interviewed refugees to find out what they missed most about their former lives. This research highlighted the rich and unique culture that once connected the communities initially. Individuals who have fled their home nations reminisce most about the relationships and camaraderie they once had with members of their community. For example, one Palestinian man spoke about how he missed sharing Friday evenings with his neighbours, where they would 'get together and chat, and their stories wouldn't stop until the middle of the night'.[22]

Understandably, some refugees may experience a culture shock when arriving in countries such as the UK, where interactions between neighbours tend to be briefer and less meaningful. Indeed, other refugees from Syria spoke about frequenting the markets in Damascus where Syrian food, handmade crafts and jewellery are sold. They also spoke of drinking coffee in local cafes whilst listening to storytellers and poets recounting tales.[23] These are just some examples of the cultural heritage that refugees often leave behind.

---

[22] (R. D. Taylor 2013)
[23] Ibid

When refugees arrive in their new host country, there is often an intense pressure to conform to the new location's culture at the expense of maintaining their traditions that have always been integral to their lives. There are two main ways in which migrants integrate into new countries: assimilation and acculturation.

Assimilation is when a minority group gradually and eventually loses all the cultural markers that sets them apart, instead of adopting the culture of a larger group. Unfortunately, this integration process is often associated with poorer mental health and psychological well-being as well as lower self-esteem.

In contrast, acculturation is a more positive process in which a minority group can maintain their cultural traditions and co-exist with the dominant culture. Although this is the more ideal form of integration, it is true certain groups within society are less willing to accommodate and appreciate other cultural norms.[24]

In the Western world, we often enjoy the cultural influences of many places but without really taking much notice of them. Therefore, it is important to celebrate and be respectful of refugees' cultural traditions and heritage. Many refugees seek to share their home country's culture through music, food and fashion. Embracing other cultures has the potential to generate a better quality of life for all. Instead of being unwilling to engage with other cultures, we should embrace them and the diverse ways they enrich our societies.

There is a perception that there has recently been a mass influx of refugees migrating unchecked into the West. This in turn has led to a rise in populism and consequently popularity in far-right

---

[24] (Cottrell n.d.)

nationalist parties across Europe such as the anti-immigrant Lega Party in Italy or the Sweden Democrats. However, this perception could not be any further from the truth. According to Oxfam, the six wealthiest countries, with the most capacity to extend shelter, education and health care, host less than 9% of world refugees. Whereas the vast majority of refugees - 84% - are hosted by poorer countries who already struggle to meet the needs of their citizens.[25]

The UN Refugee Agency (UNHCR) has stated that since mid-2020, it estimates that global forced displacement has surpassed 80 million and hosts 39% of refugees in just five countries.[26] However, where do the refugees go? Who are these five countries that host almost half of the refugees in the world?

TURKEY

Turkey has held the largest refugee population in the world since 2014. Regional instability in Afghanistan, Iraq and the Syrian Arab Republic has led to an influx of refugees to Turkey. Turkey hosts around 4 million refugees and asylum seekers, with the majority being Syrian (roughly 3.6 million). Turkey has had periods in its history of accepting refugees. Following the Greco-Turkish War of 1919–1922, the 1923 population exchange agreement with Greece saw the arrival of 350,000 Greek Muslims to Turkey. Turkey also harboured the 340,000 ethnic Turks expelled by Bulgaria in 1989.[27]

---

[25] (Oxfam International 2016)
[26] (UNHCR Turkey n.d.)
[27] (The World Bank 2021)

COLOMBIA

Colombia has more than 1.6 million refugees as a result of Venezuela's political unrest, economic instability and violence. The growing political discontent, fuelled by hyperinflation, power cuts and shortages of food and medical supplies have left over 5 million Venezuelans to seek refuge elsewhere. In addition, Colombia itself faces difficulties with displaced peoples. Cordaid Foundation highlights that there are more than 5 million displaced Colombians, people who have had to abandon their homes due to conflict or natural disasters. Unlike some of the other Americana countries, Colombia has opened its door to Venezuelan refugees. But unfortunately, over 94% of Venezuela's population have fallen into poverty.[28]

PAKISTAN

Pakistan hosts over 1.4 million registered Afghan refugees who have been displaced due to the war in Afghanistan. According to Resettlement, 36% of these refugees live in camps, whilst 63% live in urban settings, estimating that 1 million undocumented Afghans reside in Pakistan. In addition, over 5.5 million Afghan refugees have returned to Afghanistan since 2002, primarily due to the voluntary repatriation programme facilitated by the UNHCR, which saw 3.8 million refugees return from Pakistan to Afghanistan. However, due to the continuance in security concerns, voluntary repatriation is scaling down.[29]

UGANDA

Uganda is one of the largest refugee-hosting countries in Africa. It has experienced a massive influx of over 1.4 million refugees and

---

[28] (Cordaid 2019)
[29] (European Resettlement Network 2014)

21

asylum seekers. More than 62% of refugees in Uganda are from South Sudan, where people face violence, food insecurity and a lack of access to essential services and education. Another 29% come from the Democratic Republic of Congo, where Congolese escape from inter-ethnic violence and attacks on civilians. The UN states that the refugee population in Uganda has been growing since 2013, and in 2019 reported that about 200 asylum seekers arrive daily in the country.

Uganda's refugee policy guarantees freedom of movement and the right to employment, education and health as well as the right to start a business. The Government also provides refugees with plots of land so they can farm and construct shelters. It empowers refugees to become economically self-reliant while granting them the same rights that citizens enjoy.[30]

GERMANY

In 2015 Germany had taken in more than 1.7 million refugees who were moving from war-torn countries such as Syria in search of more secure futures. The German Chancellor welcomed refugees stating, "Germany is a strong country...we can do this".[31]

However, not everybody saw it as positively as Angela Merkel did. People criticised refugees entering Germany for an increase in terror attacks which resulted in growing xenophobia, and a rise in far-right political parties. Overall, however, the integration has largely been a success.

According to the Centre for Global Development, by December 2018, there were 1.8 million people with a refugee background. 75% are younger than 40 and most have higher levels of education

---

[30] (Momodu 2018-2019)
[31] (Oltermann 2020)

than other migrants. About half have found a job, paid training or internships. Additionally, it has also impacted the local German population. For example, between 2008-2015, the number of employees in companies founded by migrants grew by 50% (to 1.5 million).[32]

Although there are other countries with many refugees, such as Lebanon and Bangladesh, for example, these are the five countries with the largest refugee population as of 2021.

When you compare the figures of these countries to the likes of the UK, who according to UNHCR, at the end of 2019, housed only 133,094 refugees, you would be right to question whether or not the UK is doing enough to protect refugees and integrate them into society effectively.[33]

Contrary to the popular myth in the West, it is the less developed countries that take in and protect refugees.

So, what have we learned?

Well, hopefully, now you understand that almost all the common assumptions about refugees are wrong.

Refugees aren't all Muslims or all from the Middle East. They aren't all (or even primarily) coming to the West. They aren't coming to take your job, and they aren't the same as migrants.

---

[32] (Dempster 2020)
[33] (UNHCR 2020)

Refugees are a particular group of people who flee political persecution and conflict in their nation for safety in another state.

They come from all over the world and have done so throughout history. They are from all sorts of different cultures and religions and, in fact, largely go to poorer, less developed countries, not the West.

When we talk about refugees in the West, we should never forget these facts.

2

WHAT CAUSES REFUGEES?

Author: Let's do some basic arithmetic
Reader: Oh yeah, I'm great at maths!
Author: Great. War + climate change + political instability + economic unrest = what?
Reader: Easy...Pi!
Author: Incorrect, it equates to over 80 million displaced people worldwide.

By the end of 2020, there were 82.4 million forcibly displaced people across the globe.[34] If these individuals were to form a country, it would be the 20th largest nation globally in terms of population - greater than the UK, Thailand, and France.

So, what must have happened for there to be this many individuals uprooted from their lives?

There are numerous causes as to why and many of these factors often interlink to generate the torrid conditions that people must remove themselves from so that they can survive.

Most of us are aware that war is one of the main contributors to the displacement of people worldwide. However, many fail to

---

[34] (UNHCR 2020)

consider how the impact of conflict goes far beyond the deaths caused by intense violence. War has catastrophic knock-on effects upon the provision of clean water, access to food, housing and general infrastructure, employment, and the economy, resulting in complete turmoil for entire nations and their people.

You may think South Sudan would be free from any deep-rooted issues since the country became liberated by gaining independence in 2011, and yet, this is far from reality.

South Sudan is experiencing the worst humanitarian crisis in Africa due to a civil war that has been ongoing for six years. It is the third-largest refugee crisis, just behind Syria and Afghanistan.[35]

Over 2 million people fled to neighbouring nations, forcing a further 1.87 million to remain internally displaced.[36] Moreover, two-thirds of South Sudanese refugees are under 18 years of age, and many have been travelling alone in their search for safety.[37]

Like many other civil wars, the struggle for political power overflowed and a long period of fierce combat ensued. A division in the ruling political party, The Sudan People's Liberation Movement, followed by accusations from the president that those directly below him in the pecking order were attempting a coup sparked years of battle. The war has caused a shocking death toll of almost 400,000 and fighting in the country's main agricultural areas severely affected the supply of food, resulting in certain regions experiencing famine.[38]

Civilians have consistently been a target throughout the war. Armed militants have subjected them to physical abuse, killings,

---

[35] (UNHCR 2019)
[36] (UNHCR 2019)
[37] Ibid
[38] (Council on Foreign Relations 2021)

sexual violence, and the destruction of property.[39] Although many have fled to nearby nations, such as Sudan, Kenya and Uganda, millions remain trapped within the war-torn country and do not have the means to leave.

The UN previously deployed a peacekeeping mission to South Sudan to protect its many civilians that were under direct threat due to the conflict. They offered protection to over 200,000 civilians by providing shelter on UN bases. In addition, they constantly evaluate how to give aid to soften the humanitarian crisis, highlighting the severity of the situation being experienced there[40].

Although the widespread brutality has somewhat reduced (for the time being at least) because of a 2018 peace deal, the impact of the civil war is still being reverberated throughout the African nation and it remains relatively unstable.

In early 2021, there was an uprising in the south of Sudan and further outbreaks of violence in other areas. Political tensions remain high, but the target is to keep the peace in the walk up to the presidential election planned for 2022.

The people of South Sudan are juggling several volatile situations that put people's patience and optimism to the test. Whilst hoping to keep violence to a minimum and ensuring that the humanitarian crisis deepens no more as well as sticking to the current peace deal, a large proportion of the population cannot see stability within their country in the future.[41] Maintaining the peace deal and getting the country past the presidential poll are the most immediate hurdles. Any hope for stability demands a

---

[39] (Center for Civilians in Conflict 2021)
[40] Ibid
[41] (Boswell 2021)

complete restructuring of South Sudan's poorly constructed political system that fuels the ongoing tensions among the elites.[42]

The South Asian country of Afghanistan is no stranger to refugee crises as a result of fierce conflict.

After more than four decades of war, it is no surprise that Afghanistan has experienced large scale population movements which has caused ongoing displacement.

If we go back to the late 1970s, we can see a time when hundreds of thousands of Afghan natives fled their place of birth and crossed nearby borders to escape the violence of the Communist-led Taraki and Amin Governments.[43]

The number of those involuntarily leaving their homes only increased when the Soviet Union invaded Afghanistan in December 1979. By late 1980, more than four million Afghan people were seeking refuge in Pakistan. Over the next four years, that number grew further with more than five million refugees in Pakistan and Iran.[44]

Decades of ongoing conflict, political instability, drought, and economic chaos have left Afghanistan one of the world's poorest and most unstable nations. Hence, it has the lowest human development index ranking outside Africa.[45]

---

[42] Ibid
[43] (Amnesty International 2019)
[44] Ibid
[45] (Willner-Reid 2017)

Conditions in Afghanistan worsened in the early 21st century after the 9/11 terrorist attack in the United States. In response, America opted to invade the South Asian country to remove the Taliban from power and restrict Al-Qaeda from setting up operations, known as the 'War on Terror' which persists today. This ongoing violence and struggle for power has been a significant factor in involuntary population movements among Afghans.

Afghanistan has the second largest number of refugees originating from it, second only to Syria. Around 2.5 million people have fled and more have not been registered or sought asylum.[46] Most of these refugees are primarily in Pakistan and Iran, where they face an uncertain political situation, according to Human Rights Watch (HRW). Iranian officials, for example, deport thousands of undocumented Afghans without allowing them the opportunity to demonstrate a legal right to remain in Iran or lodge an asylum application.[47]

When Afghan refugees return home, where there are already 2 million displaced internally, they return to a country that remains plagued by war, poverty, and lawlessness. According to a 2012 report by the Feinstein International Centre, one in three Afghan children is malnourished, with rates far higher in conflict-affected regions. In addition, access to health care remains very limited, with 15% of the population without access to essential healthcare services.[48]

War has ravaged Afghanistan, leaving its economy, infrastructure, healthcare services, and political stability in tatters. Unfortunately, the country's inhabitants are most affected by all of the atrocities resulting from the war.

---

[46] (Mercy Corps 2019)
[47] (Affairs 2021)
[48] (Mercy Corps 2019)

Religious persecution is another huge contributing factor to the creation of refugees. It is defined as the systematic mistreatment of an individual or a group of people based on their religious beliefs or affiliations or sometimes their lack thereof.

Article 18 of the 1966 International Covenant on Civil and Political Rights states that everyone shall have the right to freedom of thought, conscience and religion, thus making practicing a religion a fundamental human right. Yet, religious persecution, whether it's by state or non-state actors, continues to displace millions of people each year.

The persecution towards the Rohingya Muslims in Myanmar, for example, dates back to the 1970s and its effects are still being felt today. For decades, Rohingya, an ethnic Muslim minority living in a Buddhist majority country, has been subject to institutional discrimination including exclusionary citizenship laws.

Over 600,000 Rohingya Muslims and a minority of Rohingya Christians have crossed the border into Bangladesh since violence erupted in Myanmar's Rakhine State in 2017. Renewed violence, including reported rape, murder and arson, triggered an exodus of Rohingya, as Myanmar's security forces claimed they were carrying out a campaign to reinstate stability in the country's western region. However, the United States had described the forces as showing "genocidal intent" and the international community has applied pressure to end the repression. [49]

The Myanmar Government refuses to grant the Rohingya citizenship, and the majority have no legal documentation, making

---

[49] (BBC News 2020)

them stateless. The military had seized power in 1962 and added to the exclusion laws that stripped the Rohingya people of access to full citizenship instead of replacing them with white cards, which were issued to non-Rohingyas. The Government has forced the Rohingya people to start carrying national verification cards that identify the Rohingya as foreigners in recent years.[50]

The Myanmar Government has institutionalized discrimination of the Rohingya people by imposing restrictions on marriage, family planning, employment, education, religious choice and freedom of movement. For example, Rohingya couples in the northern towns of Maungdaw and Buthidaung are only allowed to have two children. Rohingya people must also seek permission to marry, which may require them to bribe authorities and provide photographs of the bride without a headscarf and the groom with a clean-shaven face - practices that conflict with Muslim customs. In addition, to move to a new home or travel outside their townships, Rohingya people must obtain government approval.[51]

As a consequence of this religious persecution, hundreds of thousands of Rohingya people live in refugee camps, such as the 880,000 stateless Rohingya people living in the world's largest and most densely populated refugee camp, Kutupalong – with about half the refugees being children.[52]

Another example of religious persecution is the Uyghurs, native to the Xinjiang Uyghur Autonomous Region in Northwest China. They are one of China's 55 officially recognised ethnic minorities. There are about 12 million Uyghurs within the region, and most follow the religion of Islam.

---

[50] (Maizland 2020)
[51] Ibid
[52] (World Vision 2021)

Since 2014, Uyghurs in Xinjiang have been affected by extensive controls and restrictions which the Chinese Government has imposed upon their religious, cultural, economic, and social lives. There have been reports of 16,000 mosques destroyed over this period, mass surveillance and forced detention without any probable cause. Additionally, legislation such as not allowing men to have beards and women to wear veils has further entrenched this state-wide persecution.[53]

Camps have been created in the region that, on the surface, appear to be Vocational Education and Training Centres. However, these vocational centres were criticized for alleged human rights abuses by the Chinese Government specifically targeting Muslims which included mistreatment, rape, torture and 'education' programmes attempting to stop them following Islam. China has denied such allegations; however, they are widely recognized by human rights organizations as modern-day concentration camps. These camps often have Uyghur Muslims being forced to carry out manual labour and some reports have highlighted how they are force-fed pork, which Muslims are not allowed to consume. There are an estimated 1 to 3 million Muslims in these camps.[54]

This religious persecution of the Uyghur Muslims has begun to gain international recognition. However, little has been done to help the Uyghur due to China's control on information and the internet. Therefore, it is challenging to ascertain the true hardships the Uyghur people are facing.

With no signs of China curbing their persecution of Muslims in the region, it is clear that the only hope for the Uyghur people is to seek refuge in other countries. However, there are many

---

[53] (Zambrana 2020)
[54] Ibid

barriers faced by the Uyghurs, such as lack of financial capital to move or lack of willingness from potential host countries to take in Uyghur Muslims.

Turkey, however, has often been a haven for the Muslims of China, as Beijing's strict policies have resulted in a mass exodus of Uyghurs, with some 60,000 finding protection in Turkey. A large conservative Muslim Uyghur community has formed near Antalya and Istanbul, where they run their shops and restaurants. Chinese tourists visiting Istanbul often go to Uyghur restaurants, whose cuisine mixes Chinese and Central Asian. However, according to the Oxus Society for Central Asian Affairs, "Turkey is no longer a safe haven for Uyghur refugees", which of course is very troubling as it further limits the Uyghur Muslims routes to freedom.[55]

As well as religious persecution, ethnic persecution has played a role in causing refugees. If we look to the Rwandan Genocide, we can see an instance of this realised. It took place between 7th April and 15th July 1994, after continuing ethnic tension between the Hutus and the minority, Tutsis. When the Belgian colonists arrived in 1916, they introduced identity cards. The Belgians considered the Tutsis superior to the Hutus and for the next 20 years, the Tutsis enjoyed better jobs and educational opportunities.

During the Genocide of 1994, members of the Hutu ethnic majority in the east-central African nation of Rwanda murdered as many as 800,000 people, mainly of the Tutsi minority. Started by Hutu nationalists in the capital of Kigali, the genocide spread

---

[55] (Bradley Jardine 2021)

throughout the country with shocking speed and brutality as ordinary citizens, incited by local officials and the Hutu Power Government took up arms against their neighbours.[56]

By late August 1994, UNHCR estimated over two million refugees in neighbouring countries, including some 1.2 million in Zaire, 580,000 in Tanzania, 270,000 in Burundi and 10,000 in Uganda.[57]

War, political disparity, and religious persecution do cause many displaced people. However, they can also lead to economic collapses, corruption and further unemployment, in turn, leading to more displaced people. It creates a never-ending cycle that's easier to continue, rather than developing a country and making it prosperous.

What significant events could I reference when discussing the cause of refugees?

Hmmm...how about Fidel Castro's communist regime in Cuba, Zimbabwe's currency crisis under Robert Mugabe and Venezuela's current economic struggles.

These are all examples of economic deteriorations, resulting in unemployment, poverty, corruption and ultimately displaced people. And just because the cases above involve corrupt one-party countries, that does not explicitly mean that one-party governments and dictatorships cannot lead to prosperity. Many countries have demonstrated that they can marshal their nations to major economic booms even under dictator-like rule. South Korea's President Park Chung-hee and Taiwan's Chiang Kai-shek both managed such feats in the 1950s, and as such, both their economies are still flourishing today.

------

[56] (BBC 2019)
[57] (UNHCR 2000)

The most recent economy to take a giant tumble is that of Venezuela. Under the guise of former president Hugo Chavez, Venezuela saw their economy on the brink of collapse in 2013 and have continued to see it tumble downhill almost a decade later.

When Chavez became president in 1999, he saw an opportunity to capitalise on the country's number one resource, oil. This resource, of which Venezuela has the largest reserves in the world, made it easy for Chavez to fund welfare programmes aimed at redressing inequality and poverty. The rising crude oil prices in the early 2000s allowed the Venezuelan Government to make good on their promise, but they had struggled to diversify their economy. If crude oil prices burst, the economy would be in big trouble called a boom-bust cycle.[58]

And guess what? The boom did end, and it was time for the bust.

When oil prices started to plummet in 2014, the Government was ill-prepared to deal with the ramifications and had no cash reserves or meaningful investments to fall back on. Moreover, Chavez's government failed to reinvest adequate portions of the capital from the lavished years back into its state-owned oil company, Petróleos de Venezuela, so future production rapidly declined.

When Hugo Chavez died in 2013, his successor Nicolás Maduro had a huge mountain to climb. However, instead, he decided to get a helicopter to the top of that mountain and carry on running fiscal deficits (borrowing the money).

Maduro decided to fight back against protests opposing his government with force, in turn causing massive accusations of

---

[58] (Hardikar 2018)

breaching human rights from the United Nations. As a result, from 2013-2017, the Venezuelan economy has carried on shrinking well into 2020. Compounding this shrinkage is hyperinflation which had reached well over 10 million per cent from 2013-2020, which is well above the European average of 5.55% during the same time frame.

If you'd bought a million dollars in Venezuela's local currency when President Nicolás Maduro came to power in 2013, it'd now be worth just $3.40.[59] Shocking, right?

This major economic failure has seen a Venezuelan crisis marked by one of the world's highest homicide rates, food and medicine shortages and the most significant exodus in recent history. Over 3 million people have been displaced from Venezuela since Maduro took charge and fled to neighbouring countries such as Colombia. However, many displaced people are left unregistered because they are not crossing an international border like many thousands of Colombians.

This has become the largest refugee crisis in the history of South America, and poverty is reaching new lows every day. Refugee camps are being erected across South America and many governments believe the "tent cities" will become permanent ghettos. Beyond Borders, a refugee relief programme, stated that "people are losing about 24 pounds of their weight a year...eating one meal a day, so it's a major crisis".[60]

Venezuelan citizens have been displaced and their government have a long road to recovery to regain the Venezuelan people's trust. Only then will people feel safe leaving "tent cities" and returning to their nation.

---

[59] Ibid
[60] (Koh 2018)

Although the crisis in Venezuela has become one of the worst in South American history, this economic disaster has happened to many countries in Africa, sometimes more than once.

Under the leadership of Robert Mugabe, Zimbabwe had very similar traits to that of Chavez's Venezuela. Zimbabwe's major economic collapse came in the 2000s, and in hindsight, Chavez had seen what had happened in Africa and maybe should have seen warning signs for what was to unfold in his nation. Robert Mugabe became the 2nd president of Zimbabwe in 1987, his party, the Zimbabwe African National Union-Patriotic Front (ZANU-PF), winning a landslide victory. He quickly reformed the presidency from a ceremonial office into an executive one; this position gave him the power to dissolve parliament, declare martial law, and run for unlimited terms.

Mugabe gained major appeal by stating he wanted racial reconciliation and to bring the nation prosperity. But unfortunately, neither of these promises lasted long as he soon paid gangs and militias to seize white-owned farms and land. However, Mugabe claimed it was an act that was done for the good of the thousands of black families living in poverty and overcrowded conditions. Unfortunately for all parties involved, Mugabe was in fact selling the seized land to wealthy business people and ministers. [61]

As a result, the 1990s saw an economic decline as the agriculture sector failed to develop and deliver the same production levels year on year. By 2000, living standards had further declined since the 1980s, life expectancy was reducing, average wages were

---

[61] (Winter 2019)

decreasing, and the unemployment rate had trebled. In 1998, unemployment in Zimbabwe was almost 50%, but by 2005 that number had risen to a staggering 80%. To compound the corruption during this period, MPs and politicians were receiving 133% pay rises.[62]

The yearly GDP went from US$7.4 billion to US$3.4 billion over the space of 5 years (2000-2005), and then hyperinflation soon began to take over. 2007 saw Zimbabwe have the highest inflation rate globally (at 7600%) which was only compounded and by 2008 was at over 100,000%.[63] This of course increased the number of people that had been deserting the country in the years prior and those who were not able to leave had to rely on relatives abroad and foreign aid.

Many other sectors in the country were also failing. In 2008 water and sewage systems broke down, leading to a cholera outbreak with over 98,000 reported cases.[64] Additionally, the HIV/AIDS epidemic caused the average life expectancy to fall to 34 for women and 36 for men, down from 63 and 54 only ten years prior.[65]

By 2009, the country had seen over a quarter of its citizens (3-4 million) leave the country, most of whom were part of its skilled workforce. 75% of the country's population who remained were reliant on food aid. The Zimbabwean currency was left in disarray, with a loaf of bread costing a third of the average daily wage, with one British pound roughly equating to over 1.2 trillion Zimbabwean dollars.[66]

---

[62] (Umraw 2017)
[63] Ibid
[64] (C. Nicholas Cuneo 2017)
[65] (World Health Organisation 2008)
[66] (Umraw 2017)

This is yet another representation of how a failing economy can aid the mass displacement of people, whether they leave due to unemployment, poverty or corruption, the economy is the primary catalyst for leaving.

So far, we've looked at two countries led by Leninist-Marxist socialist parties, with rampant violence and corruption as a means to control a nation. In turn, this has led each of those countries to suffer economic depression and forced many to leave. Unfortunately, the following example doesn't follow the same pattern.

Lebanon...

Yes, Lebanon, a country that as of 2019 has taken in 1.5 million Syrian refugees since 2012, is facing the prospect of many young professionals seeking alternate places to call home.

Lebanon's financial crisis became somewhat predictable because of the many difficulties faced by the country. The economy had four extraordinary challenges. Firstly, public sector debt had reached such elevated levels that a default had become a question of 'when', not 'if'. Secondly, the banking sector, having lent three-quarters of deposits to the Government, had become functionally bankrupt and increasingly illiquid. Thirdly, the productive economy had experienced virtually no growth for an entire decade, a development with critical socio-political implications. Finally, and perhaps most importantly, the country was politically rudderless:

- There was no president between 2014 and 2016.
- There were multiple and lengthy delays in cabinet formation.

- The 2018 parliamentary elections took place but only after a five-year delay.[67]

By the time 2019 came around, hundreds of thousands took to the street to demand radical political change. Meanwhile, the Government was still cutting off electricity up to 20 hours a day to save money. As a result, the cabinet decided to resign rather than set out an actionable plan moving forward. The influence of these harmful shockwaves led to the implosion of the Lebanese economy.[68]

The GDP shrank by 25% in 2020 and is estimated to shrink 10-15% further in 2021. As a result, the economy may end up contracting from $60 billion to $15 billion by the end of 2021, causing many to lose their bank savings in the process.[69]

Four in every ten people in Lebanon are out of work and half the population lives below the poverty line. This becomes a crucial reason for many people choosing to leave for Europe and the USA. The health sector is seeing a steady rise in the number of doctors who are choosing to flee the economic disaster and many more could follow.
Unfortunately, the rise of COVID-19 has not made matters any easier and halfway through 2020, the capital of Beirut saw a third of the city destroyed in a chemical explosion.[70]

Following the explosion, an estimated 1,000 medical health professionals, doctors and nurses have left Lebanon. For decades, Lebanon had been known regionally for its high-quality health care, attracting medical tourism from the Middle East and even further. Unfortunately, the incident also left hundreds dead and

---

[67] (Amer Bisat 2021)
[68] (Ali 2021)
[69] (The World Bank 2020)
[70] (Collard 2021)

around 30,000 homeless. There is fear amongst the Lebanese people and the monetary facts and figures do not reveal the scars people have.[71]

Human capital is fast eroding due to a massive brain drain of the young and skilled. Equally worrying is the loss of physical productive capacity resulting from widespread business closures, which would mean that not only highly skilled workers will seek employment abroad. Much more alarming are the security consequences of the economic implosion. Lebanon's sectarian history is rife with conflict. An economic collapse provides a perfect habitat for a return of violence, of which Lebanon has seen plenty of over the last 50 years.[72]

If the situation is not dealt with soon, the currency will become further un-anchored. As a result, hyperinflation will wipe out salaries, wealth, food and medical shortages will quickly escalate, requiring rising levels of foreign support, all of which happened to Venezuela and Zimbabwe, whose economies still haven't recovered even after a decade. The security situation will inevitably deteriorate into a state of lawlessness and, at worst, an armed conflict which the country has experienced in the past.

The number of people leaving Lebanon is increasing every day. Prior to the Beirut explosion, studies show that, on average, 3,100 people were departing from the country daily and this increased following the event to 4,100 per day. The number of sea crossings also drastically grew and during the last three months of 2020, there were 21 recorded attempts to cross the sea into Cyprus.[73]

---

[71] Ibid
[72] Ibid
[73] (Ibrahim 2020)

Now that you have an idea of the desperation people are currently facing, the situation in Lebanon deteriorated further as the Government declared that over 500,000 Lebanese families have become refugees in their own countries.[74]

All of the examples above display reasons for people becoming displaced from their families, homes and nations. Several elements such as war, greed and poverty can spark an economic downturn, or in some cases, it is the economic downturn that causes these elements. Both lead to an identical problem.

A final crucial factor that causes displacement and creates migrants and refugees is climate change.

Oh, you assumed climate change was a problem for the future. So, you assumed it had nothing to do with refugees?

No. The climate crisis is already here and is already causing massive damage and displacement. Indeed, climate change has already been behind many refugee crises, even ones that seem like they happen due only to war or economic situations.

What's more, climate change will become more and more damaging and create more and more refugees in the coming years if current trends continue.

Before we get into it, though, let's talk about what climate change actually is as many people aren't entirely clear.

---

[74] (Azhari 2021)

Climate change is the increase in the temperature of the world's atmosphere caused by humans releasing greenhouse gases. These gasses absorb heat from the sun which raises the temperature of our atmosphere. The heating of the atmosphere causes sea levels to rise and increasing numbers of droughts, floods, hurricanes and typhoons to destroy communities across the world.

We essentially release these gasses when we produce electricity by burning coal, oil and gas. Our rearing of animals as livestock also releases greenhouse gases as do cars, planes and buses and when we produce concrete, clothing and nitrogen fertilisers. Humans have released vast amounts of these gasses in the last century, raising the atmosphere's temperature significantly.

What's this got to do with refugees or migrants, you might ask?

The most straightforward answer is, everything. Climate change causes refugees and migrants to flee their countries of origin in many different ways.

One of the main ways is through causing the sea levels to rise as the atmosphere heats the ice, glaciers at the north and south pole melt and dissolve into the sea. As a result, the earth's sea levels begin to rise significantly. This is problematic for people who live on low and exposed land and often leads to catastrophic disasters. They are likely to be swallowed by the sea, have their communities residing in areas covered by water destroyed and so are forced to flee to higher ground either in their country or abroad.

The consequences of climate change have already commenced, and the most remarkable event is located in the Pacific Ocean.

The sea level has drastically risen, causing the wipe out and swallowing of multiple inhabited islands and forcing millions of pacific islanders to flee to other islands.[75]

Equally, in low lying Bangladesh and Bengal in eastern India, the sea levels in the region have risen so greatly that millions have become displaced from homes near the shoreline.[76]

Another major way climate change causes migrants is through extreme weather events such as droughts, hurricanes and typhoons all of which hugely affect different parts of the world, causing massive damage to communities and displacing millions of people.

For example, droughts cause crops to fail and food to become scarce, damaging multiple regions, destroying local economies and forcing people to flee to find work, food and escape poverty. Again, this is not a problem for the future, as people are already dealing with it today.

In Somalia the refugee crisis was partially caused by human influenced climate change. Climate change helped contribute to an exceptional drought that caused crops to fail and consequently forced many Somalis to flee to Kenya and Ethiopia in 2011.[77]

Crucially, climate change has made these extreme weather events happen more often than usual across the world. Whilst, of course, extreme weather events have happened for millennia without human-influenced climate change, the scary thing is that climate change is making them drastically more frequent. Indeed, a study by Oxfam concluded that from 2010-2020, the number of

---

[75] (Warrick 2014)
[76] (McDonnell 2019)
[77] (Fraser C. Lott 2013)

extreme weather events have increased by 500% due to the effects of human-caused climate change.[78] Yes, I know, unbelievable.

A final related way climate change causes refugees and migrants is through the long term economic and political instability it causes in the regions it affects with extreme weather and flooding.

Extreme weather makes resources like food, water and shelter scarce. In addition, it destroys public services, often causing severe instability and anger which results in conflicts that displace many more people and cause refugee crises. For example, although the Syrian refugee crisis is commonly considered to have been caused by war or political persecution, many have failed to recognise that climate change has also contributed to this very process.[79]

Climate change triggered a massive 5-year drought that caused crop failures and displaced thousands of Syrians and further contributed to tensions that erupted into the 2011 civil war, leading to the forced fleeing of 5.6 million Syrians to Lebanon, Turkey and the EU.[80]

More worryingly, until we take action against climate change, the situation will only worsen. Scientists have concluded almost unanimously that climate change will only cause the displacement of millions of more people and damage more communities in the future. Some studies suggest that if global warming continues at the current rate, it will cause natural disasters and sea level to rise on such a scale that by 2050, as many as 1.2 billion people could be displaced globally. Consequently, such an unfathomably large number of people forced to seek refuge will destabilise entire continents, cause conflicts, threaten the global economy, and

---

[78] (Oxfam 2019)
[79] (Gleick 2014)
[80] (Henley, Climate Crisis Could Displace 1.2bn People by 2050, Report Warns 2020)

damage the livelihoods of billions, unless we implement a system of finding the solution needed to end climate change.

Oh, but I can tell what you're thinking; are we not solving the climate crisis now? We're building lots of solar panels and stuff at the moment, right? So surely this issue is going to be solved soon and then we won't have to worry?

I like your optimism, but unfortunately, we do have to worry.

Firstly, we are not doing enough.

Indeed, whilst the news often makes out like significant progress is being made on the issue of climate change, the truth is that progress has been painfully slow.

Globally, we have failed to make our production of energy green in any significant way. From 1973-2015, the percentage of global energy produced by solar panels and wind turbines only increased by 1%.[81] This is a problem because if we're going to decarbonise our energy supply, wind and solar will have to increase rapidly.

Although other renewable energy such as hydroelectricity and biomass exist, neither can be increased significantly beyond their current quantities. Equally, although the amount of wind and solar power created has increased in the last six years, this increase has still been minimal. Collectively wind and solar power still only represents 7% of global electricity creation.[82]

---

[81] (Gauthier 2018)
[82] (Roser 2020)

Worse still, greenhouse gas-emitting oil, coal and gas still produce around 84% of global power.[83]

Equally, little has been done to address the other causes of the climate crisis that aren't related to energy production.

Whilst some progress has been made in increasing the numbers of electric cars, buses and trains, the vast majority of transport continues to be petrol and diesel based. Indeed, a mere 2.2% of cars globally are fully electric.[84] Similarly, only 17% of buses globally are electric and 99% of these are in China, which seems to be the only country taking them seriously.[85] Therefore, our transport systems continue to pump vast quantities of greenhouse gasses into the atmosphere. Besides China, most governments have failed to provide significant funding for electric public transport to significantly subsidise electric cars or build electric charging infrastructure.

No countries have markedly worked to reduce the number of livestock bred for meat and dairy products, even though the meat and dairy industry produces 18.4% of the greenhouse gasses released each year.[86]

Likewise, no countries have addressed the significant quantities of greenhouse gasses produced through the creation of concrete or fertilisers. These issues can only be addressed by governments creating alternatives or reducing the consumption of these products. Unfortunately, however, neither has been pursued with any vigour by any national government.

---

[83] (Rapier 2020)
[84] (Kopestinsky 2021)
[85] (Marshall 2019)
[86] (H. Ritchie 2020)

Indeed, worse than these past failures, governments are still not planning to act as fast or drastically as necessary to solve the climate crisis.

Whilst Biden's climate change pledge was met with much fanfare in certain newspaper outlets, the amount of money he's committing to decarbonise US energy is minimal. Instead, more money is spent on pet food in the US than is spent to decarbonise the economy and society.[87]

Despite the Paris Climate Change Agreement, most governments have only committed to attaining carbon neutrality by 2050.[88] As we have seen, scientists predict that by that point, billions will be displaced and the world economy severely damaged.

Governments are simply not doing enough.

Despite the overwhelming threat it represents, the reasons for all this shockingly slow progress are varied (and will be discussed later in more detail).

However, the fundamental cause is that oil, coal, gas, meat, fertilisers and concrete production all remain very profitable industries. As such, governments operating in a capitalist society are reluctant to shut them down.

At the moment, profit is being prioritised over the livelihoods of billions at risk of displacement caused by climate catastrophe.

Secondly, even the minimal amounts we are currently doing to address the climate crisis are creating refugees and migrants.

---

[87] (Heron 2021)
[88] (European Commission 2020)

Indeed, the trade in minerals used in creating solar panels and wind turbines is fuelling extreme violence in the places they are extracted from and as a result, creating refugees.

For example, many minerals used to make solar panels are extracted in the Congo by terrorist groups in horrible ways. These groups force children to mine minerals such as Cobalt and Coltan in horrendous conditions with almost no pay. They then sell them to Western multinational companies like Tesla, Apple, Google and Dell for use in renewable energy and technology production.

In exchange, these terrorist groups gain money which they use to finance wars and terrorist actions. This war and terrorism create refugees and migrants who flee to neighbouring countries.[89] In the Congo, for example, 2.7 million people became displaced by conflict mineral wars like these.[90]

Likewise, the mineral trade is (ironically enough) causing significant environmental degradation in various regions.

Partly, this is because extracting the necessary minerals of Cobalt, Coltan, Cerium and Neodymium, which are used for renewable energy production, requires utilising toxic chemicals and acids to separate the minerals from the original stones. Therefore, this creates massive amounts of toxic waste, which is then dumped onto the local environment with other tech waste from old parts.

The waste produced inevitably damages natural environments in the local area which destroys the livelihoods of local indigenous communities and displaces them. Resulting in them becoming either refugees, migrants or internally displaced.

---

[89] (Dowling 2020)
[90] (Global Witness 2015)

For example, mineral extraction has created massive toxic dumps in Baotou and Ganzizhou Rongda in China and in Maharashtra in India which has displaced local communities.[91]

Equally, mineral extraction is often very water intensive. This is a problem in water-poor countries in Latin America, for example, where local farmers cannot get enough water for their local food production. This can result in food and water shortages and, therefore, displacement of local communities. For example, in Chile's Salar de Atacama, mining activities consumed 65% of the region's water. This has caused a crisis that has forced many to leave the local area.[92]

Third and finally, even if we do all we can immediately, climate change has already happened to such an extent that the displacement of millions is more or less inevitable already. We have to prepare for it and work to protect climate refugees and migrants.

Yet, as we shall see in the following chapters, across the world, governments are remaining harsh and hostile to refugees and migrants with aggressive border policies, minimal economic support and refusal to help give refugees and migrants safe access to their countries. If we don't change our refugee and migrant policy soon to support displaced people, the coming refugee crises will likely be earth shattering.

---

[91] (Maughan 2015)
[92] (Katwala 2018)

3

THE CRISIS

Reader: Okay! So, I get that refugees aren't a threat.

Author: Glad to hear it!

Reader: But at the same time, why do they need to come here? Is it really that bad in their home country?

Author: Why don't we take a look at their lives back home and explore exactly why they are forced to leave?

There are many factors that have contributed towards there currently being (as of 2020) 79.5 million forcibly displaced people in the world.[93] A large chunk of these individuals' lives has been altered as a direct result of violent wars, leading them to move from their homes in search of safety.

Yemen is currently experiencing what has been described as the world's worst humanitarian crisis, with various threats to the safety, security and well-being of the population hitting the Middle Eastern nation all at once. A significant reason for their national crisis has been the ongoing civil war. Let us look at how this conflict has impacted the country and the added damage that the COVID-19 pandemic has caused during this time.

---

[93] (Hardikar 2018)

The civil war, which began in 2015, has caused the deaths of over 12,000 civilians and extensive damage to infrastructure, including roads and hospital.[94] Airstrikes enabled by supplies to Saudi Arabia from the UK and US have damaged or destroyed half of the country's medical facilities, meaning the nation is gravely struggling to deal with its worsening health crisis. The United Nations has stated that it is struggling to provide their continued support and have made a plea for financial aid to help bolster extremely underfunded health services.

Such dire conditions have led to millions fleeing their home nation; however, Yemen also has the fourth-highest number of internally displaced people in the world. The Arab state hosts a large number of Somali and Ethiopian refugees and asylum seekers, with currently around 135,000 individuals from the nearby countries living there, adding further strain to their services.[95]

The outbreak of highly infectious diseases can have catastrophic effects on war-torn areas where healthcare facilities are already dwindling under the pressure of trying to operate over capacity.

In late October 2016, Yemen was hit with the fastest-growing cholera outbreak that has ever been recorded which persists to this day. The country is on the brink of a widespread famine which has put 5 million Yemenis at risk of starvation; almost the equivalent of the population of New York City.[96]

Before the impact of the civil war, Yemen already had one of the world's worst malnutrition rates, with the majority of the population living in poverty. The COVID-19 pandemic has had serious implications for most people across the world, however,

---

[94] (Aljazeera 2021)
[95] (UNHCR 2021)
[96] (ReliefWeb 2021)

its impact on countries experiencing conflict has been more severe. Its arrival has generated devastating consequences for Yemen, further aggravating the issue of food scarcity, namely as a result of reduced job availability and low incomes. The UN are fearful that the number of deaths caused by the pandemic could soon overtake those inflicted by the war, other diseases, and starvation over the previous five years.

With different areas of Yemen being controlled by different parties, it is difficult to get a picture of how the country has truly been affected by the disease, or trace those who have been infected. For example, whilst their government has declared 900 COVID-19 cases, rebels have said that only 4 cases have been detected in their territory. As a result of this 'perfect storm' of disasters, more than 80% of the population is currently in need of emergency aid.[97]

The conditions in Yemen are undeniably atrocious. Many organisations are currently working tirelessly to provide emergency life-saving aid to those in need, but their efforts alone will simply not be enough.

Unfortunately, many of the hardships being experienced are not unique to Yemen, numerous places and people throughout the world are enduring similar catastrophes.

In Africa, too, there are still ongoing confrontations and civil unrest which are generating refugee crises. The most recent of these is situated in Ethiopia. In 2020, a crisis broke out between the Federal Government and Eritrean forces that have invaded the

---

[97] (UNHCR 2021)

region of Tigray, causing thousands of refugees to flee to neighbouring Sudan.

The immediate cause of this crisis was the political conflict between the Tigrayan People's Liberation Front (TPLF) and the Government of Abiy Ahmed. The TPLF were the leading group that overthrew Ethiopia's military dictatorship in 1991 and established democracy in 1994, which has stood in place for almost 30 years.[98] However, in 2018, after mass civilian protests at wealth inequality, government land sales and police violence, the situation rapidly changed.

Newly elected Prime Minister Abiy Ahmed began to side-line the TPLF, removing its officials from key government posts and reducing the autonomy of regions like Tigray where the Liberation Front dominated local government. In response, the Liberation Front solidified control over Tigray, increasingly refused to obey the central government and attacked government military in the region. 2020 finally saw the tension reach its breaking point as the central government invaded Tigray to engage the threat.[99]

In November of that year, the Ethiopian Government declared war on the regional government of Tigray, accusing them of violating their sovereignty and the rule of law. Neighbouring Eritrea took advantage of this and also invaded Tigray to destroy its rivals in the region. The barbaric siege has left thousands of people dead with a further 60,000 people having to flee to Sudan, leading to millions in need of support.[100]

Ethiopians that managed to settle in refugee camps in Sudan found the conditions horribly cramped and far from liveable. One such camp, the Hamdayet camp, has a capacity of 300 but has

---

[98] (Burke 2020)
[99] (Tih 2021)
[100] Ibid

received more than 20,000 refugees.[101] This means refugees live in crowded, unsanitary conditions and are vulnerable to diseases.

The situation seemed to elevate when supply chains broke down, meaning clean water, fuel, medical supplies, and food were virtually inaccessible to those suffering. The violence in Tigray has also worsened the existing Eritrean refugee crisis. 100,000 refugees from neighbouring Eritrea have lived in camps in Tigray for some time.[102] The invasion of Tigray therefore also reduced their access to food, fuel and water. Many have reported being forced to drink dirty water and eat tree bark to survive.

It looked as though there may have been previous influences leading to this conflict, and the responsibility rests with more than just one nation.

Western countries have arguably contributed to the instability that generated this civil war and refugee crisis. Over the past 200 years they have massively impoverished the entire African continent through colonialism. In Ethiopia's case, Italy colonised its coastal region (modern Eritrea) in the 1880s and the rest in the 1930s. This drained the region's wealth and created an unstable political and economic landscape for its people.[103]

Ethiopia is a relatively poor country and needs loans from the wealthy West to develop their economy. Western governments have capitalized on these circumstances and forced unfair trade deals. These deals include 'structural adjustments', such as cutting public services and selling off publicly owned industries and farmland to foreign companies. This inequality and poverty

---

[101] (UNHCR 2021)
[102] (BBC News 2020)
[103] (W. Rodney 1973)

helped generate popular anger which brought down the TPLF, destabilised the country and helped spark the civil war.

For as long as we've had recorded history, there has always been war, persecution and turmoil. These seem to be part of the natural world, and on most occasions, they end with a victor and a victim. A group that has unfortunately found themselves on the losing side throughout their documented history is the Yazidis.

The Yazidis, a religious minority indigenous to northern Iraq, are amongst the worst affected groups that have faced exile and oppression. According to Yazidi scholars, their origins date back to around 4000 BC and can be traced to the Kurdish mountains of Iraq. However, due to vast displacement, their heritage can be seen throughout present-day Mesopotamia.[104]

As a people, the Yazidis have faced persecution for centuries by neighbouring communities and religions. It's been said that they have fallen victim to 72 previous genocides, or attempts at annihilation, and as a result persecution has become a core component of their identity.

Yazidism, the practicing faith of the Yazidis, has been tested by other religious groups on several occasions. During the 16th and 17th centuries, many Muslim societies branded Yazidism as a devil worshipping religion, due to the significance of Tawusi Melek within their religion, an angel who defies God. Serving as an intermediary between man and the divine, many people drew comparisons between Tawusi Melek and the devil.[105]

---

[104] (Asher-Schapiro 2015)
[105] (Grimm 2014)

They also faced atrocities in the 19th century at the hands of the notorious Ottoman Empire. Throughout the Middle East, Yazidis were forced to convert or suffer horrific consequences. Those who did not fall or convert were driven from their homeland, eventually seeking refuge in Europe.

Things were different 200 years ago, however, there was not as much communication or knowledge of different cultures. The world was yet to see the big picture, that working together would be a benefit. This eventually rang true for many countries and communities. Unfortunately for the Yazidi people, the bell did not ring. The 21st century did not see an end to their mistreatment.

In August 2014, the Islamic State in Syria attacked the Yazidis ancestral homeland close to the Iraqi-Syrian border, leading to hundreds of thousands of deaths, rapes, kidnappings, and refugees. Groups of ISIS fighters seized towns and villages, facing little-to-no resistance as the Iraqi Kurdish fighting forces withdrew from the region, once again leaving the Yazidis defenceless and searching for a new home. Many who managed to flee the genocide, took refuge in neighbouring countries and communities, whilst others found themselves without access to water and shade and would eventually die as a result of dehydration.[106]

By the 10th August 2014, the Syrian Kurdish forces, operating under America and Iraqi airstrikes, opened a rescue mission to guide survivors towards refugee camps in surrounding areas. Unfortunately, the effects of this attack still haunt the Yazidi people today, almost 7 years later.

But what are the lasting effects? Surely the Yazidi people have been able to bounce back?

---

[106] (Lord n.d.)

A quarter of a million Yazidis remain in Internally Displaced Persons camps across northern Iraq. Many fear returning to their ancestral lands due to continued discrimination, along with the memories of murder and destruction. This trauma has seen a sudden rise in suicides amongst the Yazidi community in refugee camps and with a lack of psychological help, there is little being done to stem this problem.

Pari Ibrahim, the director of the Free Yazidi Foundation (FYF) has described life in the camps and states that *"youth don't see a future. Adults don't know what to do on a daily basis. The memories of what happened and the lack of opportunities in the future are virtually paralysing the community"*.[107] The community's mental health has worsened with the outbreak of COVID-19 and the lockdown measures put in place. NGOs providing mental health support are no longer available as the Iraqi Government is facing a hard economic crisis and sadly, has no plans to address the refugee situation in their country.

The number of distressing situations that refugees face back home is vast, but occasionally the blame doesn't lie with a country, or militant group. Instead, countries like Bangladesh have to deal with changing climate effects and horrific weather conditions, forcing many to leave and relocate.

As a direct result of climate change, sea levels have risen to dangerous heights, which alone may cause millions of natives to resettle. On top of this, there has been an increase in deadly storms, erosions, landslides, flooding and salinisation. In Bangladesh, 5 million people were displaced between 2008 and 2014, this is equivalent to uprooting the entire population of New Zealand. We can only expect things to become worse over time

---

[107] (Jangiz 2021)

as the Bangladeshi Government states that 1 in 7 residents will be displaced due to climate change by 2050.[108]

Despite the hardship amongst the natives, Bangladesh has still managed to absorb over a million Rohingya refugees fleeing the crisis in Myanmar. This mass influx of refugees may be seen as a morally just act, but it will also increase pressure on the Bangladeshi government and struggling locals.

If more people are to be displaced, government resources and space to resettle will drastically decrease. Thus, Bangladesh may be forced to watch its citizens seek refuge in neighbouring countries or even continents.

After learning of just a tiny handful of the situations some people find themselves in, is it surprising that refugees seek to leave their homelands behind in search of a better life? I suggest we would all do the same.

---

[108] (Environmental Justice Foundation n.d.)

4

THE JOURNEY

Reader: That's horrible. But at least the hard parts are over. Travelling to safety can't be too difficult right?

Author: Think again. The journey to safety can be just as challenging and devastating.

Refugees are largely forced to use unsafe, illegal and dangerous methods to escape the horrors in their homelands.

Most have to approach illegal smugglers to transport them which puts them in huge amounts of danger as they are left to the mercy of these criminal groups. Many are lured in with the promise of safety but instead are simply robbed of their valuables. And those that *are* actually helped to gain safety are still often treated badly. Many refugee women, for example, are forced to have sex with the smugglers in return for passage.[109]

Having endured this threat, refugees then face the horrors of the journey itself.

Those who can, travel by truck and lorry overground.
Refugees travelling through the Balkans into Western Europe, for example, take these routes across borders. Relative to the

---

[109] (Freedman 2016)

alternatives, this is the safest route, but it is still extremely dangerous.[110]

The trucks are designed for cargo, not people. They often don't provide adequate air supply to the refugees inside and unfortunately,
many refugees have suffocated to death on these journeys.

In 2016, 71 Iraqi, Syrian and Afghan refugees suffocated in a truck whilst trying to reach safety in Germany.[111] In 2019, 39 Chinese refugees died in similar circumstances in a refrigerated container travelling to the UK.[112] Since 2014, over 600 refugees have died trying to reach Europe in this way.[113]

Shockingly, that is the safe option. Most refugees have to face an even worse prospect: travel by sea.

Every day refugees risk their lives taking journeys like these. Some are short like those across the English Channel or straits of Gibraltar. Others long like those across the sea between Turkey and Greece or the Mediterranean. All are mortally dangerous to those forced to take them.

Thousands die on these routes each year. Almost 20,000 refugees have drowned attempting to cross the Mediterranean since 2014. Already, within the first four months of 2021, the Mediterranean Sea has taken the lives of 453 migrants attempting to cross into Europe. In the English Channel, 300 have died crossing since 2000.[114]

---

[110] (Prtorić 2021)
[111] (Thorpe 2016)
[112] (BBC 2021)
[113] (International Organisation for Migration (IOM) 2021)
[114] (International Organisation for Migration (IOM) 2021)

These numbers are horrifying. But sometimes statistics like this can distance you from what is actually happening here. Every single number is a human being with a family, parents, children, friends, loved ones, who has lost their life because of how badly they have been treated.

As you see these numbers, think of Rasul, his wife, Shiva, and their three children, one of whom was just 15 months old. Think of how they as Kurds faced inhuman political oppression in Iran and were forced into poverty. Think of how they were so desperate to gain safety in the UK, they gave all their money to a smuggler in exchange for access to a dinghy to take them across the English Channel. Remember that in 2020, they drowned there.[115]

Refugees are under no illusions. They all know the dangers they face on these journeys, the horrors they will have to endure and that many won't survive and yet, they persevere. Not out of greed, not out of selfishness, but out of desperation. Their only option in order to escape the horrors in their homeland is to endure these journeys for the prospect of a better life.

I can tell what you're thinking. Why is it their only option? Can't they travel by safe routes? Why do they take such dangerous journeys and engage with horrible smugglers if they know how bad it is?

The answer is simple. It's because of the barriers against immigration that have been implemented.

---

[115] (The Guardian 2020)

Having now read and understood the suffering refugees experience in their homelands and on these unsafe journeys for yourself, you might be confused. You might think that wealthy countries who have the ability to care for refugees would do their best to provide easy, fast and safe access to their countries in order to gain shelter from these horrors. However, this could not be further from the truth.

Instead, most Western countries let very few refugees enter by safe and legal methods. For example, despite 5.6 million Syrians being made refugees since the civil war began in 2011, the UK has only taken 17,051 into the country via legal resettlement schemes. Whilst this may seem like a large number, it is the equivalent of only 6 people per parliamentary constituency per year![116] The USA has agreed to protect only 631 Syrian refugees in the last decade.[117]

Even for those few refugees who are given protection, they are treated terribly. Resettlement schemes are very slow and bureaucratic, taking months to decide if a refugee is worthy of support. In waiting, refugees have to remain in their homelands, enduring awful conditions in which they are constantly fearing for their lives and for the lives of their friends and families.

The USA is often represented by The Statue of Liberty on which is written the famous call to protect refugees: "Give me your tired, your poor, your huddled masses".[118] Similarly, the UK regularly celebrates its history of protecting refugees from taking in Jewish children fleeing the Nazis to giving a home to Kenyan Asians fleeing the country in the 60s.

---

[116] (Refugee Action 2021)
[117] (Statista Research Department 2021)
[118] (Hunter 2018)

Yet today they, and most of the wealthiest countries on earth, have turned their back on refugees.

Despite all this horror, some refugees survive the journey and cross the border into a Western country, a miracle of strength, courage and luck.

And finally, we can breathe a heavy sigh of relief, safety at last!

Wrong. Though refugees are forced to undergo dangerous journeys to seek safety, the unfair treatment continues even after their arrival to their host country.

Many refugees that survive sea journeys are instantly shipped back to where they came from. Those fleeing across the Aegean between Turkey and Greece often make the treacherous journey multiple times as they are repeatedly taken back to danger by Greek or Turkish coast guards.

As reported by The New York Times, the Greek authorities have taken over 1,000 refugees and left them to drown in motorless rafts outside the Greek sea territory border rather than offering them asylum. This is illegal under international law. Yet very few newspapers have reported on it and equally few nations have pressured Greece to end the practice.[119]

In Italy, the Government regularly refuses to help refugees struggling to cross the Mediterranean. Recently 130 people died after the Italian Government ignored a reported sighting of a refugee dinghy capsizing and refused to send naval support. In

---

[119] (Allen, Greece Illegally Turns Away Thousands of Vulnerable People Seeking Asylum: A Crisis of Accountability 2020)

fact, the Government actively punish those trying to help refugees. Since June 2019, they have promised to fine anyone caught helping protect refugees from drowning in the Mediterranean up to 1 million euros.[120]

In the UK, the Government has recently announced that it will aim to ship any refugees that try to cross the channel from France straight back to the country within 24 hours as well as denying them any financial support (see the following chapter for details).[121]

Sadly, the horrific treatment of the refugees that do manage to cross borders doesn't end there. Refugees that are caught by border police are often subject to significant abuse. Many are physically assaulted or thrown in jails and others report being sexually assaulted by Western police. At the US-Mexico border many refugee women have been assaulted by US border patrol and camp guards.[122] Multiple Syrian women refugees have said they too have been sexually abused by Turkish, Macedonian, German and Hungarian police.[123]

Despite all this hostility and suffering, some refugees are able to successfully gain access to Western countries and are recognised as asylum seekers. From there, they are able to apply for refugee status.

If you think this is the end of their issues, you're sadly mistaken.

---

[120] (Perrone 2019)
[121] (G. Salter, Stop The Government's Harsh New Refugee Policy 2021)
[122] (Human Rights Watch 2021)
[123] (Freedman 2016)

Whilst their claim is being processed, refugees are placed for months, sometimes even years, in horrible conditions in detention camps. The UN promises that all refugee camps should offer a safe haven for refugees and meet their most basic needs - such as food, water, shelter, medical treatment and other basic services.

However, many fail to meet these standards and refugees are often treated awfully and live in difficult conditions. The Greek camps, for example, are 31,000 people over capacity. This has increased the risk of refugees catching COVID-19 greatly.[124]

Likewise, in the US, the border camps are frequently massively over capacity. For instance, at the camp in El Paso, Texas, 900 migrants were forced to live in a facility designed for 125. In some cases, cells designed for 35 people were holding 155 people.[125]

The same is true outside of the West. In Bangladesh, as of 2019, more than 600,000 Rohingya refugees live in one of the world's largest refugee camps in the Cox's Bazaar District.[126] On top of the severe overcrowding, the camps are often very unhygienic, with limited bathroom access. In camps in Lebanon for example, multiple families often share small apartments or live in makeshift settlements that lack access to safe water, basic toilets and waste collection.[127] Equally, in the UK, the Tug Haven and Napier Barracks processing sites fail to provide refugees with consistent access to showers, soap and bathrooms.[128]

In the US, the border detention camps for migrants and refugees were also very unhygienic. One detention camp provided only four showers for 756 detainees. Many of those held are refugee

---

[124] (Ford 2021)
[125] (Dickerson 2019)
[126] (UNHCR 2019)
[127] (BBC 2021)
[128] (Dalton 2019)

children, separated from their parents and forced to live in disease ridden conditions. Whilst President Biden has promised to improve the conditions in these camps, since his election in 2020 the progress has been very slow.[129]

Moreover, these camps also often fail to provide consistent warmth and electricity to refugees. 90% of refugees around the world have no access to electricity in the camps. In 2020 hundreds of Syrian refugees in Bosnia lived for months in freezing conditions in the Lipa camp.[130] Similar cases occurred in Hungary, Greece and France in 2017.[131][132][133]

Refugee women in particular suffer in these camps. The camps often provide little safety against sexual harassment and violence, nor do they provide sufficient access to basic necessities which has an especially detrimental impact on pregnant women.[134]

Many are forced to give birth without any medical attention and then have to raise their children in cramped, unhygienic spaces. Often, mothers are forced to sacrifice their own comfort in place of their children's. Most of the Greek camps request above anything else baby milk and nappies from humanitarian workers.

The conditions are so bad that the Greek Government has been reprimanded by the European Court of Human Rights. Multiple

[129] (Aljazeera 2020)
[130] (Dunai 2017)
[131] (Smith 2017)
[132] (The Guardian 2017)
[133] (Margolis 2020)
[134] (Divers 2016)

humanitarian agencies working in the camps have declared that Greece is not meeting international safety standards and failing to meet its responsibilities to refugee mothers.[135]

Research also indicated that 55% of refugees are women who are more likely to experience sexual violence, particularly in refugee camps. They are often given tents near unknown men and left without adequate protection. In the Greek camps and at Calais, multiple refugee women reported being too scared of sexual assault to leave their tents. However, some have no choice as they may have to walk long distances for basic necessities such as firewood.[136]

Refugee women are also at risk of assault by police in these camps. They are placed under the control of the police, military or other officials who can abuse their power freely. Police are often given significant legal powers over these women with minimal oversight. Unfortunately, there have been countless instances in which these officials have abused refugee women.[137]

Even the bravest can only face so much of this trauma. In the camp at Moria on 28th of February 2021, after having her asylum claim in Germany rejected, pregnant Afghan refugee Maleka took her two children out of her tent, before setting it on fire with herself inside. Thankfully, after being rushed to hospital she was saved by doctors. However, it still stands to show Maleka's desperation as a

---

[135] (G. Salter, 5 Reasons Why Refugee Women Are Particularly Vulnerable to Violence 2021)
[136] Ibid
[137] Ibid

result of the unbelievably poor conditions that mothers experience in these camps.[138]

Not only do refugees suffer physical trauma, but they experience psychological trauma, too. Whether it is traumatic events that the refugees suffered in their home countries or their experience in the refugee camps, many suffer with mental health issues in camps and have very little or often no access to support. Yazidi camps are just one example of how previous trauma and the lack of access to support make refugee camps very difficult places to be.

250,000 Yazidis remain in Internally Displaced Persons camps across northern Iraq. Many fear returning to their ancestral lands due to the religious persecution they faced there; witnessing their friends and families murdered, communities destroyed as well as temples and holy sites demolished.

Hence, trauma that the community has suffered has seen a rise in suicides amongst the Yazidi population in refugee camps. Yazidi campaigners have been urging Iraq to implement a national suicide prevention strategy after 11 genocide survivors killed themselves within 10 days in January 2021.[139]

However, trauma is just one form of mental health issue from which many refugees suffer. Changes in circumstances in camps can also take a toll on refugees' mental health and well-being. At every juncture from their homelands to safety, refugees experience huge difficulties and immense suffering. Refugees come to the West to escape that, to survive and to have a better life. So, when we, in the West, see refugees in our countries we should have compassion and understanding for the horrors they

---

[138] (Now_You_See_Me_Moria 2021)
[139] (Hussain 2021)

have suffered. Unequivocally, we should treat them with care and not question their motivations for being here.

5

ARRIVAL

Reader: What an ordeal that was! At least they're now in the safety of Western countries.

Author: It's not that simple.

Reader: What do you mean? Western countries are some of the safest and most prosperous on earth?

Author: You're absolutely right. But despite this, our politicians, media and society don't share this wealth with refugees, nor do they support and protect them properly.

One of the main ways we fail to support refugees in our countries is in how little we do to protect their mental health.

Awareness around mental health has become increasingly prevalent over the last few years and has only accelerated during the COVID-19 pandemic. Whether it was losing a loved one, not being able to see family and friends or losing a job, the pandemic emphasised the importance of the acknowledgement of mental health disorders and how a lot of people live every day experiencing such issues.

The uncertainty around life since the beginning of the COVID-19 pandemic has affected people in different ways, but it is common knowledge that most have struggled with the associated life changes. The Office for National Statistics has shown that almost

70% of adults in the UK described feeling somewhat or very worried about how COVID-19 is impacting their lives and reported that 56% feel stressed or anxious.[140]

With an increase in understanding of mental health disorders, one therefore can understand how difficult it must be for a refugee to resettle in a country. The entire process from leaving one's home, to embarking on an often-perilous journey and resettling in a new and unknown country can cause refugees to suffer with mental health disorders. Adapting to a different environment, with different cultures and values combined, often, with unemployment are all factors which cause refugees to suffer from mental health disorders.

When refugees arrive in Europe, the procedures at reception centres focus on medical screening to check their physical wellbeing – but they don't do enough to provide psychological assessment and, if needed, support. The refugee experience is extremely challenging and research from the Mental Health Foundation shows that displaced people are five times more likely to have problems with their mental health.

Among the most common symptoms are anxiety, despair, a sense of helplessness and a loss of confidence in the future. The most severe cases suffer from Post-Traumatic Stress Disorder (PTSD), which includes symptoms like flashbacks, hyperarousal, poor sleep and concentration as well as a loss of trust in other human beings.

---

[140] (Office for National Statistics 2020)

You would think resettling in a place as 'developed' as the UK, that perhaps mental strain may be eased due to being in a safer and more secure country, however, the resettlement process often worsens the mental health disorders suffered by refugees.

Policies directed towards refugees have become increasingly restrictive in the UK and this has had a big impact on refugee mental health. Prohibitions on refugees being able to work has an impact not only financially, but also negatively impacts their sense of dignity, self-respect, self-esteem and hope.

This could leave refugees in a difficult situation: either enforced unemployment or undocumented work – both of which could have an adverse effect on refugees' mental health.

Currently, in the UK, those waiting on the outcome of their asylum claim are unable to enter paid employment. They receive just £5.39 per day to purchase food, sanitary products, and clothing. Despite ongoing efforts from Refugee Action through their "Lift the Ban Campaign", asylum seekers are not legally allowed to work in the UK.

This system that claimants find themselves in means they often endure sustained periods of unemployment. It has been recorded that being unable to work and relying on the welfare state has negative emotional effects in people such as embarrassment, discomfort, boredom, sadness and anger, so it is unsurprising that asylum seekers and refugees are more susceptible to mental health problems.[141]

However, some refugees and asylum seekers often don't have a choice and are forced into employment (either legally or illegally). Whether it is repaying debts to smugglers or sending money to

---

[141] (Lift the Ban 2020)

family back home, many refugees need to work in order to move forward with their lives. The increased legislation in preventing refugees to work often leads to refugees and asylum seekers entering into unregulated and undocumented employment. The Committee on Migration, Refugees and Displaced Persons (2002) has warned that denying asylum claimants the right to work "may force them to seek employment in unregulated, dangerous, degrading and exploitative conditions".[142] This could put refugees at the risk of suffering sexual and gender-based violence as well as exploitation and leaves them in a state of insecurity and uncertainty.

The damaging experience of being on the receiving end of racism and/or discrimination is another reason as to why refugees face mental health struggles. A University of Oxford study found that between 2016 and 2018, 32% of UK-born respondents with migrant parents perceived discrimination against their group.[143] This mistreatment from society can impact people's sense of belonging and cause them to become ostracised.

Poor mental health in and of itself is an incredibly difficult challenge to manage, let alone having to do this on top of worrying about ensuring you have a roof over your head (which is a very real concern for many refugees).

Refugee homelessness is rampant worldwide and the scale of this crisis is vast. Roughly a quarter of people using homeless shelters in the UK are refugees. That means thousands of people, who

---

[142] (EU Parliamentary Assembly 2014)
[143] (Fernández-Reino 2020)

have already experienced extreme hardship, are being failed by their new governments and left without shelter.

Doesn't seem fair? I don't think so either.

So, what's causing this crisis? Refugees face many barriers whilst gaining shelter in the UK. As of May 2021, the prime culprit for this is UK refugee law. It demands that refugees find housing only 28 days after their asylum application is accepted, otherwise they face eviction from state shelters. This means that many refugees simply don't have enough time to find private accommodation. This policy has ultimately led to thousands of homeless refugees.[144]

This same law also bans asylum seekers from working whilst their refugee applications are being processed. This means that once an application for refugee status is accepted, they often have no money to pay for a rent deposit and are faced with only 4 weeks to raise the necessary funds. This is an unattainable task for the average person, let alone someone who has involuntarily left everything behind in escaping danger. Those who do obtain private accommodation are more vulnerable to eviction than the average tenant due to minimal employment opportunities and racist discrimination from landlords and employers.

There must be some pushback against the Government so as to allow asylum seekers to work, thus increasing the time refugees have to find private housing and in providing them with the income to support themselves.

Housing is seen as a privilege; but it should be a fundamental human right to have a roof over your head.

---

[144] (G. Salter, Refugee Homelessness: A National Crisis 2021)

The COVID-19 pandemic in 2020 intensified many of the issues that refugees faced. None more crucial than job stability. The pandemic caused roughly 32% of refugees to lose their jobs, making them 4 times more likely to be unemployed than the average Briton. Many people were unable to pay their rent and therefore faced eviction.[145]

After the turmoil many people face trying to escape their homes, I think it's only fair we give them a break. They say home is where the heart is, but at this point, I think the heart just wants somewhere to live.

When someone who has been displaced eventually finds themselves in a location, they can begin to form a new life, there are countless further hurdles they must overcome on the road to achieving stability. A priority for most when establishing themselves in a new place is finding a job. Recent events have made this already challenging task a serious issue.

In an appallingly short time, the COVID-19 pandemic had a calamitous global effect, touching nearly every country and territory. As is the case with any catastrophic event, certain groups are left more vulnerable than others. One such group in this instance is refugees.

Even in normal times, those living as refugees, migrants, or the internally displaced face great physical and psychological barriers to integration. However, due to the pandemic restrictions, which have put a halt to economic activity globally, groups of individuals

---

[145] Ibid

that were once extremely vulnerable are now struggling even to survive.

Obtaining a job is not the easiest task for anyone and for refugees seeking work in a new place, it is a significantly harder feat to achieve. The barriers when looking for work in the UK range from low proficiency in English, to lack of social connections, to difficulty accessing services, to outright discrimination. This has contributed to the rate of unemployment amongst refugees being four times higher than the UK average.

COVID-19 has had a huge impact on the number of people out of work in the UK, with unemployment claims soaring by nearly 70% in April 2020 alone; the most since records began.[146] Let us explore how the pandemic may have created more difficulties for refugees during their resettlement period.

Refugees and people seeking asylum have been disproportionately negatively affected by the employment crisis which has resulted from the COVID-19 pandemic, many being placed on furlough, losing their jobs, and facing financial hardship. Employment opportunities that were previously available in the informal economy have vanished, resulting in a loss of income opportunities and an increase in economic hardships for millions.

Let's review recent research to reflect on how the barriers that refugees face to accessing employment and services have been impacted by the challenges of the pandemic in its first few months, as shown in the figures below from the Breaking Barriers May 2020 Client Needs Assessment.

Breaking Barriers is a charity that helps refugees integrate into society. They believe all refugees in London have the capability

---

[146] (Partington 2020)

to fulfil their potential and become important members of their communities through employment that matches their skills, experience, and aspiration.[147]

So, how actually has the COVID-19 pandemic impacted refugee employment and employability?

- Changing needs: Like everyone in the UK, the needs of refugees and people seeking asylum have changed dramatically during and after the pandemic. 45% report that their needs have changed during the pandemic and Breaking Barriers found that training and housing support were the top priorities going forward.

- Access to services and training: In the Breaking Barriers survey, 82% reported support with services relating to employment, training and English lessons as one of their top three needs. This highlights that refugee communities do not just need direct access to jobs, but also support with employability skills, training for work in the UK and support to improve English language skills. This issue is made even more complex by how difficult COVID-19 makes it to provide and access training like this, especially when only around half of the refugees surveyed had access to a laptop.

- Increased unemployment: Refugees were disproportionately affected by employment issues during the pandemic. 36% were furloughed, compared to 27% of the UK population as a whole and 32% of respondents who had managed to secure employment before the crisis – despite all the barriers that face refugees – lost their jobs as a result of COVID-19. UK wide unemployment rates are expected to rise from 4% to

---

[147] (Breaking Barriers 2020)

10% after the height of the pandemic – much lower figures than those we have seen from this report for refugees.

- Isolation and social connections: Social isolation is a key barrier already faced by many refugees in the UK as people seeking asylum often arrive alone, with few (if any) social connections in the UK. Therefore, when the whole of the UK had to go into lockdown, this issue was only compounded for refugees. In the Breaking Barriers report, relief from social isolation was flagged as a top need for refugee communities, alongside the need for employment and financial support. Without the opportunity to build social connections in the UK, refugees cannot integrate into the UK and will, therefore, struggle further to access employment opportunities once they are available.

- Well-being and mental health: As above, refugees have been disproportionately affected by the COVID-19 pandemic, with unemployment and social isolation exacerbating the issues refugees already face in the UK. They are therefore even more susceptible to the effects on mental health and wellbeing caused by these hardships, as we explored in more detail earlier on. As refugees are already much more likely to suffer from mental health issues than the UK-born population, this is likely to lead to an extreme mental health crisis amongst refugee communities.

- Compounding work and skills gaps: Gaps in work history is another barrier that stops refugees from accessing employment opportunities in the UK. Many refugees already have gaps in their work history by the necessity of the long journey to flee their home country; if refugees were unable to work during the pandemic, this is only exacerbated. This may be even worse for people seeking asylum who cannot work but may have had their asylum claims delayed because of COVID-19. Indeed, research shows that 45% of asylum seekers would have been essential workers during the pandemic, based on previous work experience. This has fuelled the ongoing "Lift the Ban" campaign which is fighting to allow asylum seekers to work as soon as they arrive in the UK.

- Financial impact: The Breaking Barriers report also notes that many refugees live in low-income households and as such will be harder hit by redundancies and further barriers to employment. Many households also experienced increased expenditure on weekly shopping during the lockdown due to stock shortages in supermarkets. Financial support was reported as a key need for refugee communities. Alongside immediate financial relief, employability and employment support will only become more important in preventing and alleviating poverty in refugee communities.

We can only guess how this situation will unfold as the UK's financial and employment landscape changes with the progression of the pandemic. What these statistics from the Breaking Barriers report show, however, is that refugees and people seeking asylum are already being disproportionately affected by the issues that affect the UK population.

Additional UK-wide or localised lockdowns leading to further redundancies and furloughs is likely to put heightened pressure on refugee communities. This will, in turn, make the need for employability and employment services for refugees and young people seeking asylum even more desperate.

The cumulative effect of the economic, social, psychological, and medical complications has caused unprecedented disruption to the lives of millions of refugees. While you're surrounded by your loved ones in the safety of your homes, be sure to consider those navigating their way through the pandemic with little-to-no financial security due to the backwards system that leaves refugees struggling to find and keep adequate employment so they, too, can support their families.

On top of experiencing extreme economic insecurity and poverty in the West, refugees also have to face being regularly demonised and discriminated against right across the public domain - a smear campaign spearheaded mostly by the media.

Newspapers all across the West are to blame, but it is particularly corrupt in the UK. Refugees are regularly featured in headlines in an undignified manner in major tabloids. The Sun has run headlines urgently calling for the government to "halt the asylum tide now." The Daily Mail has called refugees "the swarm on our streets" whilst the Daily Express has declared "migrants rob young Britons of jobs".[148]

UK tabloids also routinely run aggressively hostile columns. In the Daily Mail, columns have called for the government to "use gunships to stop migrants" and "send the army to Calais" to help overcome a refugee "invasion." Refugees are treated like enemy soldiers, not victims of violence.[149]

These headlines and columns are not anomalies. Studies of the British press have found that negative presentations of refugees are common. Almost 20% of stories about refugees in Britain present them as a threat to and drain on state finances and public services, whilst 15% present them as a threat to UK culture.[150]

---

[148] (Fisher 2015)
[149] (Bland, Sending Soldiers to Calais Would Show Contempt for Desperate Migrants 2015)
[150] (Mike Berry 2015)

Press in other Western countries is not much better, however. In Spain, the ABC has printed headlines branding refugees an "avalanche" threatening to overwhelm Spain.[151] The German newspaper Die Welt ran a headline scaremongering, claiming that "IS fighters want to mix with refugees so as to make their way to Europe", in effect saying that any 'refugee' could actually be a terrorist and that refugees (consciously or not) are helping to conceal them. This is not only a hugely stigmatising claim but also greatly inaccurate.[152]

European column writers also often directly perpetuate anti-refugee rhetoric. In Italy, a column was written in La Stampa declaring that refugees will "bring the jihad to Italy".[153] In Germany, the tabloid Bild ran a sensationalist story accusing 50 Syrian refugees of raping women on New Year's Eve, only to later admit they had made it up.[154]

Just like in the UK, these anti-refugee headlines and stories are shockingly normalised. For example, studies have shown that 11% of stories about refugees in Italy express concern about their threat to national security. In Germany, Sweden and Italy around 1 in 10 stories about refugees emphasise their threat to their culture and economies.[155]

Now, do you see why we must challenge this animosity?

As well as being noticeably anti-migrant and anti-refugee, the media in the West also frequently attacks the Islamic religion and culture of the majority of refugees.

---

[151] Ibid p.64
[152] Ibid p.115
[153] Ibid p.99
[154] (N. Miller 2017)
[155] (Mike Berry 2015)

In the UK, The Sun regularly runs headlines that brand Muslims as being causers of terrorism. For example, one brazenly lied that "1 in 5 Muslims [have] sympathy for jihadis", before being forced to retract.[156] Others routinely accuse Muslims of seeking to take control of British institutions and destroy 'British culture', such as The Daily Express headline that asserted that "Muslims tell us how to run our schools".[157]

Others still attack the Islamic faith directly, with Telegraph columnist Julie Birchill accusing Muslims of "worshiping a paedophile".[158]

Islamophobia is so mainstream in the UK that studies by the Muslim Council of Britain have found that 59% of stories discussing Islam are negative, with a huge 78% of the Mail on Sunday's stories about Islam being negative.[159]

EU and other Western newspapers are also very Islamophobic. Articles in the Italian and French press have been found to routinely stigmatise Islam as anti-Western. In the USA, the situation has reached worrying heights. For example, major news outlet Fox News fabricated a story declaring that Muslims had effectively conquered whole regions of England and France to govern for themselves.[160] On the whole, a 2018 Washington Post study found that 78% of US reporting on Muslims is negative.[161]

---

[156] (Worley 2016)

[157] (Bunglawala 2012)

[158] (Bland, Julie Burchill Agrees to Pay Ask Sarkar 'substantial damages' in Libel Case 2021)

[159] (Hanif 2019)

[160] (Mackey 2015)

[161] (Veen 2018)

Whether in headlines or columns, refugees and migrants are overwhelmingly presented in our newspapers as an evil force that threatens us, that wants to undermine 'British' values and take us for all we're worth. Rather than treating refugees as human beings, acknowledging the great suffering that forced them to seek protection here in the first place, and instead celebrating everything they contribute culturally and economically to our society, the press treats them extremely negatively.

What's worse is that UK politicians are just as bad. Notable figures in all our major parties have regularly attacked refugees and migrants in speeches, press briefings and online. As with Western media, politicians often talk about refugees as if they are an enemy army threatening our countries.

Former US President Trump declared recently that Minnesota will be "overrun and destroyed" by Somalian refugees if Biden were to be elected.[162]

In Europe, one of the front runners for the French presidential election Marine Le Pen has referred to refugees as a "barbarian invasion", whilst former Italian interior minister Matteo Salvini has has ludicrously claimed that refugees are trying carry out "an operation...of ethnic cleansing" of northern Italians.[163][164]

In the UK, former Prime Ministers, David Cameron, and Theresa May, have both referred to refugees as a plague-like "swarm".[165]

In the US, President Trump's remarks about refugees as "rapists" bringing "drugs" and "crime" are well known.[166] Similarly, the

---

[162] (Bennett 2020)
[163] (France24 2015)
[164] (Business Standard 2017)
[165] (BBC 2015)
[166] (BBC 2016)

Australian Immigration Minister has declared that letting "Lebanese-Muslims" into the country was a "mistake" as they bring terrorism.[167]

Finally, politicians often attack refugees for supposedly threatening our countries' economies, public services and culture. In the UK, New Labour minister David Blunkett and Conservative ministers Theresa May and Priti Patel have pushed the falsehood that refugees and migrants engage in "health tourism" by using NHS services without paying tax.[168][169][170]

Even in relatively progressive Denmark, the leader of the governing Social Democrats has said that refugees and immigrants from Muslim countries bring "anti-democratic values" that threaten "our social cohesion".[171]

Indeed, our politicians are often also as Islamophobic and hateful towards refugees' religion and culture as our press.

The recently elected Prime Minister of the UK, Boris Johnson said Muslim women who wear the burqa look like "bank robbers" and called Islamophobia "natural".[172] Former Labour party PM Tony Blair declared that people feel rightly uncomfortable about women who wear the burqa, whilst Labour MP Hazel Blears said that Muslims who have an "Islamic appearance" should expect to be racially profiled as terrorists.[173]

---

[167] (Anderson 2016)

[168] (Akbar 2020)

[169] (BBC 2013)

[170] (Mason 2016)

[171] (Bukhari 2020)

[172] (Parveen 2019)

[173] (Akbar 2020)

In the US, President Trump declared that "[he] think[s] Islam hates us" whilst associates called Islam a "malignant cancer" and fear of Muslims "rational".[174]

On the European continent, French president Emmanuel Macron Macron branded Muslims as traitors to the country by accusing them of trying to achieve "Islamist separatism".[175] In Italy, the founder of the governing Five Star party, Beppe Grillo, said Muslim Mayor of London Sadiq Khan might "blow himself up in front of Westminster" whilst Salvini said Islam is "incompatible with European values".[176][177]

Shocking, right?

Can you imagine being regularly told by the most powerful people in your country that you are an evil invading force, that your faith and culture is disgusting and that you are bringing disease and crime? Can you imagine the pain, anger and sadness this causes?

Refugees face this hateful rhetoric every day in Western countries, when all they want is to live in safety and be allowed to thrive.

Our politicians don't just attack refugees in our countries rhetorically. They also discriminate against them through the law.

They often work to deport refugees, even when they know they will face violence and imprisonment in their homelands.

---

[174] (Hauslohner 2017)
[175] (Willsher 2020)
[176] (Kirchgaessner 2016)
[177] (King 2017)

In the UK, Home Secretary Priti Patel has recently promised to deport any refugee who uses people smugglers to arrive in the country, regardless of whether the country they are being deported to is safe or not.[178]

In Denmark, the new government recently promised to deport around 100 refugees to Syria even though they will all face threats to their lives.[179]

Politicians in the US are even worse. From March 2020 to April 2021, 642,700 people were deported by Trump and Biden. Almost all of them were deported to Mexico, regardless of where they came from. Very few were given the legally mandatory screening to determine if they would face violence or persecution if deported.[180]

When they aren't deporting them, UK politicians often unjustly remove refugees' rights, financial support and housing, forcing them into poverty.

In the UK, Priti Patel recently said that she would ban refugees from accessing state financial support, gaining social housing or seeing their families if they use people smugglers to access the country.[181] This will drive most future refugees to the UK into poverty. Do you remember why? That's right, it's because, as you saw in the last chapter, most refugees have to use people smugglers to enter because the Government doesn't provide fast and safe routes into Britain. The UK Government is punishing refugees for a problem that the Government themselves have caused.

---

[178] (M. Bulman 2021)
[179] (Sly 2021)
[180] (Conley 2021)
[181] (Sona Circle 2021)

Their hypocrisy is breath-taking.

The Italian Government is similarly hostile to refugees. In 2013, they ended their migrant protection programme 'North-Africa Emergency' and expelled many refugees from asylum accommodation. While they restored it in 2015, in 2018, they again legally revoked many refugees' status and ejected them from asylum accommodation.[182]

On top of this, Italy doesn't legally protect refugees and migrants in employment. This has led to many being paid massively below the minimum wage at €2 an hour (roughly £1.70).[183] Migrants and refugees are essentially being treated like slaves in Italy, but its politicians ignore their plight.

In France, the picture is equally bleak. French politicians routinely delay financial support for refugees and initiate evictions of refugees and migrants from camp accommodation without providing either alternatives or warning. In 2020, this got so bad that the EU forced France to pay damages to them, of around €12,000 each, for failing to abide by international refugee law.[184]

Finally, our politicians also often attack the Islamic faith and culture of many refugees and migrants through legal means.

This is particularly bad in France. There, President Macron has banned those under 18 wearing a hijab in public and banned Muslim mothers from accompanying their children in public whilst wearing a hijab. He has also increased the powers of the French police to shut down mosques at their discretion.[185]

---

[182] (Sona Circle 2021)
[183] (Bellingreri 2020)
[184] (Deutsche Welle 2020)
[185] (Lang 2021)

The Government of Denmark has followed suit. They have made it the law that only a certain number of Muslims can live in any neighbourhood.[186]

It's absolutely horrifying how Refugees are being systematically attacked by UK politicians.

The result of all this rhetoric and legal violence? Hate crimes against refugees and Muslims have been given credence and encouraged in our countries.

A hate crime is when someone is attacked, verbally or physically, by members of the public for their race, religion, identity or sexual orientation.[187]

This is not a minor issue. Hate crimes can be horrifically violent and mortally dangerous for refugees and Muslims.

A particularly horrifying example you might remember is the Christchurch massacre in New Zealand in 2019. This saw a white supremacist from Australia, inspired by the anti-refugee and Muslim rhetoric of his country's politicians, slaughter 51 people at two mosques.[188]

But there are many more you likely aren't aware of. Similar attacks are horrifyingly regular across the West. In the UK, in 2018, the terrorist Darren Osborne ran over 9 people leaving a mosque in

---

[186] (TNT World 2021)
[187] (HM Government 2021)
[188] (BBC 2020)

Finsbury Park, killing Makram Ali.[189]

In 2019, Somali refugee Shukri Abdi was allegedly drowned by her classmate in Bury.[190]

In France in 2015, Mohamed El Makouli was stabbed to death by Thomas Gambett for his faith.[191] Whilst in Germany, far right extremist Tobias Rathjen shot 11 Muslims in a shisha bar.[192]

Even when they are less violent, hate crimes are still traumatising for refugees and Muslims to face. Many refugees have had to deal with constant harassment by the local population in the very areas in which they're trying to find salvation.

For example, in Bolton, the large refugee population there regularly faces verbal harassment by locals. Two Iranian refugees reported being shouted at to "go home" whilst others said they were told to "speak English".[193]

In London, refugees Khalid and Nuuriya reported how their children were often attacked and had stones thrown at them whenever they tried to play in the garden by local children.[194]

Upsettingly, attacks on refugees and Muslims by politicians and the press have only caused hate crimes to increase massively.

In the UK, from 2014-2020 hate crimes have increased from 40,000 per year to over 100,000 per year.[195] In France, 2020

---

[189] (BBC 2018)
[190] (D. Taylor, Shukri Abdi: Burnham Calls for Answers Over Drowning of 12-Year-Old Refugee 2020)
[191] (Ferhallad 2016)
[192] (Moody 2020)
[193] (Pidd 2018)
[194] (Refugee Action n.d.)
[195] (Quinn 2019)

saw Islamophobic attacks increase by over 53%.[196] In the USA in 2018, hate crimes against Muslims increased to higher levels than just after 9/11.[197]

Can you imagine how truly horrible it must be to live in fear of being attacked everyday just for trying to live your life and follow your faith?

It puts an enormous amount of strain on refugees who have already experienced so much hardship.

The West is in no way the sanctuary it should be for refugees. After suffering in their homelands and enduring a hugely dangerous journey, refugees are treated like outsiders by Western countries, too. In a truly fair and just society, refugees should be cared for, as people, just like anyone else.

---

[196] (Daily Sabah 2021)
[197] (Kishi 2017)

6

IT'S NOT MY FAULT

Reader: Ok, so I get it. I really do. This is a horrible crisis and people are being really harmed.

Author: I can hear a "but" coming.

Reader: Buuut...

Author: There we go.

Reader: But...why are you telling me? It's not my fault that refugees exist in the Middle East or Africa. What's that got to do with me or anyone else in the West? Wouldn't it be better to talk to people in the places where the problems are created and try and get them to stop creating a refugee crisis? Why isn't this book written in Middle Eastern?

Author: Well, firstly, it's Arabic.

Reader: Yeah, whatever, you get my point.

Author: Secondly, no, I don't get your point because the refugee crisis absolutely does have a huge deal to do with you and everyone else in the West. It may seem like a distant problem, but Western countries are partially responsible for the refugee crisis.

Although there are some people in Western nations who are outraged at the thought of refugees entering their country, it is important to find out the root causes that have led to people becoming refugees in the first place. In many instances, it is those same Western nations who play a significant role in the processes that create refugees.

So what examples are there of the West causing war and refugees?

Let's start with Iraq.

In 2002, President George W. Bush argued that the vulnerability of the U.S. following the 9/11 attacks, combined with the Iraq's alleged possession of weapons of mass destruction (which was later proved to be incorrect) and their support for terrorist groups such as Al-Qaeda, whom Bush viewed as the perpetrators of the September 11 attacks, made intervening in Iraq a priority.

The UN Security Council Resolution 1441 demanded that Iraq comply with the resolution and readmit inspectors and although they seemed to comply, President Bush and Prime Minister Tony Blair declared that Iraq was still hindering US inspections and retained proscribed weapons. Despite the then French President Jacques Chirax and German Chancellor Gerhard Schroder citing what they believed to be Iraqi cooperation, Bush declared to end diplomacy and gave Saddam Hussain 48 hours to leave Iraq. After failing to do so, the conflict began in 2003.

France, Germany and Russia objected to the build-up of the war. Following the invasion, it is estimated that 1 in 25 Iraqis have been displaced from their homes and according to Iraq Body Counts org, there have been over 200,000 civilian deaths since the invasion in 2003.[198]

---

[198] (Iraq War 2020)

The war has been subject to much controversy and public opinion both in Europe and the Middle East. Anti-war protests took place in the UK and US and the Bush Administration was cited for mishandling the occupation of Iraq. President Bush's justifications for the war were all proven to be incorrect. It was reported that there was no "collaborative operational relationship" between Saddam Hussain and al-Qaeda in the September 11 attacks. Equally, the US also failed to find any weapons of mass destruction.[199]

Decades of conflict and violence have resulted in more than 3.3 million Iraqis displaced across the country since 2014 and over 250,000 are hosted in neighbouring countries. The UK was one of only 7 EU countries that had a resettlement programme operating when the 2006/07 refugee crisis appeared. The Gateway Protection Programme, a scheme which aimed to resettle Iraqis employed by the British army, settled 69 Iraqis in 2007, 355 in 2008 and 432 in 2009. But it was Sweden, Finland and France who initially selected the most Iraqis for resettlement and who pushed for a more coherent European policy.[200]

Between 2007 and 2009 over 38,000 Iraqis accounted for 17% of all asylum applications in the EU, making it the largest country of origin for refugees, at the time. In the UK, principal asylum applications (excluding dependents) have averaged around 2,000 per year since 2003, although only about 10% have been granted full refugee status or humanitarian leave to remain.[201]

Although some resettlement opportunities were granted with the assistance of the UNHCR, such as resettling the most vulnerable in countries such as the United States, Australia, Canada, United

---

[199] Ibid
[200] (Iraqi Refugees: Is the UK doing the right thing? 2010)
[201] Ibid

Kingdom, Netherlands, Sweden, Denmark, Finland, Norway and Brazil, the number of refugees accepted is not justified with the West's (mostly the U.S. and UK) involvement and acceleration on the 'War on Terror'.

It is clear that the consequences of the UK and US intervention in Iraq far outweighs their involvement in resettling and accepting refugees. After fighting for over a decade in Iraq, as well as failing to help reintroduce leadership and destroying public infrastructure, the United States and United Kingdom could do far more for Iraqis where matters of resettlement are concerned.[202]

However, the West's responsibility doesn't end with Iraq. If we look to Yemen, we can again see a country in which refugees have been created as a result of Western involvement.

Labelled by UNICEF as the largest humanitarian crisis in the world, the ongoing civil war started in 2015 following the 2011-2012 Yemen Revolution and there have been continuing struggles with religious and cultural differences between the country's North and South.[203] In 2014, the Northern Yemeni based group, the Houthis took over the capital, Sanaa.

In March 2014, after President Abdu Rabbu Mansour Hadi had fled to Saudi Arabia and appealed for international intervention, the Saudi-led coalition launched a military plan that aimed to restore Hadi's rule and fight against Houthi fighters.[204]

---

[202]

[203] (Yemen Crisis 2020)
[204] (Sharp 2021)

Over six years of war has displaced more than four million people from their homes. According to the UNHCR, half of Yemen's health facilities are shuttered or destroyed, the country is suffering from years of economic decline and there is a large-scale famine taking hold - with at least 16 million people going hungry in 2021.[205]

The UK's foreign policy towards Yemen is shaped by various factors. Firstly, the UK has strong ties with Yemen's immediate neighbours, Saudi Arabia and Oman and unhindered access to energy supplies. The UK also has a colonial legacy in the South (1837-1967). Finally, Yemen is strategically located near the Bab-El-Mandeb Strait, a global maritime choke point in which an estimated 6.2 million barrels of oil per day passes through. (MEI EDU).[206]

The UK's foreign policy interests have led to a significant number of arms being supplied to the Saudi-led coalition (totalling over £5.3 billion) which, of course, is central to the war in Yemen. Over half of Saudi Arabia's combat aircraft used for the bombing raids are UK supplied, which include the Typhoon and Tornado aircraft, Pave way bombs (which were estimated at £150 million for the sale of 2,400 bombs) and missiles. The weapons provided have been used in attacks on civilian targets, such as in an attack on a community college in 2016, which used a UK-made 'Hakim A' guided missile that destroyed student dormitories.[207]

An estimated 8,750 civilians have been killed just by airstrikes, which the UK Government is supplying to the Saudi-led coalition.[208] Now, more than 4 million Yemenis have been displaced, meaning Yemen hosts the fourth largest number of

---

[205] (Yemen Humanitarian Crisis 2021)
[206] (Jalal 2020)
[207] (UK arms used in Yemen 2020)
[208] (British arms sales prolonging Saudi war in Yemen 2021)

internationally displaced people (IDPs) in the world, after Syria, Colombia and the Democratic Republic of Congo (DRC).[209]

When we muster up an image of what the Western world is, we usually think of countries that are littered with McDonalds franchises, coffee shops situated on every street corner and cities that act as the world's financial hubs. This is what we know as a 'developed country', but what of the countries that don't match up to those specifications; the 'underdeveloped' countries?

When we look at what is happening in parts of the world where there are several underdeveloped countries, more often than not, there is some form of intervention from the more developed countries taking place there.

But does that mean intervention is always a good thing?

Well, not necessarily. There have been a number of occasions when large wealthy countries have stepped in for good reason and, ultimately, it has been for the greater good. The USA's involvement in the Korean War, for example, not only helped to stem the flow of Russian/Chinese communism throughout Korea, but also helped to turn South Korea into the highly developed nation it is today.

That being said, there have been instances in which the USA has interfered in matters that were not life threatening, as was the case when they invaded Grenada in 1983. There was no threat from the Communist-led country and the several thousand Americans

---

[209] (Shortfall threatens critical aid for nearly one million displaced Yemenis and refugees 2021)

living there were safe and cared for. But the USA saw an opportunity to put someone they deemed a better fit into office and invaded anyway. That this caused many lives to be lost is not only unjust but also heartbreakingly pointless.[210]

So, what responsibility do these affluent nations have to help the little guy? Well, it's a tricky line to tread and there can be no definitive answer to that question.

If we take a look at a nation like Cuba, there are many situations that have led to their economic decline and subsequent refugees as a result.

The Cuban Revolution began in the early 1950s in an attempt to overthrow the military dictator Fulgencio Batista. Batista allowed the American mafia to control many aspects of life in Cuba and helped the wealthy landowners to become even richer. At one point, more than 70% of the land was owned by foreigners with the US owning most of Cuba's sugar industry. This came to a halt when Fidel Castro's Guerrilla force toppled the Government and kickstarted the revolution, which included taking back land for Cubans and introducing a sense of nationalisation in the country.[211]

This all took place during the height of the Cold War between the Soviet Union and the USA, which only further inhibited Cuba's prosperity. The US, at the time, feared communism, especially on its doorstep and with Castro a good friend of Soviet First Secretary, Nikita Khrushchev, things weren't looking good in their eyes.

---

[210] (United States Invades Grenada 2021)
[211] (Cuban Revolution 2021)

In the manner of schoolyard children, the US and the Soviet Union began a back-and-forth over Cuba.

The USA refused to sell Cuba weapons, so Cuba got their weapons from the Soviets.

The US didn't like that one bit and decided to retaliate by reducing their sugar exports from Cuba.

And guess what?

Cuba once again turned to the Soviets and said "hey, would you like to buy our sugar?", which the Soviets gladly accepted.

US President Eisenhower was furious and in a typical 'General of the US army' fashion, he said "Okay then, no more oil for you" and just like that, Cuba was left with no oil.

We've seen this scenario before and guess what happened? Correct, Cuba went to the Soviet Union asking for oil.

"No problem", replied the Soviets.

The only issue being that all the oil refineries in Cuba were US-owned and they refused to use Soviet oil. So, Castro knew he had to make a big splash and nationalise the American-owned refineries and not compensate the owners for their land.

Thus, the long-standing US trade embargo with Cuba was born and it still stands as of 2021. The USA embargo has unilaterally imposed an economic, commercial and financial battle against Cuba and still limits the Cuban economy to this day.

"The embargo on Cuba is the most comprehensive set of US sanctions on any country, including the other countries designated by the US Government to be state sponsors of terrorism".[212]

This helps to illustrate the point of just how damaging the embargo is and how it is an unnecessary use of power against a nation that simply cannot compete.

Cuba was significantly dependent on the US and its trade, so the Cuban economy suffered almost immediately. Because of diplomatic breakdowns and power plays by two of the world's largest superpowers, another small island nation has suffered a terrible fate.

However, by the late 60s and into the early 70s, Cuba seemed to be making good progress. With the Soviet Union still importing from Cuba at guaranteed prices, the living standards began to increase, the healthcare system became a beacon in the Caribbean region and there was an introduction of universal education. Despite this fact, Cubans, in their thousands, wanted to leave the island and many perished trying to do so. Castro could only stop his citizens seeking the Western economic systems by forcing them to stay.

This government force only compelled more Cubans to flee. When Castro did let people seek refuge in the USA, Florida mostly, he allegedly sent prisoners, the mentally ill and severely sick individuals. Which almost seems like a perfect way to continue the childish charade between the two nations.

The job of convincing people to stay grew even harder in the 80s when the Soviet Union collapsed and the exports began to decrease, shrinking the country's GDP by one-third by the 1990s.

---

[212] (Economic Sanctions 2007)

Famine soon followed and by this point, the US embargo had severely violated human rights laws.

Firstly, the USA is a major economic power in the region and the main source of new medicines and technologies, meaning Cuba was subject to deprivations that directly hinged on its citizens human rights. Secondly, by passing legislation that "tries to force third-party countries into embargoing Cuba as well" (the 1992 Torricelli Act), the US Government attempted to turn "a unilateral embargo into a multilateral embargo through coercive measures, the only effect of which will be to further deepen the suffering of the Cuban people and increase the violation of their human rights".[213]

There was a clear indication that the US was no longer concerned with communism and the Soviet-Cuban relationship but was out to cause an imposition for Cuba and maybe flex a little muscle.

Although the initial disagreement between the two nations had started due to money, the bigger picture should have been the welfare of human life. Unfortunately, this responsibility fell into the lap of the USA who swiftly dropped it onto the floor.

In 2008, the UN tried for the 17th time to persuade the US to end the embargo and, finally, was met with positive movement. Some sanctions were lifted and as Castro's brother, Raul, took charge, the country began to see prosperity once again. Raul Castro put in place some reforms and as a result the economy boomed.

2009 saw Cuba already achieve three out of eight Millennium Development Goals (MDGs) which were; universal primary education, promoting gender equality and empowering women, and reducing child mortality. In spite of Cuba's achievements, the

---

[213] (Scherrer 2003)

embargo has been a significant factor in hindering further progress on meeting the MDGs, particularly in further reducing infant and maternal mortality rates.[214]

Earlier, a US biotechnology company settled a civil penalty with the Office of Foreign Asset Control for a total of US$168,500. The firm had voluntarily disclosed to OFAC the shipment of three vaccines for infants and children between 1999 and 2002 from its factories in Germany and Italy while the company held a licence to export only one vaccine through UNICEF. This is just one example among many that acted to keep infant mortality rates at constant levels as opposed to reducing them.[215]

Overall, the relationship between these nations resulted in years of hostility, for essentially nothing, and only kept the people in the lowest social classes at the bottom, subjecting them to poverty and famine. It also managed to cause thousands of displaced people, most of whom just wanted a better life. They were forced to stay put, much like the people of East Germany, except instead of a wall, they had 175km of sea to contend with.

So, is it the responsibility of richer, 'developed' countries to help? In this case, I would argue that it has to be.

However, that same call for Western accountability and responsibility can be made in response to numerous other instances seen throughout history and across the globe.

---

[214] (Millenium Development Goals 2015)
[215] (Figaro, An Analysis on the US Economic Sanctions and the Cuban Embargo 2021)

Africa, for instance, is a continent that has felt the catastrophic effects of Western involvement and their subsequent damaging neglect. After engaging in the transatlantic slave trade whereby European countries exported African people to the Caribbean to be sold as workers to coffee, tobacco and cocoa farms, these rich, Western nations soon began ravaging the precious minerals on the African continent.

Kingdoms such as Mali, Songhai, Benin and Asante were all built on wealth from mining gold and diamonds and the Europeans saw an easy opportunity to exploit these civilisations. They did this by appeasing the leaders of these kingdoms, who would eventually aid in the enslavement of their own people (though not necessarily knowingly or willingly), and by keeping the natives largely poor and uneducated. In turn, many European countries, such as the UK, France, Belgium, Netherlands, Portugal, Spain and Denmark, were able to split kingdoms into territories so that they could more easily mine.

Unfortunately, though unsurprisingly, there are inevitable failures of large-scale, exploitative mining and its detrimental effects have been greatly felt in the continent over the last 3 centuries. Findings from reports carried out in Ghana in the year 2000, for instance, have found overwhelming evidence of human rights violations.

In January 1997, 16 local miners were severely beaten by security personnel, and others were attacked by security guard dogs. This behaviour was regular through the different mining operations throughout Ghana at the time.

"Our people have suffered beatings, imprisonment, and murder for standing up for our community rights against multinational mining companies".[216]

---

[216] (No Dirty Gold Campain Launch 2004)

Sadly, these violations existed not just in Ghana, but right across all the mining communities in Africa. For example, between 1990 and 1998, more than 30,000 people in the Tarkwa district were displaced by gold mining operations.

"Mining-induced displacement...was one of the most underreported causes of displacement in Africa, and one that was likely to increase, as mineral extraction remained a key economic driver in the whole region"[217].

Equally, in Botswana, the San people were displaced from the Central Kalahari Game Reserve as a result of opening the park to large-scale diamond mining.

The resulting physical violence and the displacement of people was tragic enough, however, the detrimental effects of the mining didn't end there. The industry itself is incredibly difficult to sustain, bringing a multitude more issues to these areas.

As a job source, mining is precarious and short-lived. Once the ore and mineral deposits are exhausted, the jobs disappear. Most large-scale projects have a lifespan of 10-40 years, after which the mining companies close up and move on to new projects.

When these large companies first come to these areas to mine, they often establish schools, clinics, centres in the community as a gesture of good will, to create the illusion that they've got the community's best interests at heart. However, once the projects

---

[217] (Africa: Conflicts and Mining-induced Displacement 2008)

have run their course, these facilities usually lose their funding. When this happens, the miners and communities are generally left to fend for themselves.

If, as it should be, it is the responsibility of these European giants to help the people whose land they've poached, then it follows that securing the futures of these communities after the big companies leave should be a priority. But, in many instances and for many companies, this isn't the case. They arrive when the money and commodities are abundant and when that dries up, they abandon, often leaving places in worse conditions than when they arrived.

The West's responsibility doesn't end with the above, however. If we return to the factors that cause refugees, we can once more see that it is the powerful, 'developed' countries that always have a significant part to play in creating the conditions that cause refugees. Yet, as the title of this chapter so clearly portrays, there exists a huge lack of awareness and accountability in these areas.

In this way, climate change and climate refugees are often presented as a crime of collective humankind. As we have seen, the release of greenhouse gasses causes climate change and extreme weather conditions that forces millions to flee their homes and communities. If we don't stop releasing these gases, billions more will be displaced.

However, it is rare to see any specific group held particularly responsible for this tragedy or, equally, held responsible for fixing it.

Newspaper articles and television programmes that address climate change in our countries regularly bemoan human selfishness, greed and lack of care for the environment. It is presented as a tragedy, but one down to 'human nature' in general - i.e., one that can't be helped. We are invited to mourn the destruction of the planet, the horrors that many will face and the refugees and migrants that will be forced from their homes, but not to pin blame on any group or demand any change.

Rather, we are told to hope and pray that every individual changes their ways equally, but only in the most banal and minimal ways possible: recycle your tuna tins! Use paper straws! Eat sausages two times a week instead of three! Not only are these ideas misleading, but they are also a recipe for disaster.

The truth is, there *is* a group of countries that bear disproportionate responsibility for climate change and the huge displacement of people this currently causes and will continue to cause in the future.

More importantly, this is a group of countries, more than any others in the world, that must be the ones to make radical changes to address climate change because they are also the ones, more than any others in the world, who are most capable of doing so.

And which countries are these?

I'm sure you can guess by now.

That's right, our Western countries have, and continue to be, the prime culprit for causing climate change and the displacement of climate refugees. More specifically, it is the wealthiest few within our countries who bear the prime responsibility for this.

Moreover, it is the same wealthy Western countries who are best placed practically to protect the climate and climate refugees.

Rather than shrugging our shoulders and saying "it's not my fault", or generally blaming "humanity" or "human nature", we in the West must acknowledge our moral and practical duty to act faster and more radically than any other country in addressing the climate crisis and protecting those displaced by it.

The fact that the West is the most responsible for climate change and climate refugees may be a shock to you.

It *is* shocking and saddening to think that the actions of our countries are responsible for destroying the planet and - as we have seen - for causing millions to be displaced and potentially billions more in the future.

You are also likely surprised because it is rare to see any of our mainstream media discussing our responsibility at all. If any countries are held up as the culprit for the climate crisis, it tends to be China or India, due to their currently high emissions. However, Western countries are both historically and currently responsible for far greater emissions than either of these countries.

Indeed, since records began, the Western countries (the 27 EU member states, UK, US, Canada, Australia, New Zealand, Switzerland, Iceland and Norway) have emitted a massive 811 billion tons of Carbon Dioxide into the atmosphere.[218]

This means that despite the fact that the West only hosts 12% of the globe's present population (and 18% of its historic population

---

[218] (H. a. Ritchie 2020)

since 1700), we are responsible for 51.4% of the world's historic carbon emissions.[219]

This is important as the climate crisis exists as a result of the historic build-up of carbon in the atmosphere. In other words, the climate crisis isn't just due to greenhouse gas emissions presently, but also those in the past. On these metrics, there is no doubt that the West bears the bulk of the responsibility.

What's more, although currently China and India are producing a greater share of global carbon emissions than they have historically, the West is still today responsible for the largest portion of carbon emissions in the world.

In 2019, the Western countries produced 11.1 billion tons of carbon dioxide in one year. This represents 30% of global carbon emissions that year, a greater share than China at 10 billion, India at 2.62 billion, or indeed any other national economy[220].

Furthermore, if we consider the relative populations of these regions, the West's emissions are even worse. The Western countries collective population is 923 million, representing only 12% of the global population. By contrast, China and India both have a population of around 1.4 billion, representing around 19%.[221] So, per person, Western greenhouse gas emissions are more than double those of China and over 6 times more than those of India[222].

---

[219] (Population By Country 2019)

[220] (Ritche 2020)

[221] Ibid

[222] (Population by Country 2019)

Finally, whilst other countries like China, India and Bangladesh do have large emissions, much of these are to a significant degree actually the responsibility of the West[223].

This might seem odd, how can emissions committed in China or India be the responsibility of Western countries?

In essence, it's because the products produced through emissions are manufactured for Western countries. China, India and Bangladesh are increasingly becoming the workshop of the world, producing much of the manufactured goods consumed in the West, often on behalf of Western companies[224].

This process began in the 1980s when many Western companies decided to produce in Asia or subcontract their production to Asian companies because it made producing their products cheaper. This is both because the wages of Chinese, Indian and Bangladeshi workers are lower than in the West and because Western brands - through a process dubbed 'monopsony capitalism' - can use subcontracting to make local firms compete for the contract to produce their goods, driving down costs for Western companies[225].

As such, many of the products that the West subcontract to these countries produce huge amounts of greenhouse gas and these are counted not as Western emissions but those made by China, India and Bangladesh even though they are made on behalf of Western companies to sell to Western consumers.

Western companies have essentially offloaded their greenhouse gas emissions to other countries even though the driving motor

---

[223] (Ritchie 2020)

[224] (Soper, Post-Growth Living: For an Alternative Hedonism 2020)

[225] (Panitch, The Making of Global Capitalism: The Political Economy of American Empire 2013)

behind them being made are Western consumers and Western companies. For example, studies estimate that as much as 9% of Chinese emissions are due to producing products for the US and 6% are due to producing products for the EU[226].

The West, therefore, bears some responsibility for Chinese, Indian and Bangladeshi emissions, too. If our governments and public decide to consume fewer greenhouse gas emitting products or insist that they are made using carbon neutral means then we could significantly reduce emissions. The fact that no Western country has thus far decided to do so indicates our partial responsibility for Asian emissions[227].

This is particularly true of the wealthy within the West. Why? Because they are the ones who own our companies and make the decisions about how much greenhouse gasses are emitted in the process of production. They also consume far more greenhouse gas emitting products than the rest of our society through excessive consumption (such as frequent private jet travel, for example).

Indeed, as Oxfam reported in 2020, the carbon emissions of the richest 1% are more than double those of the poorest half of humanity and the richest 10% account for over half of the emissions of humanity between 1990 and 2015.[228]

As we know from Chapter 3, it is greenhouse gas emissions and resulting heating of the atmosphere that is already causing millions of people to be made climate refugees and will cause billions to be displaced in the future. Moreover, it has and will continue to kill many and drive whole regions into poverty. Climate change is a deadly, damaging force that we have unleashed.

---

[226] (Kumar 2021)
[227] (Clark 2009)
[228] (Warren 2020)

Therefore, as the greatest historic and present drivers of the climate crisis, we in the West - particularly the wealthy elite - have a moral responsibility to reduce greenhouse gas emissions and protect climate refugees.

Not only do we have a moral responsibility to protect refugees affected by climate change, but we also have a practical responsibility too.

Indeed, even if the West didn't have a moral duty to make up for its overwhelming historic and present responsibility for climate change, it should still take the lead in tackling the climate crisis.

Why, you may ask?

In short, for practical reasons. Simply put, the West is by far the best placed to do so because of its wealth, political power and economic development. And, fundamentally, it is completely in our interests to prevent the destruction of the planet we rely on to survive.

The West's economies are still amongst the very largest on earth. The US and EU remain the top 2 largest economic zones in the world (as of 2021), whilst the remaining Western nations are all in the top 20.

What's more is that the West still dominates international politics and its institutions such as the UN, World Bank, IMF and WTO. Western banks and financial service companies such as Berkshire Hathaway, BNP Paribas and JP Morgan still dominate global finance, the US dollar remains the reserve currency of the world and the Federal Reserve the most important national bank on earth.

Western countries still spend far more than any other country or region on research and development surrounding renewable energy. As such, Western countries and companies have access to the most advanced renewable energy technology available.[229]

Western populations are uniformly the wealthiest on earth, have the highest salaries and spend the most on consumer items. Indeed, US consumers alone spend almost three times as much as India and China combined, whilst EU consumers spend almost 50% more than the two combined.

In short, Western economies are fully developed rather than developing. As such, our governments, wealthy companies and wider populations can afford to fund a rapid decarbonisation of our economies far more easily than other countries.

We can also afford (and are technically able to due to our developed university infrastructure) to help support developing nations to cut their own emissions and adopt green technology.

Finally, through our disproportionate international political power, we can do more than other countries to help coordinate and support the whole world to decarbonise.

With all this political and economic power, the West has a practical responsibility to address climate change immediately. It is sad that it is yet to do so significantly.

[229] (Oxfam International 2020)

Not only does the West have the means to, it has a responsibility to protect the victims of irresponsible actions that have led to the climate crisis; to protect climate refugees.

As you have seen in Chapter 3, climate change has already created millions of refugees and migrants as a result of its damaging effects on local environments. Moreover, even if we were to stop emitting greenhouse gasses overnight, we have already released so much carbon into the atmosphere that environmental damage and further climate refugees are essentially inevitable.

We can only stop the effects becoming more and more severe, not stop them entirely. As such, we must acknowledge the existence of climate refugees and truly ensure that they are 'here to stay' by ensuring that we protect them.

The good thing is, the West is in a very good practical position to protect climate refugees. As the wealthiest region on earth, it has the best economic capacity to provide economic and material support and opportunities to refugees.

On top of this, Western countries are some of the most politically stable on earth. Since the Second World War, around 80 years ago, there have been very few conflicts or moments of civil unrest across the region. As such, the West is also best placed to provide political security from violence and conflict for climate refugees.

Finally, in a darkly ironic - and arguably unjust - twist of fate, despite being the most responsible for the climate crisis, the West is likely to be the least directly hit by the extreme weather events and flooding it generates.

Scientists predict that flooding and extreme weather events will largely hit South Asia, Africa and South America rather than North America, Europe, Australia or New Zealand. As such, the

West has a responsibility to provide refugees from affected areas with safety and security in its fewer hit regions.

Western countries, therefore, have a practical duty to address climate change as soon as possible, cut emissions and protect those displaced by the crisis that they have played a large role in creating.

Why else should the West be responsible for providing support for refugees, I hear you ask?

Well, on top of all of the factors mentioned above, most of the nations that make up the Western world tend to have the political stability and economic resources to make caring for refugees possible.

At present, a very small number of countries take responsibility for a large proportion of the world's refugees.

On the flip side, where the wealth of a country is concerned, there are numerous places that are far better equipped to house refugees but who, instead, offer very little to support, or accept an incredibly limited number.

The nations that make up the EU and EEA, as well as Switzerland, could be far more accommodating. Combined, over the past decade, these countries have accepted 3 million refugees which equates to less than 1% of their populations.[230] By contrast, Germany has received almost half of the entire number of refugees who have re-settled in Europe.

---

[230] (Global Figures 2020)

Even though these joint efforts are poor, other areas in the Western world must also be questioned as to why they continue to reject those hoping to rebuild their lives within their borders. A shocking 0.25% of the United States population is made up of refugees, and just 0.19% in New Zealand.[231]

Let's take a look at why these figures are so poor, and how many of the places mentioned are actually in a strong position to help alleviate the strain being caused by the global refugee crisis.

There are various elements which contribute to how well-equipped a place is to be in the position to take in refugees. Factors such as economic development, unemployment rates, population size, and access to natural resources play a significant role.

A 2017 study by the Norwegian Refugee Council compared the number of refugees countries received in 2017 to their GDP. This was to determine which nations were contributing the most to accommodating refugees in relation to their economic capability.

The countries contributing 100% have received their "share" of refugees, according to this formula used in the study. With this in mind, Uganda obtained a score of 45,000%, meaning that they had received 450 times their share of refugees based on their economic state. Nearby Sudan was deemed to be playing the second largest role, with 10,600%.[232]

The top 20 countries playing the biggest roles were all in Asia or Africa, with Turkey being the only exception. Within Europe, alongside Turkey, Greece and Germany were the other main contributors. Other than these nations, for a relatively very wealthy part of the world, many other places are doing much less than they

---

[231] Ibid
[232] (Responsibility sharing 2020)

are capable of. For example, in Europe, the eastern European countries score the lowest, with Slovakia and the Czech Republic at the bottom of the list, at 1.3% and 1.6%, respectively. Poland follows with 2.3%.[233]

Outside of Europe, large countries with strong economies such as Japan are accepting very few refugees across their borders. Although Japan provides financial backing to the UN's refugee work, in 2017 they only received a mere 94 refugees![234]

Numerous South American nations have experienced great economic development but, unfortunately, this has not led to a similar rise in the number of refugees they opt to receive. Chile, Argentina, Uruguay and Brazil all received 1% or less of their shares. In comparison, the US received 7%.[235]

Another significant issue is that some countries have not ratified the UN's 1951 Refugee Convention, so people are not awarded refugee status. Displaced people are not guaranteed any rights set out under the convention, such as the right to work, access to education and access to the legal system. So, despite there being high numbers of displaced people from Syria and Yemen, with the vast majority of them fleeing to Saudi Arabia and other rich Persian nations, they are not technically registered as refugees.

Most displaced people flee to impoverished neighbouring countries, while refugees are helped most effectively in their own region. Therefore, it is important that wealthy countries aid displaced people by providing economic support to the countries that receive them, especially when considering they are in a far better situation to be able to do so.

---

[233] Ibid
[234] Ibid
[235] Ibid

7

REFUGEE STORIES

Reader: Okay... but everything you've said refers to refugees, you know "the group of millions of people".
Author: So, you have been paying attention.
Reader: But what about the people... like the actual individuals that make up this group? Who are they?
Author: Very good question. I'm impressed! Why don't I take you through real-life stories to give you a deeper insight into the lives and struggles of refugees and the difficult journeys they face whilst seeking refuge or asylum in a different country.

Hopefully this will allow you to empathise and come to a closer understanding of the lives that refugees leave behind, and some of the horrors they face on the road to what they hope is a better life.

Whilst reading, really try and picture yourself in their shoes and try to imagine yourself in their situation. Whilst some are fortunate enough to make it to their host country and live a better life, many others are not as lucky and their struggle continues even after their arrival.

Let's begin with Rojin's Story...

15-year-old Rojin lived an ordinary life as a young girl in Kobane, Syria. Back home she excelled at school, and, like many of her peers, she had big dreams of a successful career in law. Daughter of a shop owner, she describes her life before the war as "an ordinary but wonderful life" where she lived in a "beautiful house" with her family and would often have friends over.

The war however, completely changed Rojin's life. After being forced to flee Kobane, her father gave up his business and livelihood. The family had no choice but to live in a tent in an informal settlement in Turkey. The family slept on the cold hard floor and cooked over a fire, this became a norm for the family who had once lived in peace and comfort, this life was unjustly taken away from them.

Rojin and her siblings were very young when they were forced to flee, which meant they were no longer able to attend school. This had a huge toll on their childhood as they grew up without the ability to read or write, a fundamental right to all children. Although Rojin was a strong student with a promising future, her dream of standing in a courtroom and fighting for justice was taken away from her as the war continues to affect the lives of many children like Rojin to this day.

It has still not been possible to ensure every Syrian child attends school despite promises from world leaders in 2016. Losing the right to an education is incredibly detrimental to the development of young children. As a result, thousands of Syrian refugee children are increasingly at risk of being forced into child marriages, child labour and exploitation. [236]

---

[236] (Rojin's Story: We Lost Everything | A Young Syrian Refugee Films Her Life 2017)

Akoi's Story...

"My name is not refugee, my name is Akoi Massayan Bazzie"

When Akoi Massayan Bazzie was just 14, the Liberian Civil war tore through his nation. During the bloodiest civil war in Africa at the time, hundreds of thousands were raped and murdered, and Akoi was separated from his family and lived alone on the streets for two years. Additionally, he had to avoid being captured by rebels who would undoubtedly turn him into a child soldier while he was an adolescent in a ferocious war zone.

Akoi began wandering his country's border with Guinea in an attempt to escape the conflict after realizing he could not survive in these conditions. He gained asylum in Guinea, along with approximately 45,000 other refugees in 1991 after months of trekking through treacherous jungle terrain. This was an emotional time for him. While he struggled with the pain of not knowing when he would see his loved ones again, he also felt relief that he was still alive.

UNHCR identified Akoi as being at serious risk and that it would not be safe for him to return to Liberia, so he spent the next 12 years of his life in a refugee camp in Guinea. It was in Guinea where Akoi felt a loss of identity and simply became known as "refugee" like the thousands of his compatriots also living in the camp.

In 2004, Akoi travelled on a plane for the first time in his life to the UK as part of the original group of resettled refugees from Guinea. Despite arriving to the UK with no English language skills, his determination to build a promising future for himself prevailed. Akoi went on to achieve a first-class degree in community policy and practice from The University of Sheffield and won an award in 2009 from the Institute of Lifelong Learning in the process. His academic success did not stop there as he completed postgraduate studies at Universities in Manchester and London.

Akoi now works across the world helping those in forced migration and refugee protection. His main goals are to promote refugee cohesion and employment whilst also giving back to the society that welcomed him. His dedication to his cause is shown continually through his work since his arrival to the UK.

Akoi is a firm believer that if given the correct tools, access and opportunities, refugees have the power to succeed.

In the words of the man himself, *"My refugee story is my strength. Death made us refugees, but you can help us to be useful members of society - together we can do it".*[237]

Ahmed's Story...

The following are the four principles by which Ahmed Sinno lives his life:

- 'I never expect anything from anyone'
- 'I never retreat'
- 'I never surrender'
- 'I never give up'

Ahmed has used these four principles to overcome the incredible hardships he has faced throughout his life. Born in Beirut, Ahmed

---

[237] (My Name Is Not 'Refugee' | Akoi Bazzie Shares Shocking Experience | TEDx style SonaTalks 2019)

lost both his parents by the time he was sixteen. At the age of 24, he served as a paramedic for the Lebanese Red Cross. During an internal conflict which broke out in Lebanon between the Sunni and Shia Muslims, Ahmed was shot twice by a member of the Shia opposition. This left him paralysed.

Eight years later, Ahmed was targeted by the same people and was unfortunately, shot again. Ahmed knew that he could no longer remain in Lebanon and had no choice but to leave his loved ones behind. He left his family, friends and fiancé and fled Lebanon to seek asylum in the UK.

Despite his isolation and injuries, Ahmed persevered and managed to establish a new life in the UK. He began playing wheelchair basketball for the British League where he met new friends. He also joined the British Red Cross where he taught IT skills to the homeless and is now a volunteer and representative, and also an emergency paramedic with the British Red Cross.

Ahmed's most rewarding occupation, however, is being a part of 'Migrateful', an organisation that empowers and encourages asylum seekers and refugees to spread their knowledge and teach others how to cook dishes from their country to members of the public. Ahmed felt that Migrateful was the place he felt truly at home, with people who supported him like his own family.

Things took a turn in 2019 when Ahmed's claim to be granted refugee status was refused. Ahmed was facing homelessness. Thankfully, he received a phone call from a member of the Migrateful organisation who told him that "*no family member of Migrateful will ever be homeless*". With the help of Migrateful and the British Red Cross, Ahmed was able to appeal the decision and he is no longer facing that hardship.

Ahmed's advice to everyone? *"Never give up, there's always a way".*[238]

Ake's Story...

As a child labourer in the Ivory Coast, Ake Achi grew up working on cocoa plantations instead of attending school. In a state where children are not provided with the institutions they need for education, this is how his people lived and survived.

The Ivory Coast's unrest and political massacres deprived Ake and his family of their basic human rights, and by age 10, Achi and his sister left the country, seeking refuge in France.

Ake and his sister settled at a refugee campsite alongside a highway, where tents and small shelters were set by fellow refugees and asylum seekers. He struggled to find a sense of belonging while living as a refugee in a tent. Unfortunately, he encountered the social stereotypes and racism that many people experience.

For example, Achi's job interviews did not consist of typical interview questions regarding his skills and experience. Employers would ask him about his right to work in the country, whilst the white refugees did not get asked about their right to work.

Despite the discrimination Ake faced, he completed his undergraduate and postgraduate degree to become a lawyer and is on the way to completing his PhD. With his knowledge, he is striving to make a difference. He aims to raise awareness of the refugee crisis and protect migrants, refugees and asylum seekers.

[238] (As a Lebanese refugee, cooking has become my lifeline and my community 2020)

Ake will not allow the current system to determine the lives of future generations as he fights to abolish discrimination. Despite Ake's painful realization that *"you will only be given importance if you are born in this country"*, he still believes he can bring about change.[239]

Gulwali's Story...

Being the son of a doctor and a midwife, Gulwali Passarlay enjoyed a happy childhood in eastern Afghanistan. As a result of the invasion of American forces in his native country, his life was soon changed forever.

When Gulwali was just 10 years old, several of his family members were killed by American army soldiers who thought they were hiding weapons from them. The situation in Afghanistan continued to worsen over the next couple of years, and by the age of 12, Gulwali and his brother were receiving demands from the Taliban and their government. The Taliban wanted them to fight for their cause, but the government wanted them to become informants.

To keep her sons safe, Gulwali's mother paid smugglers thousands of dollars to bring them to Europe where they could start a new, more secure life. During their journey, the brothers felt isolated and more afraid after they were separated by the traffickers early on.

---

[239] (Modern Slavery | Exposing Systemic Racism in the UK | Ake Achi | TEDx style SonaTalks 2019)

He arrived in the UK over a year after leaving his home and was reunited with his brother and uncle who were already in the UK. But it wasn't all plain sailing from here. At first, officials did not believe he was 13 years old, rather they assumed he was at least 16 years old. It took Gulwali two years to prove to the UK government that he was a young boy in order to receive the support he was entitled to.

As a result of Gulwali's experience, he believes wars contribute greatly to refugee crises and must be recognized as such. His life would have been very different had the invasion of Afghanistan not occurred, and he would still be living in his country of birth today.

Gulwali, who has now lived in the UK for over a decade, still believes that *"Europe partly created this crisis, so its politicians can't just shut borders, build barbed wire fences and sit on their hands while people die."*[240]

Nour's Story...

Nour Mouakke moved to the UK in 2009 and studied marketing at Durham University. He then began working in Newcastle's suburbs. While aspiring to land his dream job in London, he worked as a door-to-door salesman and then a kitchen porter.

He eventually struck gold and gained a position as global account manager at Intercontinental Hotels Group. He devised an innovative method to save companies thousands of pounds during his two-year probationary period. The concept focused on

---

[240] (Story of Resilience, Courage & Determination | Refugee | Gulwali Passarlay | TEDx style SonaTalks 2019)

automated meeting and event scheduling, transforming the manual process into an automated one. One problem with this idea was that he was not able to establish a start-up company on a two-year visa.

Nonetheless, Nour continued to work hard and was able to secure a permanent role and sponsorship from Intercontinental Hotels Group. Although he had achieved this, his gap-in-the-market idea still persisted in his dreams. Nour eventually gave up everything he had achieved to pursue his dream.

During this time, war had broken out in Syria and Nour was granted refugee status in the UK although he was unable to see or contact his father and four younger siblings. Nour was completely alone.

He decided to move to Bulgaria to work on his start-up company which he named 'Wizme'. He invested every penny he had to start the company, but it didn't succeed like he had hoped. Nour's failed business resulted in his homelessness in 2017. He had no family to lean on during this difficult time.

However, this did not stop Nour from striving towards success. Fortunately, he was given the opportunity to head to France and present his business idea to 120 business owners. With less than two months to prepare for this opportunity, even Nour's closest friends doubted him. He brushed their concerns aside and told them "I will manage". A week before the event, he was able to create a prototype and on the day of the event, Nour successfully pitched his idea to a number of business owners who were willing to invest in his company.

As of 2019, Nour's company 'Wizme', had hired 11 engineers (8 of whom still live in Syria). Nour's team in Syria give him a more rewarding, fulfilling sense of accomplishment. He did not just fill a gap in the market when creating his company, he was able to provide opportunities for the less fortunate and allow them to develop advanced skills in software engineering which will ultimately lead to a better life.[241]

Imad's Story...

"Don't ask me where I'm from; but ask me what I can do"

Imad Alarnab opened his first restaurant in Damascus in 2000, then steadily built up a small empire consisting of three restaurants, cafés, and juice bars. It took just six days however, at the height of the Syrian war, for them all to be destroyed. As the city grew increasingly war-torn and dangerous, Imad's empire crumbled. To find a better life for his family, he fled Damascus, and made his way to the UK in 2015.

Having arrived safely in the UK, Imad got to London, where he was granted asylum, and he was able to bring his family over to join him. At first, he worked as a car salesman, although at heart he was a chef who dreamt of running his own restaurant again.

However, he was not given the opportunity to prove himself in any of the restaurants he applied to. In no time, Imad was running successful pop-up restaurants in London, which sold out every night and received rave reviews. He was then asked to create collaborative menus by many people who had not given him a chance before.

---

[241] (Success is an Attitude | Wizme CEO | Nour Mouakke | Refugee | TEDx style SonaTalks 2019)

A recent campaign by Alarnab raised thousands of pounds for the charity 'Choose Love', which works with refugees.

He then continued to raise money on Crowdfunder to fund his restaurant. In London's bustling Kingly Court on Carnaby Street in London, he opened his first UK restaurant called 'Imad's Syrian Restaurant' after raising £50,000.[242]

---

[242] (Life as a Refugee trying to find Opportunities | Imad Alarnab | SonaTalks | Inspiring Story 2021)

8

WILL IT BENEFIT US ECONOMICALLY?

Reader: The thing is though...

Author: Argh! Get out of my bed!

Reader: But I've got a question about refugees?

Author: Can't I answer your questions in the morning?!

Reader: No, it has to be now.

Author: Ok, fine!

Reader: Good. So, I understand that refugees are suffering and it's partly our fault. But my worry is that won't it be really costly if we let loads of refugees and migrants come into our countries? How can we afford it? Won't I suffer economically if we do?

Author: Quite the opposite. Supporting refugees and migrants into the country will benefit everyone economically. At least, if it's done well...

Refugees are a burden on local and national economies, right?

Wrong...very wrong!

Before we delve into the vast economic benefits that refugees have brought and continue to bring to the Western world, let's debunk some of the false claims that bounce around certain social spheres.

You may have heard people claim that refugees are a strain on local resources; overwhelm health facilities and schools; reduce the availability of land; and place a burden on social and administrative services. Some also strongly believe that refugees take jobs from nationals and drive up the cost of housing, goods and other services.[243]

In reality, the economic benefits that refugees can offer, especially in the long term, heavily outweigh any form of negative impact that may possibly be generated. When arriving in new countries, migrants are often constricted and cannot work whilst waiting for the outcome of their asylum claim. The support they receive is wholly inadequate - a measly £5.66 to live off per person per day.[244]

If we take a look at Canada, refugees report higher rates of employment, higher incomes and pay more taxes compared to other immigrant groups.[245] This just goes to show, if given access to land, the labour market, and freedom of movement, refugees can have a positive economic impact by creating jobs, services and facilities, or equally, by contributing to agricultural production and the local economy.[246]

The West should take note of policies that have been applied in Uganda. The country allows refugees to "self-settle", meaning they do not have to remain in camps and can choose where they live. This enables refugees to be more independent and self-reliant and therefore do not have to rely on aid, thus making them more able to contribute to the communities they operate within.

---

[243] (S. D. Miller 2018)
[244] (Facts about refugees 2021)
[245] (Miller, 2018)
[246] (Miller, 2018)

In America, once refugees have joined the workforce, they often create new jobs and, as a result, have increased the median average of incomes over long periods of time. One study found that within the
first 25 years, their median income tripled to $67,000, which is $14,000 higher than the national average.[247]

More substantial incomes ultimately mean there is more money to go into taxes and businesses which in turn positively impacts the economy as a whole. On top of the economic benefits created as a result, the increase in refugee income also gives refugees a sense of purpose and financial independence. By improving their own lives, refugees can create economic benefits that also improve the lives of residents of their new country.

Research surrounding resettled refugees also shows positive contributions to local economies. Further data about refugees in the United States highlights that despite an initial cost in assistance for refugees resettling in the nation, over the years, refugees are a net gain to the economy. For example, in Ohio refugees have been an asset to the local and regional area over the years; refugees tended to find employment within five months of their arrival and were able to work their way out of requiring government assistance within the first few years of arrival. The total economic impact of refugees in the area was $48 million created and 650 jobs occupied in 2012. Moreover, refugees were situated above average in socio-economic integration compared to national norms.[248]

For those across the pond and in Europe who are afraid that the continued influx of refugees may become economically unstable, if a similar effect occurs as in the countries neighbouring Syria, this will be far from the case.

---

[247] (Are Refugees Good or Bad for the Economy? 2020)
[248] (Miller, 2018)

A study from the World Bank showed that, as of 2015, Syrian refugees in Turkey had increased the country's average wages by creating formal jobs outside the agriculture sector. Around this time, the Lebanese economy also grew beyond expectations over the previous two years, with the World Bank estimating a 2.5% growth in 2015 alone, which was the country's highest growth rate since 2010.[249] Also, there is evidence to suggest that the situation in Europe is in fact a strong one. For example, a 2016 Tent Foundation report found that in the European Union, each euro invested in refugee support programmes produced two euros of return in economic benefits over time. As refugees are given the opportunity to become entrepreneurs, innovators, taxpayers, consumers and investors, they create jobs, raise productivity and wages of local workers, lift capital returns, stimulate international trade and investment, and boost innovation, enterprise and growth.[250]/[251]

Research into the economic impact of refugees in Europe between 1985 and 2015 showed that in just two years of an increased inflow of refugees, the economy in the 15 countries studied became healthier and unemployment decreased.[252] Refugees generated demand for goods, created jobs and paid taxes. They were thus able to offset the cost of the government support they needed on arrival and contribute towards a net gain and overall economic growth.

During periods of tightened immigration policy in much of the Western world, it is worth considering the words of Michael Clemens, an economist at the Centre for Global Development: *"If*

---

[249] (How Refugees can benefit the economy 2015)

[250] (Are Refugees Good or Bad for the Economy? 2020)

[251] (Miller, 2018)

[252] (Migrants and refugees are good for economies 2018)

you slash immigration for cultural or security reasons, you will pay an economic price".[253]

All the cases for economic growth mentioned above have yet to touch on the subject of demographic ageing which, of course, is a huge drain on resources.

This issue has been investigated by many countries and various methods have been proposed worldwide to encourage higher birth-rates and lessen the impact of an ageing population. For example, if you are pregnant or have a young baby in Sweden, you are entitled to fewer weekly working hours and an increase in paid parental leave.[254] And in Russia, parents have the chance to win money and prizes in return for having children.[255]

In South Korea also, the Government is incentivising people to have children by awarding them with grants.[256] Even the smallest nations are trying; Singapore rebranded their national holiday to 'National Night' in an advert in collaboration with Mentos Mints in which (through the form of a tongue-in-cheek rap) citizens are encouraged to show their patriotism for their country through reproducing.[257]

It appears governments will go to great lengths to avoid having decreasing populations and with the average rates of over 65s in most countries increasing, meaning fewer workers, it seems a valid

---

[253] (Migrants and refugees are good for economies 2018)
[254] (Sweden's support for parents with children is comprehensive and effective but expensive 2020)
[255] (Russians given day off to make babies 2007)
[256] (Why the South Korean Government Is Paying Families To Have More Babies 2017)
[257] (Singapore uses rap to try to boost birthrate 2012)

stance to take. Therefore, it seems clear that it's the time to nurture a young economic workforce.

Many countries today are experiencing an ageing population, where the number of people over 65 is increasing faster than any other age group in the population. As of 2021, Japan, Italy and Portugal had the most aged populations, but the UK is not far behind. In the UK, over 12 million people are over the age of 65 and with improvements in medical care and life expectancy, this is only projected to increase. In fact, according to the UN World Population Prospects, by 2050 one in four people living in Europe and Northern America will be aged 65 or over.[258]

So why is an ageing population such a problem?

In the UK, 55% of welfare spending is paid to pensions and spending on this age bracket is expected to increase by £32.8 billion every year. With a larger proportion of the population being of retirement age, this means that there are fewer workers who can support government spending on pensioners. In short, the Government is increasingly spending more on the older population whilst receiving less tax revenue from younger people of working age.[259]

What has all this got to do with refugees, I hear you ask?

In general, the refugee population is much younger and therefore still of working age. 73% of asylum seekers are between the ages of 18 and 65, with the majority being in the lower end of that age bracket. In fact, just 0.6% of the refugee population is over 65 years of age. For this reason, encouraging the employment of refugees could solve two problems at once. Society could integrate

[258] (Could refugees help solve the problem of ageing populations? 2020)
[259] (Challenges of an ageing population 2021)

and support refugees to rebuild their lives in their host country whilst relieving some of the stress inflicted by the ageing population.

In addition, the UK could gain access to the diverse set of skills that refugees offer. For example, a study by Deloitte found that 38% of refugees held a university degree and according to the Nuffield Foundation, nearly half of all refugees coming to the UK held some type of qualification. Furthermore, refugees bring a diversity of thought, innovation and a variety of skills that they can contribute to workplaces in their host country.[260]

Lebanon currently has 1.39 million refugees that have been granted asylum, putting it 3rd on the world list. The countries that take the top two spots are Turkey and Jordan and, based on the fact that Turkey is 78.3 times larger than Lebanon, and Jordan 9 times larger, it could be argued that Lebanon should be ranked 1st. The population is relatively small, meaning 1 in 4 people in the country are refugees. This is a massive statistic and coupled with the knowledge that 73% of refugees seeking asylum are aged between 18-65, there is potential for positive change.[261]

There are a number of different refugee communities that have settled in Lebanon over the last 60 years, including Palestinians, Kurds, Syrians and others in the Levant region. This influx of different communities has led to segregation throughout the country which may be a factor as to why refugees are still being overlooked.[262]

---

[260] (Could refugees help solve the problem of ageing populations? 2020)
[261] (Palestinian Employment in Lebanon - Facts and Challenges 2012)
[262] Ibid

The CEP (Committee for Employment of Palestinian Refugees in Lebanon) conducted a study in 2012 detailing the work and education of Palestinian refugees. Some highlights of this study showed that the Palestinian labour force shared similar characteristics with the Lebanese in terms of activity rate, sector and employment status. Palestinian unemployment rates are almost equal to that of the Lebanese.

Where the situation differs is in salary, healthcare, paid sick leave and pension; namely, that Palestinians receive less money and poorer care compared to Lebanese nationals. This indicates that the Palestinians are certainly willing and ready to work but are still being discriminated against due to their heritage. This community also has a much lower percentage of high school graduates compared to the Lebanese, perhaps due to the need to work from a younger age to support the rest of their families.[263]

An intriguing statement in the CEP study reads: *"The Palestinian workforce is poorly educated, young and lacking in skills."* As stated earlier, the majority of refugees seeking asylum are young and eager to work. There is a clear opportunity to profit as a nation by utilising this group of underdeveloped youth. By providing adequate education and pushing for not only Lebanese but also refugees and descendants of refugees to learn skills and trades, the country's economic future could benefit greatly.[264]

Another community of people, the Syrian refugees and settlers, have also been excluded from pursuing their potential in Lebanon. The Lebanese Labour Law, introduced in 2014, after the influx of Syrian refugees, restricts Syrians from working in sectors outside of agriculture, construction and cleaning services. This came as a shock to the many Syrians who were qualified

---

[263] Ibid
[264] (Palestinian Employment in Lebanon - Facts and Challenges 2012)

doctors, nurses and other healthcare professionals. The Lebanese Government may have overlooked this community at the time, but as of 2020, with COVID-19 ravaging the country and the already dwindling healthcare workforce only continuing to shrink, they may be forced to amend this outdated law. Thus, it may be time for Lebanon to finally utilise a qualified workforce that is already within its borders, hopefully leading to a reduction in refugee segregation and poverty. If the law is changed and the country does see significant improvements, the next step could lead to the full integration of these communities.[265]

Lebanon originally allowed those crossing the border to remain unregistered, meaning there were no legal obligations to pay fair wages or provide humane care for these people. They now have a system in place to register refugees, which is a step in the right direction. This allows for significant data to be collected to aid things such as educational budgets, healthcare workforce numbers, pensions and more.[266]

Although 2020 was a difficult year for the whole world, Lebanon had the opportunity to revolutionise how other countries view refugees and show the beneficial impact which they can have on society if given an equal opportunity.

So, back to the question in hand, could refugees really make a difference to demographic ageing?

Realistically, the number of refugees arriving in Europe would be too small to make a dramatic difference on the issues caused by the ageing population across the nation. At the height of the refugee crisis in 2015, the number of people arriving in Europe made up just 0.1% of the EU population and therefore could not

---

[265] Ibid
[266] Ibid

single-handedly solve this problem. However, it is typically in rural areas where the most aged reside and it is believed that these smaller towns could benefit the most from the youth of the refugee population.[267]

Whilst it is unlikely that welcoming refugees could solve the problem of aged populations, they could become a part of the solution if they are recognised as an economic asset.

Refugees have, however, had a great history of creating thriving businesses and bringing innovative ideas into society that have benefited the economy and created jobs. Refugees are often highly skilled and experienced and due to their experiences have often developed enormous resilience and adaptability so are able to fill many gaps in the markets.

The rhetoric that refugees are a burden on the economy and take jobs from hard working nationals could not be further from the truth. Refugees bring a wealth of experience or entrepreneurial spirit which can bring employment opportunities to the hosting country.[268]

In Uganda for example, 21 percent of refugees own a business that employs more than one person – 40 percent of whom are Ugandan nationals.[269]

Furthermore, in Australia, although people from the UK and India – most of whom arrived on Visas – contributed the largest share of $38bn earned by migrants from data collected in 2009-

---

[267] Ibid

[268] (5 Key Benefits to Hiring Refugees 2020)

[269] (How refugees can actually create jobs for locals in growing cities 2018)

2010, it was migrants who arrived as refugees who reported the highest proportions of their incomes that year "from their own unincorporated businesses". Nearly 10% of humanitarian migrant incomes in 2009-2010 were generated by their own businesses, almost twice the figure recorded in other categories, such as skilled and family migrants.[270]

The ideas and businesses that refugees bring could result in nearly $1bn a year added to the Australian economy within ten years, according to a report by the Centre for Policy Development (CDP) in which it states that, "an increase in refugee businesses results in jobs for both refugees and locals as well as increased local and international trade".[271]

In the United States, refugee entrepreneurship rate outshines those of other groups. The United States was home to more than 180,000 refugee entrepreneurs in 2015 – meaning that 13% of refugees were entrepreneurs, compared to just 11.5 percent of non-refugee immigrants and 9.0% of the US-born population. The businesses of refugees also generated $4.6bn in business income that year.[272]

Haroon Mokhtarzada arrived in the US when he was just 3 years old after his parents fled the Russian invasion of Afghanistan. In the rise of the dotcom era, Haroon and his brothers Zeki and Idris started Webs, the first major company that allowed users to easily design their own websites using templates. The company grew and by 2006, Webs had raised $12 million dollars in venture capital funding and by 2011, the company was bought by Vistaprint for

---

[270] (Refugees are Australia's most entrepreneurial migrants 2015)
[271] (Refugees are the most entrepreneurial migrants in Australia 2019)
[272] (Refugees in the U.S. Had More Than $56 Billion in Spending Power in 2015 2017)

$117m – by then Webs had roughly 60 employees and produced roughly 50 million websites.[273]

In Britain, many refugees have come and thrived in their own right. Indeed, there may even be some entrepreneurs that you may not have known were refugees who have created ideas and businesses that many Brits use today.

Laxmishanker Pathak, a refugee from Kenya who created Pataks, a range of curry pastes and spices which is used in households across the UK. Pataks now supplies to 90% of Britain's 10,000 Indian restaurants.[274]

Montague Burton, a Jewish Lithuanian who came to Britain in 1900 and founded one of Britain's biggest clothing store chains, Burton. The retailer had over 400 stores in the UK.[275]

Sieng Van Tran fled his home country Vietnam and spent two years in a Singapore refugee camp before arriving in London in 1981. Whilst studying at Middlesex University, Tran came up with iLearn.To, the first profitable UK internet learning company in 1999. iLearn.To delivered over 500 online courses.[276]

Sukhpal Singh Ahluwalia fled the brutal regime of Ugandan President Idi Amin with his family at just 13, and came to London. He founded Euro Car Parts which he sold for £225m in 2011.[277]

Razan Alsous founded Yorkshire Dama Cheese, a multi-award-winning cheese and dairy company which she set up after she left

---

[273] (Afghan Entrepreneur is Behind one of Maryland's Most Successful Technology Startups 2017)
[274] (5 refugee entrepreneurs who have thrived in Britain 2014)
[275] (5 refugee entrepreneurs who have thrived in Britain 2014)
[276] Ibid
[277] Ibid

everything behind and fled Syria with her husband and 3 children in 2012. Razan had a pharmacy degree and despite searching for jobs, the lack of references and work history in the UK made it difficult for her to find one.

Raza used her business acumen by taking advantage of her surroundings. High quality milk from Yorkshire, a £2,500 loan from the Local Enterprise Agency and her experience in microbiology, Raza started manufacturing cheese in 2014 and the business has been a success ever since. After four months of production, the company won a Bronze Award in the World Cheese Award and has continued to grow. Raza opened the company's factory in 2017 which was attended by Princess Anne.[278]

It is clear that refugees enhance the economy through innovative and entrepreneurial measures. Whether refugees think that they are on their own and have to start something themselves in order to make it, or whether they bring their values and ideas from their home countries, they have shown on all continents that they add value to their host countries by adding new ideas, creating jobs and stimulating the economy.

But, but, but.

Yeah, I can tell you're not entirely convinced that refugees and migrants are good for your financial situation, are you? Let me guess why.

---

[278] (Refugee Action 2021)

Do you, by any chance, happen to think that migrants and refugees are stealing your jobs and making you unemployed?

Or maybe you think refugees are the reason your wages are so low?

You might even think that they're the reason house prices and rents are so high?

Is that what you're thinking? How original!

To be fair to you, it makes sense why you'd believe this.

Many major newspapers across Europe and the US have repeated this line over and over again and figures in almost all the West's major political parties - on left and right - have supported this idea.

You're hardly alone in this view.

However, this argument is incredibly misleading and damaging. It must be debunked.

For those of you who aren't aware why refugees and migrants are being blamed for these things, let me explain.

The argument goes like this:

Refugees and migrants come into Western countries from much poorer countries with little or no knowledge of the language or the workers in the local area. Because they are from poorer countries, they are used to much lower wages and worse working conditions than is the norm in the West. On top of this, Western currencies are much stronger than those in their homelands and therefore even if they are paid a relatively low wage in the West, when they send that money back to relatives in their homelands, it will still be able to buy much more than an average wage in the local economy when converted to local currency. As such, refugees are willing to take on jobs for far less pay and in worse conditions than the local population.

This means that local workers are undercut by refugee and migrant labour as employers are free to keep wages low and worsen working conditions through unsafe workplaces or unsecure zero hours contracts because refugees and migrants will often always be willing to take on these jobs. This forces the local population to have to accept lower pay and worse working conditions if they want to have a job.

On top of this, the argument is that refugees and migrants are also very disconnected from the local workforce because of lack of local language knowledge. Therefore, in an attempt to improve pay and working conditions, it is often difficult to get them to unionise with local workers. They are similarly blamed for increasing demand for core necessities such as housing and healthcare, thereby driving up prices and availability for existing citizens.

The result? People who make this argument demand we close our borders and keep refugees and migrants 'out' to protect local workers. They have been incredibly successful in convincing people (like yourself) that refugees and migrants are to blame for high house prices and low wages.

Now, we shouldn't dismiss this argument out of hand. What has made this such a compelling and persuasive case for so many people is that it does have an element of truth to it.

Employees across the West *do* employ migrant and refugee labour because they can pay them lower wages and keep them working in unsafe conditions on insecure contracts. For example, in the waste management sector in the UK cheaper migrant labour from Eastern Europe is disproportionately utilised over local labour because it helps businesses cut wage costs and force people into zero hours contracts. This enables employers to increase their profits as well as making it easier for them to fire workers who resist. They also force their workers into very dangerous conditions which have led to many injuries and even the deaths of some workers like Rafial Swiadek and Zbigneiw Galka.[279]

Moreover, wages have stagnated or declined for much of the Western population over the last 40 years in real (purchasing power parity) terms.[280] More are unemployed and live on very minimal unemployment support. Equally, inequality has grown massively with workers gaining a smaller and smaller share of the national income relative to the top 1%.[281]

Likewise, house prices and rents have hugely increased in real terms for everyone in the last 30 years, particularly in urban centres. This has forced many into homelessness or into poverty as they spend most of their wages on mortgage or rent costs.[282] Crucially, this increase *has* occurred roughly during the time when

---

[279] (Does migration undermine workers' rights? 2017)

[280] (What Is Purchasing Power Parity (PPP)? 2021)

[281] (Shaikh 2018)

[282] (Real UK House Prices since 1975 2021)

refugees and migrants have come into Western countries in larger numbers.[283]

However, hidden within this truth is a dangerous and damaging lie.

What is this lie? Simple, it's who we are told to blame.

We are told not to blame the wealthy employers who exploit the desperation and insecurity of refugee and migrant labour to drive down wages, job stability and working conditions in order to maximise their already lucrative profits. That would be ridiculous!

Neither are we invited to point our fingers at the politicians across the West who allow employers to get away with these practices. Those same politicians who sold off public housing, cut public services and income support and who prevent unions from fighting back with aggressive anti-union laws. Obviously, because it has nothing to do with it!

Nor are we instructed to accuse the financiers whose reckless greed and malpractice caused the 2008 financial crash whose effects were still being felt over 10 years on.

No. Instead we are told in no uncertain terms that it is refugees and migrants who are to blame for your suffering. Yes, that's right. It's those people from across the poorest regions of the earth, who have experienced extreme suffering and hardship travelling long distances in horrible conditions in a desperate attempt to escape violence, climate disaster, poverty and persecution to achieve a better life for themselves and their families. They are to blame for your suffering. Those refugees and migrants, who even in the

---

[283] (Migration and Immigrants in Europe: A Historical and Demographic Perspective 2021)

West work for pittance, without job security and often at risk of death or injury.

That makes sense!

Keep them out!

The inaccuracy and callousness of such an argument should be obvious.

It is largely because of the acts of politicians, employers and financial services companies that the average worker's real terms wages have stagnated since the 1980s. Governments across the West have, since the 1980s, weakened unions' abilities to strike and organise, thereby preventing them from acting to force employers to raise their wages.

For example, they have in the UK, Australia, US and other countries outlawed the right of unions to engage in 'solidarity strikes' or 'secondary action' as it is known in legal terminology. This is where unions strike collectively to support each other's demands (rather than only striking when their specific workplace is affected by the issue in question) to add greater pressure to the government and capitalists to concede to the demands.[284] They have also forced unions to give a long notice before they strike, which limits their ability to put pressure on their bosses or the economy to help them achieve their demands.[285]

Alongside this, the shifting of the nature of the economy from concentrated industrial labour to scattered modern service labour has acted to increase the difficulty with which workers can unionise. Both trends have helped decrease union membership

---

[284] (What is secondary (or sympathy) industrial action and is it unlawful? 2021)
[285] (How to Go on Strike & Give Notice of Industrial Action 2021)

across the West and limited workers' ability to demand their wages increase or even keep pace with inflation.[286]

Western governments simultaneously removed regulations on investment bankers and encouraged them to freely engage in speculative and rash investments. This greedy and high-risk behaviour caused multiple financial crises, such as the 2008 crash, which impoverished workers across the world, driving down their wages.[287]

Finally, governments also enable Western companies to keep wages low in the West and subcontract production of goods to India, China and Bangladesh, where workers can easily be paid less. Simply, this has reduced the relative wages and job opportunities for Western workers.[288]

Likewise, the price of homes and rents have increased largely because of government and elite action. Western governments have sold off public housing, allowed private landlords to hoard them, allowed financial speculators to buy up housing as assets without using them. This is not so much a case of there being a lack of supply of housing per se.

In San Francisco for example, a city with a huge homeless population, there are far more empty homes than there are unhoused people wanting housing. Likewise in the UK, there are 5 times more empty homes than unhoused households. Rather, the issue is that governments have allowed housing to be built by financial speculators without requiring them to make them affordable or to sell them to people who will actually live in them.

---

[286] (Panitch, The Making of Global Capitalism: The Political Economy of American Empire 2013)

[287] Ibid

[288] (Milanovic, Global Inequality: A New Approach for the Age of Globalization 2016)

Why would people buy houses if they didn't want to use them? Because owning housing is in and of itself a source of wealth. Housing prices are constantly rising and so owning housing delivers a good return on the capital invested. As such, very wealthy individuals or investment groups buy up properties solely as assets rather than to use them.

By hoarding homes - a commodity that basically everyone wants - without actually using them the supply of housing is reduced and prices increase further, providing money to the buyer. This speculation and the refusal of governments to build public housing outside of the market has massively reduced the supply of affordable housing for the poor, forcing many to either get into crippling debt to buy, to pay massive amounts of salary on rent or to simply become homeless waiting years to gain access to the small supply of council housing.[289]

The number of unemployed people and workers on insecure zero-hours contracts has massively increased because governments across the West have refused to outlaw these terms and have refused to empower unions.[290]

On top of this, the declining rate of economic growth in the West has led to many businesses cutting staff. In response, Western governments have not attempted to address this with public spending and taking businesses into public ownership but have instead further aggravated the issue with spending cuts and public sector redundancies.[291]

Put simply, migrants and refugees aren't to blame for the poor conditions of Western workers, it's the fault of politicians and the super-rich. No wonder politicians and wealthy newspaper

---

[289] (Bano, The Solution to the Housing Crisis: More Council Houses 2021)

[290] (Benanav, Automation and the future of work 2020)

[291] Ibid

magnates are keen to deflect the blame for their own mistakes and greed onto the most vulnerable communities.

As Russell Brand memorably remarked when Nigel Farage blamed migrants for the poverty in which many British workers live, "Nigel Farage's mates in the city farted, and he's pointing at immigrants – and holding his nose".[292]

We shouldn't be blaming some of the most exploited and abused communities on earth for having the temerity to attempt to improve their situation. We shouldn't be trying to bar their entry. It's not refugees' or migrants' fault that employers are able or willing to cut costs by driving down wages and working conditions.

It certainly also isn't migrants' or refugees' fault that government policies and the acts of economic elites have led to rising house prices, homelessness, the stagnation of worker's wages, reduced public services and rampant inequality. Instead, we should be looking at those groups that have actually caused this situation - politicians, bankers and exploitative companies.

We should be seeking to remedy these economic problems and improve the conditions of all workers - both locals and refugees and migrants - by forcing them to change the law and improve their practices.

Refugees and migrants should be given the legal right to work immediately and ensure that they have the same employee rights as local workers. This will ensure that they can't be so easily forced into horrible working conditions and prevented from unionising to improve those dreadful working conditions.

---

[292] (Russell Brand & Nigel Farage clash over immigration 2014)

Zero hours and unstable job contracts should be ended so that refugees, migrants and local workers are always guaranteed stable, secure employment rather than vulnerable, exploitative contracts.

Anti-union laws brought in across Europe since the 1980s that make it hard for workers to organise and strike to improve their working conditions should be removed. This will help refugees, and local workers empower themselves by enabling them to strike easily if employers don't pay them adequately or try to force them into dangerous working conditions.

Regulations should be placed on banking, finance and Western companies, preventing them from freely shifting manufacturing production and capital to countries like China, Bangladesh and India where labour is cheaper.

Government should invest more heavily in businesses, infrastructure and renewable energy and take companies into public ownership to help grow the economy and create secure jobs.

Finally, the Government could increase funding for public services, like the NHS, and increase affordable housing. This will help to improve healthcare for the population and reduce the price of homes and rents to ensure that those who struggle to afford current prices are guaranteed housing.

Crucially, the housing crisis cannot be solved simply by building more houses for the market as this would enable the same speculators to simply buy up the housing as assets so that it becomes inaccessible to the poor as well as preventing prices from ever being lowered.

Instead, public owned housing should be built so that their cost is insulated from market price inflation and they remain cheap and affordable for those who need them.[293]

By doing all this we can create an economy that is beneficial to migrants, refugees and local workers alike. One that doesn't pit local workers and migrants against each other and drive down wages and worker conditions but instead helps provide economic security for all.

---

[293] (Bano, The Solution to the Housing Crisis: More Council Houses 2021)

9

WHO HAS CULTURE?

Author: Are you proud of your culture?
Reader: Why wouldn't I be?
Author: Do you know where it comes from?
Reader: My ancestors, right?
Author: Errr, sort of. But many elements of 'your' culture actually come from immigrants and refugees.

When we talk about culture, we often look for things in our family heritage or something that we feel defines us. But culture is something that is ever-evolving and will continue to adapt to the changing demographics in each country. Europe and large parts of the Western world are a melting pot of different cultures and customs. Throughout history, people have been travelling between countries, spreading their way of life and the history of their ancestral land and traditions.

Whether this be through food, fashion or art, it all adds up to create a unique splash of unification. This unification comes through a shared patriotism with the country one resides in, and it does not discriminate based on race, sexual orientation or religious beliefs.

So now that we know that culture spreads by those who travel the globe, let's look at how refugees and immigrants of the last 100 years have influenced and evolved cultures. A group that has been known to emigrate, through both voluntary and involuntary means is the European Jewish population. The Jewish communities of Eastern Europe suffered a terrible fate at the hands of the Nazis during WWI and were in turn forced to seek refuge in other parts of Europe and the Americas.

Around 50,000 Eastern European Jewish immigrants fled to the UK and joined over 200,000 other Jewish refugees who had fled Germany, Austria, and Russia from 1880 - 1919. The Jewish communities in the UK began to assimilate their culture into the wider English culture around them, divulging into the textile, real estate, and food industries.[294]

When it comes to food, fish and potatoes are a common combination for many countries in Europe and further West, but no such combination embodies a culture quite like battered fish and chips does. The UK is synonymous with fried fish and chips and has a fanbase that spreads from Charles Dickens (who mentioned 'fried fish warehouses' in *Oliver Twist* 1838) to Queen Elizabeth II. It is also the only meal that was not rationed during both WWI and WWII; which shows just how much it means to the British people.[295]

What may come as a shock, is that it was created by Jewish immigrants who journeyed to England in the 16th century. The idea of fried fish had existed in places like Portugal, Spain and Holland prior to its sightings in England, and was frequently sold on the streets by Portuguese Sephardic Jews.

It wasn't until nearly 200 years later, that the perfect counterpart was found: chips. The dish is a cornerstone of British culture in

---

[294] (Events of 1901 2021)
[295] (Fish and chips, the quintessentially British dish 2021)

the same way that the Monarchy is, but probably a lot less polarising, and has become a mainstay for both nationals and tourists alike.[296]

Another particularly special asset Jewish people brought with them to the UK (and East London in particular) was the beigel. The Beigel made its name in East London in the 19th century and still gathers a bustling attraction of tourists and locals today. You would be hard-pressed to find someone in the West who hasn't heard of a beigel, let alone consumed one. This soft ring of dough has not only become a staple in London and other parts of the UK, but is part of everyday life in places like New York and other American cities with large Jewish communities. Large food corporations have played a part by mass producing the product, but an independent beigel market still thrives, especially in parts of East and North London.[297]

So Jewish settlers created some food that we still eat today, is that it? No, no it's not.

If you've ever been to the UK or Hong Kong, then you would have definitely heard of the brand; Marks and Spencer. The company was co-founded by a Polish-Jewish Immigrant (Michael Marks) in 1884 and has been involved in British society ever since.

- They provided healthcare to their staff in the 1930s, which was not common, and predated the NHS by a decade.
- They advocated for women's education and workplace involvement before and during WWII.

---

[296] (Little known history of fish and chips 2020)
[297] (Celebtrating East London's Jewish Community on Passover 2014)

- M&S introduced free cervical screening for women over the age of 35, and this was expanded to women over the age of 25 in 1967. Screening was not yet available on the NHS.
- The 'Marks and Start' work-experience initiative for disadvantaged people was the biggest company-led work experience programme in the UK and Ireland in 2004. The initiative helped disabled people, homeless people, lone parents and the unemployed youth.[298]

The company has become a quintessential part of British culture, despite being the product of a Polish-born immigrant. M&S has been intertwined in British history over the past 130 years through its initiatives, charitable work, and mouth-watering television adverts, and still boasts over 78,000 employees as of 2021.[299]

There are constantly evolving cultural traits in the UK, and for some of those bringing these traits, their impact on the British people is only just beginning.

One such person is Fatma Al-Baiti, who has created a series of pop-up brunch shops called 'Meet me at Fatma's'. The food is centred around traditional Yemeni cuisine with its own twist and has been inspired by *'a certain tradition practised in our household and the cities I was born or raised in'*. Fatma is originally from Yemen, but after arriving in the UK to study for her master's degree in 2014, was unable to return to her country due to the conflict that was unfolding there. Fatma, however, is keen for Yemen to be known for more than just conflict and instability.[300]

---

[298] (M&S Employee Welfare 2021)
[299] (Quintessentially British brands 2021)
[300] (Meet Me at Fatma's: An Inspirational Story of Refugees in Entrepreneurship 2021)

'I noticed that what people know about Yemen is limited to the war and the current political unrest. I wanted to inform them that there's more to Yemen than a conflict'. Beyond the war, she says *'Yemen is a beautiful country with a rich culture and very diverse cuisine that needs to be rediscovered with open minds and hearts'.*[301]

Sharing Yemeni culture has been something in which Fatma has definitely succeeded. Tickets to each pop-up brunch sell out fast, and so far, she has introduced hundreds of Londoners to Yemeni cuisine. She says, *'refugees are often highly skilled and deserve the opportunity to be employed so they can start giving to their new society'.* Although Fatma's journey is at its early stages, her hard work and desire to share her way of life may lead to society embracing and embodying parts of those traditions, and so in turn, adding to the already diversified culture in the UK.[302]

Refugees are mostly associated with war, persecution and natural disasters. But despite the hardships that refugees endure, along with all of the suffering comes unique and amazing art that we can see throughout the entertainment industry. Whether it's individuals who make music that resonates with people across the globe, or raising awareness for worldwide issues through the skills they possess, refugees have had a major impact in film, music and entertainment.

When people hear the band Queen – they are hearing one of the greatest bands ever. Inducted into The Rock and Roll Hall of

---

[301] Ibid
[302] Ibid

Fame in 2001, Queen have made numerous famous hits and have left a legacy that continues to define pop music to this day. Freddie Mercury, who was lead vocalist of the band and who "embodied the band's identity, its triumphs and failings" was a refugee.

Mercury was born Farrokh Bulsara in Stone Town, the British Protectorate of Zanzibar on 5 September 1946. His family were from the Parsi community of western India and had origins tracing back to Gujrat. In 1964, Mercury and his family fled from Zanzibar to escape the violence of the revolution against the Sultan of Zanzibar, in which thousands of ethnic Arabs and Indians were killed. Freddie moved to Middlesex and after studying his passion, music, he, along with Brian May and Roger Taylor, formed Queen in 1970.[303]

The newly named Freddie Mercury and his band would go onto produce an era defining sound and some of the greatest rock albums and songs of all time, such as Bohemian Rhapsody. Freddie Mercury's musical success and brilliant stage presence made him a global superstar. Along with his amazing voice and great song writing ability, Mercury also inspired the band to get involved with charity concerts such as Live Aid 1985 – which raised $127 million in famine relief for African nations. His musical legacy has influenced subsequent generations of musicians from Lady Gaga to Nirvana. Mercury continues to exert a huge cultural significance in the UK and was named one of the Greatest Britons by the BBC as well as being posthumously awarded the BRITs "outstanding contribution to British Music".[304]

A more contemporary example, however, can be found with chart topping singer Rita Ora, who has used her prominence in the

---

[303] (Queen's Tragic Rhapsody 2014)
[304] (Britannica 2021)

industry to act as a well-known activist. In 1991, following the outbreak of the Yugoslav wars, Ora's Albanian heritage meant she risked persecution by Yugoslav forces. Her family managed to escape her hometown, Pristina, on one of the last planes out of Kosovo and settled in London.

Showing great musical ability from a young age, Ora gained a place at the prestigious Sylvia Young Theatre School. This kick-started her career in the industry and she has since been nominated for five BRIT awards and seven MOBO awards. Ora is greatly revered in her native Kosovo and in 2015 was awarded the title of Honorary Ambassador of Kosovo for her work. She is a real role model for many refugees and acts as UNICEF Ambassador working on various projects concerning refugee rights such as her campaign on the Syrian refugee crisis.[305]

Entertainment is something that can be universally enjoyed. However, often the perspectives we showcase are by a limited few. Refugees can offer a unique perspective which enriches and diversifies our culture. Entertainment is a valuable tool in informing the public, with artists often using their work as a platform to explore issues related to the refugee experience.[306]

Comedians such as Shappi Khorsandi, for instance, humanises the refugee narrative in confronting it with humour and light. Khorsandi came to the UK as a child during the Iranian Revolution as her father's satirical work put her family's safety in danger. She has found a source of comedy in British life, identity conflict and discrimination showing that life as a refugee is not simply defined by tragedy and loss. Her creative talent has also

---

[305] (Refugee Action n.d.)
[306] Ibid

been channelled into her novels *Nina is Not OK* and the soon to be released, *Kissing Emma*, as well as her memoir *A Beginner's Guide to Acting English.*[307]

⊚

Work within the entertainment industry has allowed comedians like Khorsandi to shift perspectives and challenge misconceptions about refugees in an entertaining way. Refugees are able to further influence the public sphere by using their voice to focus attention on issues they value. This success and public image of refugees in the industry has been used by many to enhance philanthropic efforts.[308]

Refugees have also become major figures in the film industry around the world. Mila Kunis, known for her roles on *That 70s Show* and the movie *Ted*, came to Los Angeles from the Ukrainian SSR in 1999, when she was just seven. Her family were Jewish and anti-Semitism attacks were rising in the country – along with religion suppression. Kunis had stated that "after the Holocaust, in Russia you were not allowed to be religious".[309]

Kunis has been awarded and nominated for respectable acting awards such as winning the 2014 MTV Movie Award, 2018 People's Choice Award and the 2011 Saturn Award for best supporting actress for her role in *Black Swan*. Along with major roles in movies, Kunis is involved in supporting charity organisations such as Comic Relief and Artists for Peace and Justice, a social non-profit organisation which encourages peace and social justice and deals with poverty in different communities around the world.[310]

---

[307] Ibid
[308] Ibid
[309] Ibid
[310] (Who is Mila Kunis? 2021)

The entertainment industry is made up of all different types of people from all walks of life. Over time, the entertainment industry and even more so the world, has been impacted by refugees who, having been given the opportunity, use their experiences, skills, wisdom and abilities to make significant and meaningful impact. Whether it's a generational singer, songwriter, a pop-star or a film star - refugees have been noteworthy assets in the entertainment industry and to popular culture in the Western world.

As well as bringing so much to Western food, music and film, refugees have also contributed so much to the art, architecture and literature the West enjoys.

For hundreds of years, some of the most successful and impactful visual artists have been refugees who have developed and portrayed their work through the refugee experience.

In the 1870s refugees brought the famous impressionist art movement to the UK.

That's right! We owe those iconic paintings of French landscapes: canals, fields, parks and marketplaces, with their kaleidoscopes of bright colours and visible sharp brushstrokes, to refugees.

Indeed, Impressionism was brought to the UK and the Netherlands by refugee artists like Claude Monet and Camille Pissaro who fled France after the Franco-Prussian war broke out, to escape violence and political persecution.[311]

---

[311] (Hobsbawn 1997)

The style was also partially developed due to the refugee experience. When he sought refuge in the UK, Claude Monet was exposed to the work of English artists J.M.W. Turner and John Constable, both of whom helped inspire his use of colour and depiction of water. Indeed, the defining painting of the impressionist movement *Impression, Sunrise*, from which the movement takes its name, draws heavily from the atmospheric, foggy seascapes of Turner particularly.[312]

Imagine if Monet had been treated like modern refugees and deported back to violence in France? Preventing him from being exposed to Turner's art and maybe even causing his death? Some of the most ground-breaking art in history may never have been created or become so widespread!

Refugees also helped create some of the most striking art of the 20th century, too.

In the 1930s and 1940s some of the most famous artists were forced to flee the violence of the Fascists of Germany and Spain. Jewish artists like Lucian Freud and Frank Auerbach fled persecution in Austria and Germany respectively as Fascists gained power, gaining safety in the UK.[313]

Likewise, Spanish artist Salvador Dali and Dutch artist Piet Mondrian were both forced to flee France for the US by the Nazis.[314] Dali in particular, completed some of his most famous surrealist works, such as *The Elephants*, after being granted sanctuary in the US. Some of his most iconic paintings would never have been created if the US had refused to protect refugees from the Nazis.

---

[312] (Lobstein 2002)
[313] (Lucian Freud 1922-2011)
[314] (Salvador Dali - Salvador Dali Museum 2014)

These four artists were some of the most ground-breaking of their time, having a huge impact on the movements of Cubism, De Stijl, Surrealism and Expressionism. Salvador Dali and Lucian Freud had a particular impact on surrealism with their unsettling works such as *The Persistence of Memory* and *Girl with a Kitten*. Piet Mondrian was one of the main developers of De Stijl with its block colours and sharp line abstract work, whilst Frank Auerbach's Expressionist pieces make him one of the most famous artists still living.[315]

More recently, refugee artists such as Mona Hatoum have also brought new and diverse cultural influences and experiences to Western art.

Mona Hatoum is a famous Lebanese-Palestinian artist whose family was made refugees by the ethnic cleansing of Palestinians from West Palestine by Israeli colonists.[316] After gaining sanctuary in England, however, Hatoum was able to establish herself as a ground-breaking artist in the area of video and sculptural installations. Works like *So Much I Want to Say* consists of still images of her face in close-up, with a pair of male hands covering her mouth which prevent her from speaking. Through it she expresses the experience of living in the West as a person from a developing country, being an outsider, being excluded and how the perspectives and struggles of non-Western peoples are ignored and silenced in the West.

Much the same is true of literature.

---

[315] (Piet Mondrian 1872-1944)
[316] (Who is Mona Hatoum? 2016)

Refugees have contributed hugely to this area, providing the West with some of the most moving, gripping and engaging stories and ideas. However, they were only able to do so because they were protected from violence by Western countries and allowed to work in relative safety.

As with visual arts, refugees have been contributing to literature for centuries.

In 1851, famous French writer Victor Hugo was forced to flee violent persecution by the dictator of France, Louis Napoleon, for criticising his crackdown on democracy. He was able to gain sanctuary in the British territory of Guernsey, where he wrote his most famous work *Les Misérables*.[317] This historical drama depicts the experience of Parisians living under and fighting back against poverty and persecution in the years of the Bourbon Monarchy and explores universal themes such as justice, religion, love, redemption and social struggle for freedom. *Les Misérables* is known worldwide and in 2012 was adapted into a musical film starring Hugh Jackman, Russell Crowe and Anne Hathaway.[318] Without the protection granted to him by Britain from persecution, he may never have been able to write this epic work.

And yes, the same is also true of many famous 20th century writers.

Playwright Bertolt Brecht produced some of his most famous works, such as *Mother Courage and Her Children, Fear and Misery of the Third Reich* and *Galileo* whilst gaining sanctuary from the Nazis in Scandinavia and the US. He developed the distinct realist style of *Epic Theatre,* which aimed to engage a working-class audience in contemporary ideological and

---

[317] (Victor Hugo - Exile (1851-1870) 2019)
[318] (The Editors of Encyclopædia Britannica 2019)

political debates and to present the world as it is rather than to provide escapism and fantasy.[319] His works are considered by many to be the greatest of the 20th century, exploring the horror and pointlessness of war, the nature of fascism, the creative and destructive power of science and the struggles of ordinary working people.

Likewise, Russian writer Vladimir Nabokov produced his famous novel *Lolita* after gaining refuge in the US from the Nazis.[320] This story controversially explored the narrator's attraction to an underage girl as well as the complexities of the 'American dream' and the coercion and power dynamics within modern Western sexuality. It is one of the most notable works of the mid-20th century and continues to have a significant cultural impact, having inspired the work and persona of musicians such as Lana del Rey and Katy Perry, for example.[321]

More recently, award-winning bestselling writers like Loung Ung and Khaled Housseni were only able to write their bestselling works due to the protection they gained in the US from violence in their homelands in Cambodia and Afghanistan. Loung Ung's work *First They Killed My Father* details the horrifying impact of the Khmer Rouge on Cambodia.[322] Khaled Hosseini's bestselling novels *The Kite Runner, A Thousand Splendid Suns* and *And the Mountains Echoed* explore the history of Afghanistan, the experience of refugees, familial relationships and struggles for redemption.[323]

Once again, the above examples act to prove that choosing to protect refugees can massively enrich the host country's culture.

---

[319] (Gossard 2013)

[320] (German dramatist. In: Encyclopædia Britannica 2019)

[321] (Vladimir Nabokov, Biography, Books, & Facts. In: Encyclopædia Britannica 2019)

[322] (Flanagan 2018)

[323] (Gandhi 2018)

Refugees and migrants have also contributed hugely to the architecture of Western countries, helping define its cityscapes and designing many of its iconic buildings.

Refugees have been contributing to our architecture for centuries. If we look as far back as the time of King William III in the 17th century, we can see that a refugee was centrally involved in redesigning one of England's most iconic palaces: Hampton Court. Daniel Marot was an architect, furniture designer and engraver who was forced to leave France by the violent crackdown of Louis XIV against Protestant Huguenots. He was granted asylum in the Netherlands and England and went on to design many areas of Hampton Court and most of its furniture.[324]

Refugees and migrants have continued to have a huge impact on our architecture in more recent times. In the 1930s as the Nazis began to persecute the Jews within its borders, Peter Moro fled to seek sanctuary in the UK. There, he was able to have a huge impact on the theatres of the country, designing both the Royal Festival Hall in London and the Nottingham Playhouse.[325]

Similarly, internationally renowned architect Zaha Hadid migrated from Iraq in the 1970s to the US to study and escape the violence of the Baathist party. There she trained as an architect and became a pioneer in her discipline, helping develop the field of Modernist architecture through combining it with Russian Supremacist and Futurist styles. She has designed iconic buildings across the West: including the Bergisel Ski Jump in Austria, the Contemporary Art Centre in Cincinnati, the Bridge

---

[324] (Hosseini 2019)
[325] (Powers 2011)

Pavilion in Spain and the London Aquatic Centre for the 2012 Olympics.[326]

Throughout history, refugees and migrants have contributed so much, with such great value to Western art, architecture and literature.

When we see all these examples it is impossible not to consider how the West treats refugees today and ask "what if"?

What if we had shunned, harmed, turned away and deported all these historical refugee and migrant artists, architects and writers when they had asked for protection in the West?

What if this prevented some of the most iconic artists of the Impressionist, Modernist, Cubist, Surrealist and Expressionist movements from creating their great works or spreading them to wide audiences? Their creators denied the opportunity to develop their craft and showcase their work, refused safety and thrust into deadly violence and poverty with no hope of thriving and every likelihood of death.

What if Victor Hugo was denied asylum, died in France and was never able to write *Les Misérables*? Bertolt Brecht never able to write *Mother Courage*? Daniel Marot never able to design Hampton Court and Zaha Hadid never able to create her modernist designs all across the West?

What if our current refugee and migrant policies are doing just this, preventing the modern Claude Monets, Vladimir Nabokovs, Anish Kapoors, Piet Mondrians and Mona Hatoums from

---

[326] (Hadid 2016)

creating new ground-breaking creative movements and flourishing in safety?

As we move into the future, let us push for all refugees to be protected from violence and allowed to thrive so that no future artist, architect or writer is denied an opportunity to create and enliven our culture.

Equally, sport plays a big role within the cultural identity of people and the places they are from. Refugee athletes learn and develop their sporting attributes in their home countries, and upon being displaced, they continue to hone their skills in their host nations and often bring success, global attention, and accolades with them as a result.

It is not always plain sailing for uprooted athletes, however. Countless refugees have to temporarily put their sporting endeavours on hold, or abandon them completely, as they try to regain stability and rebuild their lives.

There are numerous sports stars from refugee backgrounds - probably far more than you realise - and many more in the early stages of their sporting careers that have recently been displaced.

For lots of us, sport is a leisurely activity that we play or watch for fun, however, for others, it can be so much more than that. Not only does sport have the power to unite people through playing in a team or supporting the same club, but also as a temporary outlet and form of therapy during times of immense hardship. Many refugees speak of how sport has helped them through the torrid situations they have faced and how it has given them hope for the future.

It is worrying to think that some of the world's future big sporting names may be lost due to the factors that cause refugee crises.

Why don't we have a look at some stories of refugee athletes at different stages of their careers and acknowledge and appreciate the impact they have had on the West by implementing their cultures in this part of the world through sport.

The Refugee Olympic team showcases a huge mix of highly talented individuals who wish to represent the millions of displaced people across the world at the upcoming Tokyo Games and beyond.

For some background information; during the height of the European Migrant Crisis in 2015, the president of the International Olympic Committee (IOC) announced the first-ever Refugee Olympic team would be taking part in Rio 2016. The team consisted of 10 athletes from multiple countries, and they competed under the Olympic flag and anthem. After the breakthrough moment of the Refugee Team competing at Rio 2016, the IOC developed an initiative called Olympic Solidarity which assists 55 athletes with their training to help them qualify for the upcoming Tokyo Olympic Games. The Refugee Athlete Scholarship-holders come from 13 countries (21 host National Olympic Committees) and represent 12 different sports.[327]

Now you know more about the history of the Refugee Olympic Team, let's take a glance at a couple of young talented hopefuls who we may see competing at the next Olympics and learn of their journey to this point and how they have used sport to also give back and help others.

---

[327] (Refugee Council n.d.)

Yusra Mardini was born in Damascus, Syria, in 1998. She is a gifted swimmer who specialises in the 100m butterfly and 100m freestyle disciplines. She currently lives and trains between Hamburg and Berlin in Germany. The story that has led her up to this point is quite remarkable and shines a light on the kind of resilient human being she is.[328]

In August 2015, Yusra decided to flee her place of birth alongside her older sister after their home was destroyed during the Syrian Civil War. A turbulent journey saw them travel to Turkey via Lebanon, and from there they would ride a dinghy across the Aegean Sea to Greece with 18 other migrants. Fifteen minutes into their journey, terrifyingly, the engine failed, and the small boat began taking onboard water. Being a professional swimmer, Yusra opted to jump into the water with a few others to alleviate the weight on the boat, which was already three times over its capacity. After treading water for more than three hours the engine kicked back into life and they reached Lesbos, Greece. Yusra and her sister settled in Berlin in September of 2015.[329]

Yusra's swimming abilities were soon acknowledged in Germany and she was selected to be a part of the first Refugee Olympic Team. Since then, she has spoken at the United Nations General Assembly and has become the youngest ever Goodwill Ambassador for the UN Refugee Agency (UNHCR). Her story is in the process of being made into a film.[330]

The young swimmer's talents arguably helped save the lives of many on her journey to Greece. Her story and sporting achievements have led her to many great opportunities, and with them, she is now helping millions of others with the new platform she has developed. Yusra made it through the tumultuous journey

---

[328] (Refugee Olympic Team 2021)
[329] Ibid
[330] Ibid

so many other similar refugees have to face and is now contributing great benefits to society. Although her story is remarkable, it makes us think that there must be so many others similar to Yusra out there who could also have a positive impact upon their communities that may never make it far enough to be heard.

Another Olympic prospect is weightlifter Cyrille Fagat Tchatchet II. Cyrille moved to the United Kingdom in 2014 when his weightlifting pursuits saw him compete for his birth nation Cameroon at the Commonwealth Games in Glasgow. He was fearful of returning to his home country and decided to run away from his team base during the multi-sport event.[331]

He endured a tough start to life in the UK as he battled homelessness, whilst waiting three years until his asylum claim was accepted. Cyrille believes that weightlifting, combined with professional mental health support, saved him during his lowest points. He went on to obtain a first-class degree in Mental Health Nursing to "give back some of the support" he had received. Whilst studying, Cyrille won multiple British, English, and BUCS weightlifting championships and hopes to continue his successes by qualifying for the Tokyo Olympic Games. Cyrille's sporting prowess helped him get his life back on track, and now he is a qualified mental health nurse, he is helping others in the UK who may be struggling like he once was.[332]

These are just two examples from a giant pool of extremely skilled athletes that are refugees. There are so many more displaced individuals who also have hopes of showcasing their sporting abilities on the world stage, however unfortunately, plenty of them will never be able to do so for reasons out of their control.

---

[331] Ibid
[332] (Refugee Olympic Team 2021)

With such people in mind, let us explore the life and journey of a well-known refugee athlete competing at the very top of their sport.

Francis Ngannou made history by becoming the first African to win the heavyweight championship after defeating Stipe Miocic at UFC 260. As talented a fighter Francis Ngannou is, his journey to becoming a heavyweight champion showed qualities of great determination and fight from a young age – all of which he takes into the ring.[333]

Ngannou was born in the village of Baite, Cameroon on the 5th of September 1986. Ngannou's parents divorced when he was just six years old and he was sent to live with his aunt where he grew up in poverty in which he struggled for basic necessities and received little formal education (Ngannou went to a school 6 miles away from his home and had to walk 2 hours to get there). The struggle led Ngannou to experience a very lonely childhood. He described himself as "staying in retreat" and limited socialising with his classmates due to the frustration of not having basic items such as a pen or a book – and sometimes even clothes and shoes.[334]

From the age of 11, Ngannou started working in a sand quarry to provide for his single mother, siblings and aunt. He even worked as a motorcycle taxi driver. However, Ngannou's passion for boxing and determination to bring his family out of poverty, led him to head to Europe to pursue a fighting career.[335]

---

[333] (Francis Ngannou: From The Underdog To The Favourite 2021)
[334] Ibid
[335] Ibid

Ngannou's 14-month journey to Europe began by travelling through Nigeria and Niger towards North Africa. In his quest to reach Algeria, Ngannou found himself having to drink from a well infested with dead animals and birds and failed to cross the Sahara Desert on six different occasions.[336]

After arriving in Tarifa, in the south of Spain, Ngannou was caught by the authorities and spent two months in prison for illegally crossing the Moroccan-Spain border by sea. After his release, Ngannou received refugee status and ended up in France.

However, having no money meant Ngannou slept rough on the streets of Paris, dreaming of pursuing a boxing career by approaching gyms that would let him train.[337] Ngannou made ends meet by working at a homeless shelter called 'La Chorba', where he chopped vegetables. His life took a turn for the better when the director of the La Chorba Foundation introduced him to Didier Carmont, who ran a boxing training centre in Paris.[338]

Ngannou was introduced to Mixed Martial Arts and went on to receive a professional UFC contract. His 13th fight in the UFC saw him be crowned the heavyweight champion in March 2021, beating Stipe Miocic who many consider to be the greatest of all time in this weight category.[339]

Ngannou made his dream of becoming a professional fighter a reality and went on to be a world champion. However, even before the rise to success and acquiring his title, Ngannou's journey highlights just how much of a great fighter he has always been.[340]

---

[336] Ibid

[337] Ibid

[338] (Francis Ngannou: From The Underdog To The Favourite 2021)

[339] Ibid

[340] Ibid

It ponders the question; how many future Francis Ngannous are out there that we just don't know about yet?

Ngannou's story highlights the importance of opportunities. Sport offered an opportunity for Ngannou when he reached France, now he uses his resources to encourage the youth of Cameroon to aim high as well as inspiring numerous youngsters across America, where he now lives. More must be done to provide accessible opportunities to refugees, so they can continue the cycle to motivate and educate the youth around them, and who knows, many more sporting stars may be born as a result.

Individuals like Francis Ngannou are an example of refugees who now reside in the Western world and have brought great sporting success. Athletes like Francis, alongside other well-known names such as Mo Farah and Alphonso Davies, should not only be credited for their achievements on the track, on the pitch, and in the ring, but they also deserve to receive great acknowledgement for the journeys they have endured to get to this stage.

Sport is a fundamental aspect of culture. Stories like the ones mentioned above highlight the wealth of talent that exists globally and the great impact sport can have on both individuals and communities as a whole. We should nurture athletes, and give particular credit to those from refugee backgrounds, whilst also considering the thousands who may never make it due to the unfair and extremely harsh conditions that strip them of the opportunity to fulfil their ambitions.

10

SOCIAL AND SCIENTIFIC IMPACT

Reader: I thought this book was about refugees, what has this got to do with science? I'm not interested, bye now.
Author: Hold on! Just listen for a minute. There are a vast number of pioneering scientists, inventors and philosophers who were once refugees, did you know that? Refugees have a huge beneficial impact on society as we know it, so this issue has a lot to do with science actually.

There is an extensive number of Nobel prizes, Copley Medals and Franklin Institute Awards that have been presented to individuals who have fled their country of birth. Science has been impacted profoundly by immigrants and refugees throughout history, and the same will likely hold true for the future.

Though it may be difficult for regular citizens to acquire knowledge on complex scientific theories without prior academic expertise, it is important to recognise the individuals who, through their life-long devotion to scientific discovery, have enabled us to understand the world as we know it today.

Albert Einstein, a German-born immigrant whom you are probably aware of, was among the most brilliant scientific figures in history. Einstein himself had to escape one of the world's deadliest regimes. Because of his Jewish heritage, Einstein was no longer permitted to teach in Germany during the Nazi regime in the 1930s and fled to several European countries before deciding to settle in America. His general theory of relativity laid the groundwork for modern science. He was affectionately known as a 'cartoonist's dream come true'. In spite of being displaced, Einstein thrived in his scientific apprehensions, an opportunity that is rare for many able and intellectual refugees today.[341]

$E = mc^2$. Most people haven't the 'energy' to study this equation, but that doesn't really 'matter'. Arguably the most famous equation of all time, but rarely understood by the 'masses'...[342]

Pop culture has made this equation synonymous, and you have most likely heard of it. It may even be difficult to fully comprehend the concept, but one can still appreciate what it has brought them over the years. If Einstein hadn't published his physics in 1915, we might still be lost in the woods without a GPS, nor would we have the popular Science Fiction stories and movies about black holes and space travel that saturate the entertainment industry.[343] The most popular understanding of relativity comes almost exclusively from Sci-fi cinema and the 1968 Planet of the Apes movie (adapted from Pierre Boulle 1963 novel 'La Planète des Singes), which crudely explained time dilation (an effect of Einstein's predicted relativity).[344]

Einstein has contributed substantially to our understanding of the world today, and his impact has been undeniable.

So, what about the sciences that are not exploited in Hollywood movies? Or scientists who aren't imitated on Halloween?

---

[341] (Albert Einsten's Life As A Refugee 2019)
[342] (Einstein's Theory of Special Relativity 2021)
[343] (8 ways you can see Einstein's theory of relativity in real life 2017)
[344] (5.4: Time Dilation 2020)

George Radda was one of those scientists who, while his name may not fill the same place as Einstein's in people's minds, had a huge impact on the study of pharmacology and was incredibly influential. You can thank him if you've ever had an MRI scan for helping you locate a diagnosis for your ailments, even if you've had to suffer through the loud noise!

Radda was a biochemist who developed nuclear magnetic resonance (NMR), a powerful tool for biomedical imaging. As a result of his extensive work in NMR, cell membranes and enzymes, he developed the first clinical NMR unit, which laid the foundation for medical imaging and paved the way for the lifesaving MRI machines of today.[345]

All of Radda's work was sadly preceded by his experiences in Hungary as a young man. The country came under the influence of László Rajk's Marxist-Leninist ideology during the 1950s. As a result, 20-year-old Radda was smuggled out of the country through the Danube River. As the Hungarian revolutionists pushed back against communist rule in 1956, the country's youth were subjected to retaliation worse than before. His journey ultimately ended in Oxford, England, where he studied chemistry after reaching safety.[346]

Radda was among the many notable scientists in their fields who failed to gain the public's attention. Although Einstein may have been popularised by cartoonists because of his distinct appearance, he is nonetheless recognised for his scientific capabilities. Though we can't expect every scientist to achieve such fame, studying past scientific achievements should be encouraged more.

---

[345] (George Radda Biography 2021)
[346] (Gurman 2021)

So, being an expert in science isn't all that is required to gain attention from the public eye. Perhaps having an array of talents in multiple fields such as the Arts and Literature, as well as in science, will give someone the recognition they deserve. An example of this is Congolese novelist and chemist, Emmanuel Dongala. Born in the Republic of the Congo, Dongala had a PhD in Organic Chemistry, published four novels, produced a collection of short stories, founded a theatre company, and he even wrote a play. Amazing.[347]

After earning his bachelor's and master's degrees in the USA, he headed for France, where he earned his PhD. Dongala then returned to the Congo and worked as a teacher whilst striving to become the Dean of the Republic of the Congo's State University. He held this position until 1997, when civil war broke out in the Congo. Thousands of people were killed in the conflict that followed, but Dongala managed to find a way back to the USA with the help of a friend and fellow author, Philip Roth. Once again, he resumed working as a teacher, this time at Bard College in New York.[348]

During Dongala's second stay in America is where most of his literary success was achieved. His many works, initially written in French, have been published and translated in over a dozen languages. In the case of his novel *Le Feu des Origines* (The Fires of Origins), he received the Grand Prix d'Afrique Noire and the Grand Prix de la Fondation de France awards. Furthermore, his novel *Johnny Mad Dog,* was selected by the Los Angeles Times for one of its Book of the Year awards and was adapted into a feature film in 2008. Emmanuel also wrote short stories whilst living in the Congo, many of which were banned from publication

---

[347] (Emmanuel Dongala 2021)
[348] (Goodreads: Emmanuel Dongala 2021)

as they satirised the communist state that was in power at the time.[349]

His success ventured past his literary writings as he became the founder and president of the National Association of Congolese Writers, and the Congolese chapter of PEN International (Writers Association). This was an excellent addition to his Guggenheim fellowship award and Fonlon-Nichols Prize for literary excellence.[350]

Dongala was once asked, "What are your reasons for writing?" to which he replied, "Why do people make love?". Does this sound like a man who has been told that he must choose a single path in life?[351]

The interdisciplinary work of Emmanuel Dongala proves that you should not feel compelled to choose between a science or art career if you have a passion and talent for both. It is remarkable that Dongala continued to strive towards success whilst seeking refuge from war in his home country.

As well as their scientific contributions to society, refugees have also contributed significantly to the technology and engineering industries of our time.

It is a huge misconception that most refugees are unqualified and lack the relevant experience and skills that are required for high-level professions.

---

[349] Ibid
[350] Ibid
[351] Ibid

The inspiring story of Loay Elbasyouni is a particularly noteworthy one. Born and raised in Gaza's Beit Hanoun city, Loay's journey to becoming a NASA engineer was far from easy. Due to the ongoing political turmoil taking place in his home state for decades, academic and career opportunities were limited.

Numerous stories surface yearly of bright and capable students who are unable to take up offers from top Western universities, this is due to the travel restrictions the Israeli government has placed upon them.[352] The same misfortune applies to the young people who excel in sports as they are blocked from competing internationally due to its military occupation.[353] It is also far too costly to move to another country in search of greater job opportunities and is further complicated by the difficulty to obtain visas.

From an early age, the Palestinian refugee from Gaza dreamt of studying aeronautics and space engineering, however, as Elbasyouni's birthplace is not even recognised as a country, he knew a space programme would not be available to him. He acknowledged that pursuing aeronautics in Palestine would not be possible. Motivated by his desire to help people and 'make a difference in the world', he decided that electrical engineering was the path he would pursue.[354]

As a result of Loay's impressive levels of intelligence, he was awarded a scholarship to study at an American university in 1998. Upon his arrival in the US, however, he realized that settling was not straightforward as he continued to encounter difficulties. In an interview, Loay recalled a time when he would work 90

---

[352] (Gifted Palestinian dreamers defy Israel's occupation nightmare 2021)
[353] Ibid
[354] (Gaza refugee designs first NASA helicopter to fly on Mars 2021)

hours a week at a Subway fast-food chain just so he could afford to sustain living in the US.[355]

After a few years, Elbasyouni achieved both a bachelor's and master's degree in Electrical Engineering at the University of Louisville. After his studies, Elbasyouni worked for various engineering firms in the States. Then, in 2012 he started a new role at AeroVironment, in which he took part in developing lightweight electronic aircrafts. Just two years into this job, NASA contracted AeroVironment. As a result, Loay became the lead electronics engineer for a team that helped develop a helicopter sent to Mars in July 2020, eventually landing on the red planet in February 2021.[356]

The resilience, hard work, and intelligence of Loay Elbasyouni have undoubtedly impacted the world. While Loay's journey from Gaza to NASA is unique, others, like him, are unable to break free from the turmoil in their home nations and are not given the opportunity to reach their full potential.

When talking about the people from his home community, Elbasyouni importantly and passionately reiterates, *"We are just people like anybody in the world...We want to live in peace and succeed. Build a prosperous future for our children, and live in a free, safe and peaceful place."*[357]

If ever you hear someone say that refugees are unqualified to work, tell them all you've read about Loay Elbasyouni, a Palestinian refugee from Gaza who, despite all of his trials and tribulations, played a critical role in the first helicopter flight to Mars. How inspiring!

---

[355] (From Gaza to Mars 2021)

[356] Ibid

[357] (Gaza refugee designs first NASA helicopter to fly on Mars 2021)

Among the most successful individuals in the world is Sergey Brin, one of the co-founders of Google. He, too, is a refugee from an impoverished background, and never shies away from his roots.

Anti-Semitism was still rife in the Soviet Union when Sergey was growing up in the 1970s. Brin's father, a talented mathematician, knew he would not be able to pursue the career of his dreams whilst living in a country that persecuted Jewish people. In 1979, Sergey's father made the difficult decision to emigrate to the United States, feeling as though he were an outsider in his birthplace and wishing for a better life for his family.

Sergey remembers the early battles of his life in the US. He was a young boy attempting to learn an entirely new language whilst also struggling to abide by the religious aspects of his Jewish ethnicity. After three years at a Hebrew School, Sergey begged his parents to stop sending him there, in which they eventually agreed.[358] Instead, he went on to study at Eleanor Roosevelt High School in Greenbelt and later graduated from the University of Maryland with a degree in Computer Science and Mathematics at just 19 years old. Being one of the top achievers of his year group, Sergey was offered the prestigious National Science Foundation graduate student fellowship, in which he finally completed his PhD in Computer Science at Stanford.[359]

It was at Stanford University in 1995 that Sergey met his future business partner, Larry Page. The two initially clashed and engaged in highly intellectual debates around computer science, but with this came mutual respect. Both Brin and Page had similar backgrounds, both were the sons of academics and both from a

---

[358] (The Story of Sergey Brin 2007-8)
[359] (On the Origins of Google 2004)

Jewish descent (although neither fully engaged with the religion, nor did they have a bar mitzvah).

Soon, Sergey and Larry developed their fiery relationship into a true friendship, their love for data and computer science was at the forefront of their lives. Sergey and Larry spent so much time with one another, trying to find multiple ways to extract mass amounts of data from the internet. The pair even adopted a collective identity, "LarryandSergey".[360]

Sergey and Larry soon realised that it was possible to use the link between different web pages to rank their importance. Alongside this, they developed an algorithm that used backlinks to connect multiple web pages and, in turn, generate a search engine that would quickly bring up the most valuable site and more in-depth than any other of its kind at the time.[361] Thus, what seemed to be a revolutionary discovery at the time, is now the fundamental basis of most search engines. Larry and Sergey chose to name their invention Google, a misspelling of a maths term "googol" (1 followed by 100 zeros), and likely, a nod to their geeky nature.

Larry and Sergey knew they had come up with something big, but it was a matter of convincing others that it could be as influential as they thought. Sounds simple right? Not quite...

Initial interest in the project was low. Alternative search engines such as AOL and Yahoo! were much more popular and offered a good reliable service for much less than $1 million, so people were not overly interested. Even so, they truly believed in what they had developed and opted to drop out of Stanford to focus on Google on a full-time basis.

---

[360] (The Story of Sergey Brin 2010)
[361] (The Birth of Google 2005)

Sergey and Larry got their first big break in 1998 when Andy Bechtolsheim, the cofounder of American computer tech company Sun Microsystems, wrote "Google, Inc." a cheque for $100,000.[362] It took a couple of weeks for the pair to overcome the slight issue that "Google, Inc." was not yet incorporated, but once they had completed the required paperwork, they were all set.

Over the coming years, Sergey and Larry secured interviews with well-known publications such as Playboy and featured on the cover of Time Magazine[363], the stock price of Google rocketed. Sergey and Larry's creation became a global phenomenon that has undoubtedly had a significant impact on the way in which people surf the web today.

Unsurprisingly, Sergey Brin is now a very wealthy and influential individual, with Forbes listing him as the 9th richest person in the world, in 2021, with a net worth of just over **$100 billion**.[364] A multi-billion-dollar refugee, amazing!

Stories like Sergey's and Loay's are crucial, they need to be told and shared so the stigma and misconceived ideas surrounding refugees can be changed. We need to recognise refugees as individuals who have the potential to become leading figures in all industries, to support the economy and society as a whole. In doing so, we must address the recurring question that many individuals are concerned with amidst the current refugee crisis': are refugees coming to 'your' country to take 'your' jobs?

There is an urgent need for us to start considering refugees as people who can potentially impact the world for the better and to accept that we all deserve a fair chance in life to do so.

---

[362] (Von Bechtolsheim 2009)
[363] (The Story of Sergey Brin 2007)
[364] (Today's Winners and Losers 2021)

Refugees are becoming increasingly prominent figures in the political realm. Many refugees that enter the political world often use their position to ensure that refugees are adequately represented, and their interests are looked after. Whether they experienced hardships on their journey or witnessed atrocities, politicians that were once refugees have had a significant impact in directing policies to support refugees and the disadvantaged.

So, who are some of these refugees in politics?

Ilhan Omar is the first Somali American in the US Congress, and the first woman of colour to represent Minnesota and, along with Rashida Tlaib, is one of the first of two Muslim women to serve in congress. In the American political realm, being a Muslim woman and a refugee defies all odds. Omar's life changed during the Somali Civil War in 1991, the war created a brutal environment, "[...] one day you're all family and next day some members no longer have the right to exist".[365] Choosing to escape the conditions in her home country, Omar and her family found themselves living in the squalid Dadaab refugee camp in Kenya for four years before seeking asylum in the US in 1995.[366]

Since she began her position in office, Ilhan Omer has courageously stood up for the rights of refugees, workers, and people of colour. Together with colleagues like Alexandria Ocasio-Cortez and Bernie Sanders, she has worked tirelessly to promote progressive policies in the US. These include 'Medicare for all', ensuring that US citizens have access to affordable healthcare. Through her campaigning efforts, Omar has transformed the initial nature of the policy into a well-established policy which is supported by the majority of US citizens.

---

[365] (Triumph in Adversity: Ilhan Omar 2021)
[366] Ibid

Furthermore, she has consistently increased the minimum wage for workers and successfully convinced Biden's Government to provide 1.9 trillion dollars to support working-class people who have lost their jobs due to COVID-19. In addition, Omar is a fierce defender and advocate for refugees and people of colour (POC) across the world.

She fought against the horrific conditions of Latin American refugees and migrants who were subjected to camps at the border between Mexico and the US under the direction of then President, Donald Trump. Omar has also continued to ensure that new president Joe Biden closes these camps and provides sufficient shelter to migrants. Most remarkably, she has done this despite facing ongoing scrutiny and recurring racial abuse and even death threats. Her fight for social justice and against racism and classism has never wavered, even after white supremacists stormed the capitol and threatened her life.[367]

Pnina Tamano-Shata, the first Ethiopian born minister in Israel, is another woman who defied the odds and told her story during her political rise. Tamano-Shata was born in 1981 in Wuzaba, a small village in the Gondar region of Ethiopia. Tamano-Shata was amongst the hundreds of thousands that fled the country's economic misery and political repression during the peak of the Civil War. Leaving her home at the age of 3, Pnina fled to Sudan before immigrating to Israel, searching for the true homeland of her ancestors.[368]

Just over three decades after leaving her birthplace, Pnina had managed to gain a foothold in the political career she was seeking. After serving in the Israeli armed forces, her next mission was to achieve a degree.

---

[367] (Triumph In Adversity: Ilhan Omar 2021)
[368] (The Story Of Pnina Tamano-Shata 2021)

However, as an immigrant, Pnina was informed that she could not attend because the institute could not provide Ethiopians with accommodation to study Law. Not disheartened by the discrimination, Pnina chose to study at the local Ono Academic College, and finally earned her degree in Law, which she believed to be fundamental to evoke change in Israeli society.[369]

By 2012, her political career began to take flight as she joined the Yesh Atid party and became a Knesset (Israeli parliament) member. This newfound experience in the Knesset served her well, and she was driven by the ability to carry out reforms and brighten the path to a just and moral society. However, her success did not stop there. Pnina became a member of the Blue and White party (a coalition party) in April 2019 and was elected twice more. The latter of these elections saw her appointed as the minister of Aliyah (immigration of Jewish peoples to the holy land) and integration as of May 2020, becoming the first Ethiopian-born Israeli to achieve this status.[370]

Lord Alf Dubs is a widely respected figure amongst the Labour Party. A child refugee from Nazi-occupied Prague, Czechoslovakia, Lord Dubs fled to the UK via the Kindertransport, a British government initiative allowing Jewish children to gain refuge in the UK. Lord Dubs is the former Chair of Liberty, a trustee of Action Aid and the Immigration Advisory Service and former director of the Refugee Council.

In recent years, Lord Dubs has achieved prominence in his advocacy of refugee rights in the Lords, most notably through his

---

[369] Ibid
[370] Ibid

amendment to the 2016 Immigration Act. Named in his honour, the Dubs Amendment allowed unaccompanied Syrian children to seek protection in the UK. Lord Dubs also continues to focus on post-Brexit policy towards Britain's approach to refugees. In an interview with Sona Circle, Lord Dubs said that he hopes the UK will negotiate the continuation of the Dublin Treaty, which allows asylum seekers who seek refuge in one European state to reunite with family members in another European state.[371]

Ok, so there are refugees in politics. What impact have they had?

The presence of refugees in politics impacts the way that refugee-related issues are addressed when in a position of influence. Ilhan Omar, Pnina Tamano-Shata, and Lord Dubs are just a few prominent refugees who have faced great hardships and succeeded in becoming influential figures seeking to promote change for refugees as well as people from disadvantaged backgrounds.

Their impact in society goes further than that.

Their success and where they arrived at today can only be described as inspiring. In a society that generally limits women, especially in politics, Ilhan Omar raised the standard for women. It is inspiring to see how she began her journey by seeking refuge following a civil war in Somalia to then becoming one of America's first Muslim politicians who is an advocate for refugees, women and Muslims across the world.

Again, when reflecting on Pnina Tamano-Shata's journey to becoming the first Ethiopian born minister in Israel, it is very inspiring. Israel has previously been criticized for its treatment of the Ethiopian-Jewish community, so to see Pnina's efforts within the Israeli government is inspiring for the future generations of the Ethiopian community in Israel.

The contributions of refugees to Western society have not only been profound through politics, but they have also been among the most pioneering, inquisitive, and inspiring thinkers in the social sciences, philosophy, and religion. Refugees have significantly impacted how we conceptualize society, its development, where we belong, and the reasons for acts we perform. Refugees developed, researched, and wrote about history, philosophy, religion, psychology, anthropology, economics, and sociology. Their ideas have therefore inspired countless social movements, discoveries, and debates over thousands of years and have shaped our world today.

Now, let's take a look at philosophy and religion.

Of course, we don't typically think of it in this way, but did you know the founders of the two largest religions over the last 2,000 years were both refugees.

Surprising, right? Yes, both Jesus and Prophet Muhammad, upon whose words Christianity and Islam are based, had to flee across borders to escape political persecution.

In the New Testament, we learn that Jesus and his family fled to Egypt when King Herod decided to kill every child for fear that one of them would dethrone him.[372]

---

[372] (Matthew 2:13-23)

Likewise, the Quran also states that Prophet Muhammad fled the political persecution taking place in his homeland Mecca. The rulers of the city repeatedly attacked his people, and, after an assassination attempt, Muhammad was forced to flee to the city of Medina.[373]

There has been an incalculable effect of both teachings on the world, both historically and currently.

It is estimated today that 2.3 billion people follow the words and teachings of Jesus, while 1.8 billion adhere to the teachings of Prophet Muhammad as a guide to their faith and practices.[374]

Over half of the world's population is made up of the religious followers of these two refugees!

Jesus' instruction to "love thy neighbour as thyself" and to "turn the other cheek" as well as to treat the poor and vulnerable well is an inspiration for those striving to improve the world.[375]

Similarly, Prophet Muhammed states, "Do not do evil to those who do evil to you, deal with them with forgiveness and kindness," he also said, "among the best deeds are to feed the poor." His words have encouraged billions to prevent war and violence among people.[376]

You may think that there are no other individuals that could have an impact more significant than Jesus and Prophet Muhammad on the world.

---

[373] (Muhammad completes Hegira 2010)
[374] (Christians remain world's largest religious group 2017)
[375] (Matthew 22:36-40, Matthew 5:38-40, Matthew 25:40)
[376] (Islam Daily 2016)

However, there is one who comes close. A refugee that goes by the name Jean Jacques Rousseau, one of the founders of the philosophy of liberalism.

Rousseau was born in Geneva, Switzerland, in 1712, when Kings and Queens ruled most of the countries of Europe. However, because Rousseau's ideas were highly radical, he was exiled multiple times from his home in Geneva and forced to flee to France before being exiled from France and forced to flee to Britain.[377]

According to Rousseau, man's nature is inherently good. It was the monarchy, the structure of the church, private property, inequality, and culture that corrupted society. In *The Social Contract*, Rousseau argued that a society where all had the right to vote, had free expression, had the rule of law, had protection from poverty and had freedom of religion would allow man to express his good nature and achieve individual freedom.[378]

The ideas of Rousseau had a significant impact on the French Revolution and the rise of republican democracy in Europe and across the globe. Several French revolutionaries viewed him as their founding father and placed his ashes in the Parisian Parthenon in his honour.[379]

More than 200 years later, we live in a world that is indebted to his ideas. Around the world, monarchies have been replaced by liberal democracies.

In recent decades, refugees and migrants have continued to influence philosophy and shape the world.

---

[377] (Years of seclusion and exile of Jean-Jacques Rousseau 2021)

[378] (Rousseau 2019)

[379] (E. Hobsbawm, The Age of Revolution, 1789-1848. 1977)

For example, Audre Lorde and Fatema Mernissi have had a huge impact on Feminism, particularly the modern and inclusive forms of Feminism that advocate for the experiences of women from minority ethnic backgrounds that are often underrepresented.

Audre Lorde's family were migrants who came to the United States from Jamaica in search of a better life. Lorde grew up to become one of the most influential theorists of Black Feminism, exploring the ways in which racism and sexism intersect as a form of discrimination against black women. Lorde argued relentlessly for a world in which black women were treated equally and strived towards an inclusive feminist movement in which the struggles of black women were also recognised to establish collective freedom.[380]

Fatema Mernissi was born in Morocco but moved to Paris and then Massachusetts, where she studied and developed the influential ideas that many are familiar with today. She challenged both Muslims and non-Muslims who claimed that Islam was incompatible with female empowerment, referring to the teachings of Prophet Muhammad, the Quran, and historical examples to support her arguments.[381]

Like Audre Lorde, Mernissi also criticised white Western feminists for ignoring the lived experiences of non-Western and non-white women. She too strived for an inclusive feminist movement that brought Muslim women together with the Western feminist movement to fight the patriarchy under which many women are subjugated.

The two drew upon their experiences as migrants in understanding the variety of women's experiences worldwide and

---

[380] (Audre Lorde 2021)
[381] (Gross 2015)

promoting an inclusive feminist philosophy that those from the West and white backgrounds often did not.

Also, did you know that refugees have been hugely influential in the discipline of psychology?

Sigmund Freud, one of the most famous psychologists to have lived, was a refugee.

I know what you're thinking - "Isn't he that weirdo who thinks about having sex with his parents?" - and to be fair, you're not entirely wrong. However, there's much more to him than that!

Freud was born to a Jewish family in Vienna, where he lived and worked until the 1930s. However, with the rise of fascism in Germany and Austria, he was forced to flee his country and reside in Britain for safety.[382]

A pioneer in the field of psychoanalysis, Freud explored how childhood experiences and subconscious instincts influenced people's thoughts and behaviours.

However, modern psychology has rejected Freud's ideologies and theories. Some have even called him 'Sigmund Fraud'![383]

It is undeniable, however, that he has had an impact on the whole field of psychology. His focus on childhood development and its effects on one's character, his practice of having regular sessions with an analyst to explore unconscious behaviours, and the idea

---

[382] (Jay 2018)
[383] (Alliant International University 2019)

that animalistic instincts have an effect on human behaviour are all key elements of modern psychology that Freud pioneered and helped develop.

In addition, his work had a major impact on popular culture and understanding of the mind. Concepts like "ego", "projection", "inferiority complex", "slips of the tongue," "defence mechanisms", and the "subconscious" are all Freudian terms. Freud's exploration of familial power dynamics and incestuous desire in the infamous "Oedipal" and "Electra" complexes have hugely impacted popular culture.[384]

In addition, Anna, his daughter who fled Nazism along with him, also had a significant impact on psychology. She was a prolific writer who contributed significantly to the field of children's psychology and the concept of "defence mechanisms."[385]

Recently, another refugee broke free of the white, European origins of psychology and explored how European colonialism affected black people. Franz Fanon was born in Martinique and migrated to France to study. During the Second World War, the racist French colonial authorities forced him to flee to Dominica. As a result of racism and being made a refugee, he developed radical, anti-imperialist ideologies.[386]

Fanon's ideas in psychology and politics were innovative and challenging. Even so, while acknowledging his impact, he criticized Freud for being too focused on the experience of white Europeans, for generalizing about the rest of the world, and for favouring one-on-one therapy over group therapy.

---

[384] (SACAP 2019)
[385] (The School of Life 2014)
[386] (Macey 1996)

Throughout his famous works *Black Skin, White Masks,* and *Wretched of the Earth,* he made the argument that the experience of cultural and political subjugation to European empires affected the psychology of black people greatly. He argued that it had created in them a deep-rooted sense of inferiority that encouraged many (including, he acknowledged, himself) to put on a façade of whiteness - to adopt mannerisms, language and habits of white people - in a futile attempt to appease their masters.[387]

Only by embracing their heritage and freeing themselves from the political oppression of European colonialism could people of colour escape this sense of inferiority and gain a sense of self-respect and strength.

In addition to significantly impacting our understanding of the relationship between politics, colonialism, race, and psychology, Fanon also influenced the world we live in through inspiring anticolonial liberation struggles around the world. Frantz Fanon's work directly inspired Algeria's independence struggle against French colonialism, as well as the Black Panther Party in the US, who helped end segregation.[388]

Finally, refugees have also had an enormous impact on the study of history, economics, and sociology, helping shape all three disciplines. Moreover, their ideas in these areas have inspired social movements that have changed the world.

There is one refugee in particular who had the most significant impact on this area: Karl Marx.

[387] (Drabinski 2019)
[388] (Abu-Jamal 2020)

Also known as the big-bearded man who looks like Father Christmas.

Marx was born in Trier in modern Germany but was forced to flee to Britain in 1849 when the Prussian Kaiser cracked down on dissidents.[389] He wrote all of his major works in Britain and they have hugely impacted sociology, history and economics.

Marx has indeed been regarded as the founder of sociology, which studies social structure, changes, and social causes of behaviour. He is very likely the first thinker to correctly discuss the systems of society and concepts we take for granted today, such as socio-economic class and how it impacts your perspectives, culture, and political activities.

He has also had an equally significant impact on the study of history.

Historians have tended to focus on elite political figures such as kings, queens, bishops, presidents, and prime ministers, and how their actions affected society. However, Marx turned this on its head. In works like '*The Eighteenth Brumaire of Louis Napoleon*' and '*The German Ideology*', Marx focused instead on how the poor and working-class groups had impacted historical development through social movements, rebellions and protests and explored their experiences. This was a ground-breaking change in perspective that gave birth to the field of "social history", which is now arguably the most dominant form of history practised.[390]

---

[389] (Wheen 2001)
[390] (Marx 2021)

Marx challenged fellow historians who believed that ideas and culture are what caused historical change. In his view, social structures, technology, economic systems, and social groups play an equally (if not more) important role in shaping history than ideas and culture.

Lastly, Marx had a profound impact on economics and capitalism.

He stated in his most influential text, *Das Kapital*, that capitalism suffers from several problems that lead to frequent crises, such as stock market crashes, recessions, unemployment, and rising inequality.

Specifically, Marx pointed out that in a capitalist economic system, capitalists are encouraged to decrease workers' wages as much as possible, which impoverishes them. There are two major problems with this. Firstly, it angers workers, leading them to strike or revolt, causing a crisis in the capitalist system. Secondly, workers don't have enough money to buy the products capitalists sell, resulting in 'overproduction'. When more goods are produced, than consumed, this leads to stagnant growth, underinvestment, falling profits, unemployment, and stock market crashes.[391]

These issues could only be resolved if workers took control of the economy, took control of their workplaces, and redistributed wealth so that all of them were protected from poverty.

Marx's ideas have had a huge impact on the world that continues to this day. Political parties and social movements worldwide have been inspired by him to either reform or overthrow capitalism and

[391] (Marx, K., Fowkes, B. and Mandel, E. 1990)

replace it with an economic system that protects the poor and workers from poverty.

Moderate, social-democratic reformist projects like the UK Labour Party's NHS and welfare system, German SPD's policies and the strike actions of Trade Unions draw inspiration from his ideas.[392]

Equally, Marx's work has inspired more revolutionary activities such as the overthrow of the Russian Tsar in 1917, the Spanish revolution in 1932 and anti-colonial revolutions against imperialism in Algeria, South Africa, Vietnam, China, and Cuba.[393]

Marx certainly could not have written his books if he did not seek refuge in Britain. All of Marx's best works, including the *Communist Manifesto* and *Das Kapital,* were written in London. All of his writings drew on the knowledge Marx gained from reading British thinkers like Adam Smith and David Ricardo, from his contacts in Britain and from the resources he had at the British Museum, where he wrote.[394]

Whilst he is a polarising figure whose work is often misrepresented, misunderstood, or contested, his impact on world history and status as a great and influential thinker is undeniable.

The impact of refugees and migrants on this area doesn't stop with Marx, however.

Other schools of economic thought have also been influenced by migrant economists like David Ricardo. David Ricardo was not a

---

[392] (E. Hobsbawm 1997)
[393] (E. Hobsbawm 1995)
[394] (Marx, K., Fowkes, B. and Mandel, E. 1990)

migrant directly, but his family moved from the Netherlands to the UK just before his birth.[395]

Ricardo is one of the founders of classical liberal economics. He argued that the best way of organising an economy was a capitalist free market where anyone could trade and freely compete to produce the most desirable product. He believed this would help promote innovation, economic growth and profit for the whole of society.

He was also particularly impactful in his arguments for a central bank. While many contemporaries, including Adam Smith, believed the best way of running finance was to have lots of commercial banks competing. Ricardo, however, argued that a national central bank was the best way to secure economic stability and prevent frequent stock market crashes. Ricardo arguably won this debate, with most nations of the modern world having a central bank, as Ricardo suggested.[396]

Modern neoclassical economists owe a lot to his ideas.

Likewise, in the twentieth century, many refugees have contributed significantly to the study of history.

For example, the most influential British historian of the twentieth century, Eric Hobsbawm, fled Germany during the war. Most university modern history courses are centred on his series of books on western history from the French Revolution to the fall of the USSR. The social history he helped pioneer focuses on the experiences of the often ignored poor and their impact on history through social movements. In addition to that, he helped

---

[395] (Stead n.d.)
[396] (Stead n.d.)

found *Past & Present*, arguably the most influential historical journal in the world.

Refugees have also impacted the study of history by revolutionizing its focus from white, Western, and European history to the experiences of people who have lived and continue to live in Africa, Asia, Latin America and the Middle East.

As an example, Guyanese historian Walter Rodney contributed to studies of African history. Rodney migrated to Dar es Salam in Tanzania to study African history. Following his political persecution at the hands of the Jamaican Government, which denied him the right to live in the country, he became a refugee.[397]

It was only through migration that Rodney gained in depth knowledge of African history which would inform his great work *How Europe Underdeveloped Africa.* In it, he explores Africa's rich history and highlights the continent's cultural and economic developments preceding European invasions. He successfully shows that, contrary to European viewpoints, Africa has not always been underdeveloped. On the contrary, Africa had been a thriving society before European colonialism, which actively underdeveloped it.

Likewise, Palestinian historian and cultural theorist Edward Said has helped challenge the western image of the middle east and provide a new interpretation of the history of Asian and Arab peoples.

Born in Mandatory, Palestine, Said was forced to move to the US by the Israeli invasion and the ethnic cleansing in the region.

---

[397] (W. Rodney 2018)

His experience of both the Middle East and the West enabled him to challenge ethno-centric, prejudiced, and inaccurate portrayals of the Middle East. In his most famous work, *Orientalism,* he highlights how Western colonialism has helped generate a specific cultural view of the Middle East and Asia as backward, mystical, uncultured, and inferior to the West. He concludes that this viewpoint has to be dismantled as it is profoundly racist and only serves Western imperialism.[398]

What do you think of our immigration system after reading all of that?

Many of the most influential, inspiring, and informative writers, inventors, and scientists whose ideas have shaped our world were refugees. Their significant works were born out of their escape from persecution in another country and their encounter with people there who inspired and taught them a lot. With blinding clarity, history shows that turning away refugees and migrants is both self-defeating and prevents exceptional thinkers from spreading their ideas.

We should instead celebrate refugees and make sure they have everything they need to thrive.

---

[398] (Edward Said 2006)

11

WHAT CAN WE DO AS INDIVIDUALS?

Reader: There's not much we can actually do, is there? Businesses and governments are the ones responsible, right?
Author: Well, you'd be surprised at just how powerful you really are!
Reader: Oh yeah? Tell me more.
Author: Gladly.

There are many things you can do as an individual to help refugees in your local communities. It doesn't even have to take a lot of your time.

As an example, there is a lot you can do to protect refugees from homelessness.

The issue of homelessness is one of the biggest challenges refugees face in the UK. More than a quarter of those sleeping rough in our major cities are refugees, and thousands more are without a permanent place to live. As a result of fleeing horrific conditions in their home countries and enduring long journeys for a better life, so many refugees are left homeless.

Thankfully, there are some organisations working on this issue. Room for Refugees provide safe, temporary housing and support to refugees and asylum seekers. From 2002 to 2019, they provided shelter for more than 104,000 refugees and other vulnerable individuals.

Community Housing Network NACCOM is another group that is dedicated to supporting refugees. Asylum seekers and refugees in need of housing are accommodated by their members across the country who sign up to provide this service. In addition, they provide data and research about the scale of the UK's homelessness crisis and urge the government to take action.[399]

Refugees at Home is a UK charity which connects those with a spare room in their home with refugees and asylum seekers in need of accommodation. So far, it has placed 2,345 guests for a total of 182,072 placement nights. Even though this may be a temporary fix, many councils are trying hard to make long-term changes through the Refugee Council Private Rented Scheme.[400]

The Refugee Council works to support refugee rights in many ways. One of their key projects is their Private Rented Scheme. The programme helps provide refugees with deposits for private housing and encourages landlords to provide housing without deposits to refugees.[401]

Each of these organisations contribute greatly to alleviating the homelessness crisis. But we need to change the policies of the National Government to really solve the issue. Governments need to provide housing for everyone who needs it. Council houses can be constructed, and vacant properties can be used. The only way to effectively end homelessness is to guarantee housing as a human right.

---

[399] (NACCOM 2021)
[400] (Refugees at Home 2021)
[401] (Refugee Council 2021)

Migration isn't easy. Accepting change isn't easy. Starting a new life isn't easy.

Refugees face a wide range of challenges when it comes to integration and acceptance within their communities. It is no secret that xenophobia and racism are two of the most pertinent issues that plague societies around the world today.

Adding to the various difficulties that refugees face is growing anti-refugee and anti-migrant sentiments, which have profound implications for refugees' social welfare and mental health as they migrate to and settle in new host communities. The current political climate and emerging policies on immigration in various western countries, has propelled refugee resettlement programmes into the everyday consciousness of the public through news and social media. Researchers have observed that refugees are often unwelcome in many communities as a result of the "rampant Islamophobia, racism, and anti-immigration rhetoric."[402]

The rise of populist, nationalist governments has boosted hate speech and xenophobic rhetoric.

From Hungary to the United States, political actors in power have resorted to anti-refugee and anti-immigrant stances that promote fear and distrust of foreigners. In some cases, leaders are expressing a complete denial of any need to respond to the world refugee crisis, by insinuating that most asylum seekers' claims are

---

[402] (Sona Circle 2021)

WHAT CAN WE DO AS INDIVIDUALS?

false and tearing down the basic notion that people have the right to flee for safety.[403]

Hundreds of thousands of refugees embark on long, perilous journeys every year, for the opportunity of a 'new beginning', only to be greeted by the stigma of their past, encroaching into their hopes of a new life with a clean slate.

Mental health is often stigmatised amongst the general population.

This is extended to a much greater degree towards the refugee communities who have often experienced traumatic events due to political, religious, environmental or social circumstances. The trauma caused by these events often begins before the event itself, that causes millions to flee from their homes, communities and countries every year.

While many of the required changes are at a macro-policy level, individuals who form a part of the general population have the power to bring about many small changes, which combined, can have a great impact.[404]

By acting together, we can change the historical trend of systemic oppression, discrimination and intolerance towards refugees and immigrants.

---

[403] Ibid
[404] Ibid

So, what can we do on an individual level to show our support and change the narrative of refugees and asylum seekers within our communities?

To start with, we can embrace diverse cultures. A small change in attitude can go a long way. An appreciation for different cultures, cuisines, fashions, languages, skin tones, and even physical appearances can help us understand so much more about the world we all live in. As human beings, we all have many similar shared values and ethics. If we can learn to embrace diversity, then understanding and empathy for others will follow naturally.[405]

We can support refugee businesses. By contributing to refugee businesses such as those supported by The Entrepreneurial Refugee Network (TERN), you could help support refugee integration. This could be as simple as buying bread from a refugee owned or supported outlet such as Breadwinners. You may not realise it but by doing these little things, you're helping someone feel like they are a valued part of a community, showing that the community is as much theirs as it is yours.[406]

We can employ refugees. Employing refugees is great for businesses. Aside from adding new skills and diversity to your business, it also creates a healthier work environment as different cultures and ideas working side by side produce the best results.

We can work together.[407] No two refugees have the same experiences. Each individual has needs and requirements which are based on their unique characters and experiences. It is therefore essential that we all collaborate and cooperate to

---

[405] (Sona Circle 2021)
[406] Ibid
[407] Ibid

understand the different ways in which we can best support refugees and asylum seekers in our communities.[408]

This is why there are so many diverse organisations which all have one thing in common, a shared commitment to supporting the skilled and dependable refugee workforce.

Is there a way you can offer support on a wider scale? Absolutely.

There are organisations and charities that act globally in offering assistance to nations that are struggling with refugee crises.

One of these places is Yemen. Previously, we looked at the ongoing humanitarian crisis occurring in the Middle Eastern country and the impact it is having upon the displacement of its people. Now we are more aware of the details surrounding the Yemen Civil War, let us talk about a number of the organisations and charities helping to stabilise the area and aid their recovery.

Firstly, The International Committee of the Red Cross has been working to deliver food, clean water, medical assistance and essential household items such as blankets and soap to those in need in Yemen. For example, in 2020, they provided 52,000 food parcels and 63,000 blankets to its inhabitants.[409]

Oxfam has been providing agricultural assistance, clean water and sanitation services. They provide families with food vouchers and have developed cash for work programs to simultaneously provide

---

[408] Ibid
[409] (British Red Cross 2021)

food assistance and to support local businesses. Oxfam is also currently working to educate communities about the spread of COVID-19 and how they can protect themselves from the virus.

Additionally, the Save the Children movement has been working to combat the effects of the famine in Yemen by treating malnourished children and pregnant or breastfeeding women. They also provide psychosocial assistance to help young people cope with the humanitarian disasters they have witnessed. 380 of Yemen's schools have been attacked, damaged or occupied by militant groups[410], so Save the Children is running temporary learning programs so that children do not miss out on an education.

Lastly, as well as providing food, medical aid and improving access to education for Yemeni children, The International Rescue Committee is calling for a ceasefire between parties involved in the Yemen Civil War so that aid can be effectively delivered to those who require it.

The humanitarian organisations in Yemen are making substantial efforts, but this is just a snapshot of what they're doing. Given that you are now more aware of what these bodies do, maybe you would like to play a role in offering assistance? These organisations have clear instructions on their websites about how to donate and what they plan to do with the funds they raise.

Ethiopia's northern region of Tigray is another area experiencing a severe humanitarian crisis as we discussed earlier. In our previous discussion, you may recall that the Ethiopian

---

[410] (VOA News 2021)

Government declared war on the regional government of Tigray[411], accusing them of violating their sovereignty and the rule of law. Neighbouring Eritrea took advantage of this and also invaded Tigray to destroy its rivals in the region. Thousands have been killed, 60,000 people have fled to Sudan and millions require support.[412]

There are many ways you can help this crisis by supporting the established organisations currently operating there.

Since June 2021, the UNHCR has appealed for donations in order to increase their supplies, which means they are prepared to respond to worsening situations between federal and regional forces in Tigray, as well as civilians there.

Refugees in Sudan are being sheltered in transit centres near the border, which are unable to accommodate the growing numbers. The UNHCR is cooperating with the Sudanese authorities to provide necessities, such as food and water, and are also working 24/7 with the goal of setting up a new refugee site.[413]

You can also help the situation by attempting to create change at the core. The Western world should take responsibility for the damages it has caused over the past 200 years through impoverishing Africa via colonialism.

Getting involved in the Stop the Maangamizi campaign and signing their petition is one way to do it. As stated on their website, "The campaign aims to urge the UK Government to commit to a holistic process of atonement and reparations... this includes recognizing and addressing the longstanding legacies of slavery,

---

[411] (BBC News 2020)
[412] (Medecins Sans Frontieres 2021)
[413] (UNCHR 2021)

colonialism and neo-colonialism, such as the racial discrimination of majority world peoples, socio-economic inequality and environmental injustice."[414]

It is well known that Greece is a nation that hosts many refugees and asylum seekers, with around 120,000 living in numerous camps as of 2021.[415]

We believe it is important to consider the conditions within these refugee camps on internationally recognised days, such as Mother's Day. Specific calendar dates such as these are often some of the most cherished occasions for many people across the world. It is a time where close friends and family come together to celebrate and enjoy each other's company. Mother's Day serves as an unavoidable reminder to parents living in refugee camps of the hardships they are experiencing and the past lives they have left behind.

There are many ways you can help refugee women who are trying but struggling, to care for both themselves and their children on a daily basis in the squalid conditions of the camps.

Choose Love is a UK-based non-governmental organisation that provides aid to "refugees and displaced people with everything from lifesaving search and rescue boats to food and legal advice."[416] Through their website, you can buy vital supplies like soap, milk, hot food, baby essentials and nappies.

---

[414] (stopthemaangamizi.com 2021)
[415] (UK 2021)
[416] (Choose Love 2021)

Choose Love also provides "Women's Support", through purchases from their shop, refugee women and girls can gain access to vital services and information for those that are most vulnerable.

Another service is a charity called Global One, a female, Muslim-led international charity. They acknowledge the hardships and trauma of giving birth and raising a child in refugee camps. Global One has constructed a kit for mothers and babies who live in such a place. The "vital Mother" and "Baby Box4Life" contain everything a mother needs for the first 6 months after giving birth.[417] Using the right products, maternal deaths can be avoided to a great extent. Global One's maternity boxes will ensure women have access to quality maternity care, and thus improve displaced people's lives.

In addition to all of the above, you can also sign the #EuropeMustAct petition, that calls for relocating asylum seekers fairly, overseeing Greek refugee camps, and registering European legal, medical, and protection personnel to work within the Greek camps.

Furthermore, you can protect refugees by joining a political party that is devoted to improving their treatment.

Government policy and politics play an important role in the refugee crisis. Political conflicts, in one way or another, usually lead to people becoming refugees. We will be able to solve the refugee crisis comprehensively only by changing governmental policy at the national level. Politics is always an important part of how refugees are treated when entering a country.

---

[417] (Global One 2021)

Often, political parties are reluctant or totally unwilling to support refugees or migrants for ideological reasons or fear of electoral defeat. As we have seen, in many Western countries like Denmark, France, the UK and the US, politicians from both right- and left-wing parties have been outwardly hostile to refugees and migrants and have refused to protect them.

Often charities and businesses can only do so much to support refugees and migrants, to get them access to safety, jobs, housing and financial support. Helping to solve this issue may feel overwhelming without large scale support from the government and national policies.

In spite of this, there is still so much you can do to help. How? You may ask. The answer is simple, direct action.

Direct action is where you personally help protect refugees and immigrants. This can be doing work to help protect and support refugees in your local community or in the camps across Europe and the world where refugees and migrants seek shelter.

One of the best ways to help refugees is to take direct action through your local community and get involved with unions.

Among the best of these unions is a renter's union.

As we have seen, homelessness is one of the biggest issues refugees face in the west, particularly in the UK. In most of Britain's major cities, a quarter of those sleeping rough are refugees and thousands more are without a permanent home.[418]

---

[418] (C. Miller 2019)

Refugees who have housing are often at risk of being made homeless. This is because they have unstable employment. As a result of the COVID-19 pandemic, 32% of refugees have lost their jobs, which is four times the national average. As a result, it becomes difficult for many refugees to pay their rent, leaving them vulnerable to eviction.[419]

You can help protect refugees and migrants from homelessness by joining, supporting or creating a renter's union in your area. Renter's unions are organisations that provide legal and physical protection for their members – both refugees and others – against eviction or discrimination by landlords and social housing associations.

Renter's unions gather tenants and create a network that collectively works together to protect their members from exploitation. This includes eviction, disrepair, unfair charges or extortionate rent and also pressures landlords to agree to the members demands.

These unions can be very effective at reducing evictions and preventing homelessness for their members, including refugees. In the event that a landlord tries to evict a tenant, the tenant can contact the members network, which will then prevent bailiffs from entering the building and evicting the tenant. A bailiff is not legally entitled to arrest individuals, so they are forced to withdraw, and landlords are then able to negotiate with the tenant instead of forcing them to leave.

They also are very effective at protecting renters' legal rights. Many renters - both refugees and others - rent housing that has fallen into disrepair but are unable to get their landlords or social

---

[419] (Salem Media n.d.)

housing associations to address this. Others have their deposits effectively stolen from them when landlords refuse to release it even though the tenant has done nothing wrong to the house. Renter's unions provide legal advice to their members and provide support to claim their money back, through sending formal letters to landlords, initiating legal cases and engaging in direct protests to encourage landlords to negotiate.

They also pressure the Government to ensure everyone has access to housing and prevent evictions and homelessness. For example, the ban on evictions that the UK Government has put in place since the pandemic hit is partly due to the pressure renter's unions have exerted on the Government.

Through their work thousands of people have been protected from an eviction. Thousands more have been able to force reluctant landlords to finally deliver necessary repairs to their housing, return deposits and cancel unfair charges.

They have also managed to reduce the extortionately high rents across Europe. Renter's unions in Germany have successfully fought for rent caps that make renting far more affordable than in many other parts of Europe thanks to longstanding, well established renters unions. In Berlin, for example, an average tenant pays half as much as someone in London.

If you live in the UK there are many different unions you can join and support depending on your location. In London, the London Renters Union is the best organisation to join, with branches all over the city.[420] If you live anywhere else in England or Wales then contact Association of Community Organisations for Reform Now (ACORN).[421] If you live in Scotland, then you can contact

---

[420] (London Renters Union 2021)
[421] (ACORN, Union for the Community n.d.)

Living Rent.[422] You can find contact details and further information on their website.

If you live in Germany, there are also many renter's unions you can join. Most of them belong to the Deutsche Mieterbund group - an umbrella organisation that represents 3 million renters. On their website, you can find the union that represents tenants in your local area. For example, the Berliner Mieterverein represents Berlin's tenants. The Mietenwahnsinn Alliance is also very active in Berlin.[423]

In Madrid, you can join the newly formed Sindicato De Inquilina or the Sindicat De Llogaters in Barcelona. In Ireland, there is the Dublin Tenants Association, the Warsaw Tenants Association in Poland, the Bond precaire Woonvormen in the Netherlands and Habita in Lisbon, Portugal.[424]

You can help refugees and migrants find housing by joining these associations in your local area.

Aside from renter's unions, you can also help refugees by getting involved in workplace unions.

As we have seen, refugees and migrants are often highly exploited in the workplace and denied safe working conditions, decent pay or job security. As a member of a union, you can exert pressure on all levels of management, your industry and even the government to improve the wages and working conditions for refugees and migrants.

How can I do this? You may ask.

---

[422] (Living Rent n.d.)

[423] (O'Halloran 2019)

[424] (Stringer 2019)

The answer is: strike action.

Your employer, industry and government may suffer economic harm if you threaten to stop working until your demands are met. As a result, they have great incentive to comply with your request and let you get back to work.

For instance, if you work with refugees and migrants who earn less than yourself or are forced to do unsafe work or are on zero-hour contracts, you can team up with other workers in a union and threaten to strike unless they are given safer, better paid and more secure work.

Even if you don't work with refugees directly, you can still help to protect them.

You can go into refugee workplaces and teach them about trade union tactics and their legal rights so they can unionise and fight for better pay and conditions. As a result, you give refugees the tools and knowledge they need to organise and threaten to strike if their employer does not improve their pay and work conditions.

Some unions in Europe have already started working to protect migrants and refugees.

For example, the confederation of British trade unions: the Trade Union Congress (TUC) and other members of the European Trade Union Confederation (ETUC) has committed to assist the inclusion of asylum seekers in society, and particularly in the workplace, with access to work and equal employment rights since 2015.[425]

---

[425] (Brooks 2021)

Other trade unions across Europe like the Belgian Confederation of Christian Trade Unions have helped organise refugees and asylum seekers into unions and provide advice on their legal rights and how they can fight for higher pay and safer work conditions.[426]

Of course, there is more to be done. Despite the hostile environment toward refugees we have seen in the West and the widespread exploitation of migrant workers, trade unions have been unable to defeat it entirely.

However, this can change. Joining a trade union to improve refugees working conditions through striking and unionising refugees can help them fight for themselves.

You can find the union that represents your trade through an online search. For example, if you're from the UK, you can find all major unions on the TUC website.[427] Though it is unlikely, if there are no unions that represent your industry then you can also establish one yourself. Through unionisation, you can do a lot to improve the working and living conditions of refugees and migrants.

Another way to directly help refugees is through starting or getting involved with an anti-raids group in your local area.

Glasgow's incident on Thursday, 13th of May 2021, gripped the whole of the United Kingdom. Lakhvir Singh and Sumit Sehdev were deported out of the UK by immigration enforcement police at 9am in the morning. Amazingly, the people of Glasgow came together and prevented the van from leaving. After a standoff lasting hour, immigration enforcement relented, and both Singh and Sehdev were released to return home.

---

[426] (Statista Research Department 2021)
[427] (TUC n.d.)

In the media, commentators and individuals marvelled at this miraculous and spontaneous uprising that prevented the callous deportation of two migrants who had lived in the local community for years and were simply trying to celebrate Eid peacefully.

This resistance, however, was not in fact spontaneous or miraculous, but the result of months of planning and organisation by a Glasgow anti-raids group called the No Evictions Network.[428] Prior to the raid, this group had established a network of locals prepared to resist whenever a raid took place and connected up with businesses, refugee charities and refugees and migrants living in the area who might need assistance. A local citizen who saw Singh and Sehdev being forced into a van called for this extensive network of people who came to help.

We, too, can carry out similar efforts in our communities since this incident was not an unrepeatable miracle.

Anti-raid groups exist across the country and work as networks to help inform refugees, migrants, their colleagues and friends of their rights and support in resisting attempts to deport them. An anti-raid group can be joined easily, and you won't have to commit a lot of time to it. The most important thing is to follow up on potential border police raids to prevent refugees from being deported and be available to physically stop them. You have the right to refuse to comply with border police, even though this may seem scary. However, they do not have a legal right to arrest you.

As an example, the anti-raids network in the UK has been doing exactly that. The network connects anti-raid groups throughout the Southeast. It has existed since 2012 and includes anti-raids

---

[428] (Delahunty 2021)

groups in the London boroughs of Haringey, Newham and Peckham and also in Brighton.[429]

Furthermore, as a response to the events in Glasgow, new groups were set up in Tower Hamlets and Hackney through the organisation of Haringey. There are also anti-raids groups in Bristol, Leeds, Sheffield, Edinburgh and, of course, Glasgow itself.

If you are unaware of the groups in your local area, then contacting the anti-raids network team is a good idea. It may be the case that there isn't an anti-raids group in your local area. In which case, you can set one up yourself! The anti-raids network and Haringey anti-raids websites both provide helpful advice on how to do so effectively.

Finally, volunteering directly with refugee charities is another great way to help refugees. These charities help to protect refugees on their journey to another country and also support their integration into communities.

By doing so, you can directly help refugees and migrants gain safer access to protection.

This can take many different forms.

The best way to help refugees and migrants who are being mistreated by border police and in camps is by volunteering for groups that act as legal observers. In doing so, we help protect

---

[429] (Anti-Raids Network n.d.)

refugees' legal rights and prevent abuse by border officials and camp staff.

For example, Channel Rescue gets volunteers to monitor the condition and treatment by border police of refugees crossing the English Channel from the continent. They provide them with supplies, rescue them from the sea if they are in danger and work to ensure that their legal rights are not violated.[430]

Similar work is done by human rights groups in refugee camps across Europe, documenting violations of rights. They then use this documentation to work in the legal, public and media spheres to make sure asylum seekers, refugees, and migrants' rights are respected and that asylum seekers are not left in horrible conditions without hope.

Another method is to volunteer directly in refugee camps to help distribute necessary supplies such as food, water and medicine and build shelters, toilets and shower blocks.

Several organisations need volunteers to assist them in this vital work. In Greece, organisations like Khora, One Happy Family, Sea of Solidarity, and Za'atar offer essential supplies and services to refugees from the ongoing Middle Eastern refugee crisis.[431]

In addition, the Help Refugees/Choose Love organisation works to provide similar services in Calais, Serbia, Bosnia, and Greece, whilst Go Overseas offers multiple opportunities to help refugees in Bangladesh, the United States, and elsewhere.[432]

---

[430] (Channel Rescue 2021)
[431] (Doyle 2018)
[432] (Choose Love 2021)

Last, but not least, you can volunteer for several charities that protect refugees from destitution in countries where they seek asylum and integrate them into communities.

In the UK, there are a number of organisations like this.

In Dover, Samphire helps refugees gain economic security, shelter, and English language proficiency, as well as educating the area about refugees and their experiences to counter misinformation.[433]

In London, Hackney Migrant Centre and Akwaaba both provide refugee families with food and a shared community space where they can make friends and socialise.[434]

Volunteers from Refugee Councils provide refugees and migrants with useful skills such as English lessons and assistance in accessing vital services such as hospitals, shopping, and transport.[435]

Organisations such as REvive Greece and Schoolbox help refugees in Greece to integrate into society, escape the difficulties of the camps and simply have fun. REvive Greece, for example, teaches refugee children coding skills, while SchoolBox provides education and creche services for refugee children to play and make friends.[436]

There are many great organisations where you can volunteer and directly support refugees. You can search for them online!

---

[433] (Samphire 2021)
[434] (Akwaaba 2021)
[435] (Refugee Council 2021)
[436] (REvive Greece 2021)

I hope that you've been inspired and shown that you're not powerless but can have a positive impact by getting involved and helping refugees and migrants in so many ways.

There is always something you can do, no matter what your circumstances are.

The task may seem insurmountable, but do not despair. As a Chinese proverb says, *"a journey of a thousand miles, begins with a first step."*

12

WHAT CAN BE DONE POLITICALLY?

Reader: Surely though, the refugee crisis won't be solved unless governments get involved to support them?
Author: Yeah, you're quite right!
Reader: So, what do governments need to do?
Author: A lot! Here are some ideas.

As I've said all along, the only way to truly and comprehensively address the refugee and migrant crisis is to change national government policy.

As good as local initiatives from businesses, individuals and communities are, none of them will be enough to solve the crisis unless they result in a change in policy at the national and international level.

Of course, it is on us as members of the public to make governments change policy by engaging in public campaigns, taking direct action in our communities, supporting charities or working within political parties. However, to do this effectively we need to have in mind what we are fighting for, what our plan is at the national level and what we want changed in government policy.

Only this will comprehensively protect refugees and migrants and enable us all to thrive.

The first thing governments should do to help is provide safe and fast access to safety in their countries for people seeking refuge.

The UK's departure from the EU marks a shift towards an ever more hostile and precarious environment for asylum seekers. The aim of the Conservative Government has been to impose policy that cracks down on illegal entry into the UK, with a stern rhetoric set to ensure that migrants caught will be sent back to where they had travelled from – put so eloquently by Prime Minister Boris Johnson in August 2019 - "we will send you back".[437]

The UK's policy towards border control and illegal crossing has been
to clamp down on people accessing via the English Channel. The hostile stance towards asylum seekers from the Government has meant a rise in asylum seekers risking their lives to access the country on small boats.

The UK and France agreed a Joint Action Plan in 2019 to strengthen efforts against migrants illegally entering the UK through the English Channel. The agreement saw 6 million spent on new security equipment such as CCTV and night goggles, increased beach patrols and intelligence sharing. Additionally, in July 2020, the UK committed £750 million to border security in response to Brexit and in August 2020, appointed former National Crime Agency commander Dan O'Mahoney as 'Clandestine Channel Threats Commander' to intercept small boats in the English Channel. Despite this, by the end of December 2020, a

---

[437] (Timberlake 2021)

total of at least 8,417 people had crossed the channel by small boat – quadruple the number from the previous year.[438]

Refugee Rights Europe, who have analysed the UK's policy response to small boat crossings describes the policies from the Home Office as having a "long track record of giving way to increasingly dangerous migration journeys across the channel" and also criticises the UK's post Brexit strategy as being a continuation of "misinformed and inhumane" immigration politics.[439]

Along with reforms on policy focusing on accessibility, additional reforms must also be made regarding the widely criticized accommodation that the Home Office places refugees in.

More than 25,000 people pass through the detention centres of Britain each year, in conditions which have been described as being worse than of that in prison. People are confined in their rooms up to 13 hours a day and describe life in the detention centres as deeply depressing.

The High Court's decision to rehome an asylum seeker who was placed in Napier Barracks in February 2021 has shed light on the poor conditions refugees and asylum seekers face, even in a 'developed' country such as England. The court had heard evidence about unsafe and unsanitary living conditions in which fourteen men shared one room, a lack of heating, as well as the unattended impact of a recent fire which had caused one man to sleep on the floor.

Bella Sankey from Detention Action, an organisation who defends the rights of immigrants detained in detention centres stated

---

[438] Ibid
[439] Ibid

"Priti Patel's experiment with segregated refugee ghettos is a divisive poison to community relations and is re-traumatizing survivors of genocide, rape and torture".[440]

Britain's accommodation for refugees and asylum seekers needs significant reforms. Fewer than 50% of detainees are actually removed from the UK and Home Office statistics show that 55% are released back into the community, which renders the entire incarceration period pointless. Yet the experience and trauma of these centres remains with those who are released for life as many don't recover from the horrors they faced.[441]

One of the most important ways governments can better protect refugees and migrants in our countries is through giving them proper economic support and shelter, thus lessening their vulnerability to experiencing poverty and abuse.

Across the West, refugees and migrants are banned from working whilst they seek asylum and are given pitiful income support. This is particularly bad in Ireland and Lithuania, where asylum seekers have no right to work at any point. However, it is not much better in the UK, US, Germany, France and Australia where asylum seekers have to wait 12 months to work and in the remaining European countries, they have to wait 6 months. Even after that period, asylum seekers struggle to get work because governments often only allow them to work if it can be proven that no local citizens can do the job instead.[442]

---

[440] (D. Taylor, Asylum Seeker Cannot Remain at Kent Army Barracks, Court Says 2021)
[441] (D. Taylor, Worse Than Prison: Life Inside Britain's 10 Deportation Centres 2018)
[442] (Migration Watch UK 2013)

Moreover, refugees are not guaranteed housing and struggle to find private rented accommodation as the lack of income support and opportunity to work means they often cannot raise funds for a deposit. Additionally, they have little local knowledge of the area and so often fall victim to discrimination by landlords and estate agents, making finding and securing housing very difficult. The result of all this? Many refugees and migrants across the West are extremely poor and often homeless.[443]

Further, the lack of financial independence, housing and security also leaves many refugees and migrant women in particular vulnerable to violence and mental health issues.[444] As such, protecting refugees requires us to drastically change government policy and ensure refugees are provided with proper material security, housing, and income support.

In the short term, one of the most important immediate policies to help achieve this would be to lift the ban on asylum seekers being able to work, as called for by protestors in London in 2020.[445]

Refugees should be able to start earning and supporting themselves immediately rather than having to wait the minimum 6-12 months as they presently have to in the West. This would mean that when refugees' applications for refugee status are accepted and they are expelled from state accommodation and have their state income support removed, they would not become as economically vulnerable.

In turn, refugees will be less likely to fall into poverty and homelessness and will be better integrated into their community. They will already have a stable income to support themselves, to

---

[443] (G. Salter, Refugee Homelessness: A National Crisis n.d.)
[444] (C. Miller 2019)
[445] (Lift the Ban 2016)

put down a deposit and buy key supplies. As a result, they will be more integrated into the local area as they will better know the people and geography of the region through their work.

However, whilst this policy would help, singularly, it is not enough to address all the elements of this issue. Even if the ban was lifted, many refugees would still struggle to get well paid work as they often lack local knowledge and struggle with a language barrier. If they do find work in Western countries, they often lack the same employment rights as local citizens and are much more vulnerable to exploitation by employers (like being paid below the minimum wage). Equally, many refugees are children and below the working age or have been so physically and emotionally scarred that they cannot work.

Moreover, this would do little to address the vulnerability of refugee women against violence and mental health issues.

Finally, lifting the ban only affects those who can claim asylum. Migrants, as we saw in Chapter 1, under Western law, are legally not considered equally deserving of protection as refugees despite many of them being displaced for equally horrific reasons (floods, droughts, economic poverty). These people would still be banned from working if the ban on asylum seekers working was to be lifted.

But *all* people deserve protection.

Therefore, in the long term, to truly protect all asylum seekers, refugees and migrants from poverty, homelessness and abuse, three fundamental policies must be put in place at the national and international level.

The first of these would be to guarantee housing as a human right by building more social accommodation. This would mean ensuring that if anyone - refugee, migrant or local - is unable to afford rented housing, they would be provided with state council accommodation. This would protect all refugees and migrants from the horror of homelessness and rough sleeping.

Crucially, it would also enable vulnerable refugee and migrant women to escape the risk of violence against them - either on the street or in a domestic setting with their partner. In the latter case, if they have managed to get rented housing with a partner, refugee and migrant women are often too scared of being homeless to leave an abusive home - providing them with guaranteed housing would enable them to leave the place of abuse more easily.[446] In order to do this, Western governments would have to build a significant amount of new social housing to provide for those who need it.

The second policy would be to provide all refugees and migrants with more significant income support and access to public services (such as healthcare and psychological support). This would ensure that refugees and migrants are not driven into poverty and, in turn, bad health but instead are guaranteed material support. In this instance, governments would have to allocate more money to public welfare and healthcare services.

The third, would be to build more rape crisis shelters and women's refuges. This would specifically address refugee and migrant women's risk of violence and abuse by providing safe spaces with trained professionals who can administer sufficient and appropriate support. These centres have had funding cut in recent years in places like the UK.[447] The Government should not only return that funding but should also provide even more to

---

[446] (G. Salter, 5 Reasons Why Refugee Women Are Particularly Vulnerable To Violence n.d.)

[447] (Whitehead 2021)

ensure that all women are better protected from violence and abuse and its damaging psychological and physical impact.

Another important way governments can help refugees and migrants is to help them integrate into their communities by providing them with appropriate and adequate resources. This will not only benefit themselves, but also the communities that they are a part of.

One of the main difficulties in smoothly starting a new life in the Western world for many refugees is the language barrier. The level of English for many displaced people arriving in the UK ranges greatly; some may have proficiency in English and want to improve, whereas others may have no knowledge of English at all. A good level of English is a key skill for many jobs, but it is also beneficial to allow individuals to be more independent and social whilst integrating into the UK. There is a responsibility for governments to aid new inhabitants in developing their language skills, otherwise, how do we expect them to truly become a part of the new community they are living in?

Currently in the UK, there are a number of services on offer that aim to enhance migrants' English skills, but these are often provided by charities. Refugees who have been awarded resettled status in the UK are given funding for eight hours a week of free English for Speakers of Other Languages (ESOL) during their first year in the UK. However, this provision is cut to four hours a week of language classes after one year, once you enter mainstream provision services in the UK and claim jobseeker's allowance. If you are claiming other "non-active" benefits (as the UK

Government calls them), you will not be able to access funding for ESOL courses, due to recent changes in legislation.[448]

So, the UK Government provides some assistance but not too much! Don't get greedy now.

Fortunately, there are numerous other services from charities and local groups that are willing to help alongside the Government services. Mostly these are free, but some do come at a cost.

Lots of organisations and charities that work with refugees in the UK also provide free English lessons. Some of the organisations that do so include the Refugee Council, Barnet Refugee Service and English for Action.

Similarly, dotted around the UK are designated places named "City of Sanctuary". Such areas offer refuge to people who are fleeing violence and persecution. In the UK, Brent, Lancaster, Morcombe, Leicester and Coventry are all Cities of Sanctuaries that offer language courses or support for refugees and people seeking asylum, usually for free.[449]

A lot of these organisations will also run community reading, discussion or listening groups that can help improve skills in a relaxed setting alongside the more formal structured lessons.

Without support from the Government (namely, through funding) many of these organisations may struggle to continue to provide their services in the future which will have a very detrimental impact on migrant populations. The UK Government must provide greater assistance to help integrate refugees into the country, however, this seems unlikely when taking into

---

[448] (Allen, How Can Refugees and Asylum Seekers Learn English in the UK? n.d.)
[449] (City of Sanctuary UK 2021)

229

consideration the direction of current policy around the treatment of migrants.

As we have outlined above, there are ways people can strengthen and hone their English skills with the help of charities and local groups, but ultimately more can always be done and we must continue to fight for this.

Another area that deserves further attention is the provision of, and access to, medical services specifically designed for displaced people. For many refugees, their traumatising experiences means that they require particular and specific medical attention.

A large proportion of migrants witness highly traumatic events which result in them having to flee. Many lives are then lost on the journeys to "safety" before people must overcome the grave difficulties in establishing a new life in host countries. Harsh policies and treatment of migrants make it extremely difficult for countless people to secure employment, resulting in high levels of poverty and poor mental health.

The European Migrant Crisis, which peaked in 2015, saw increased pressure and challenges for healthcare services. The accessibility to healthcare for migrants was impacted because of legislative, financial and administrative barriers. This consisted of things such as lack of cultural mediation services; lack of reliable information on the health history of migrant patients; lack of knowledge of entitlements and available services; lack of organisation and coordination between services.[450]

---

[450] (Antonio Chiarenza 2019)

Regularly, the impact upon child refugees and the support they need after their relocation is overlooked. Worryingly, the majority of mental health practitioners have not received training in how best to help traumatised children from other cultural backgrounds.[451]

There needs to be more focus on the aid young, displaced people receive. Under 18-year-olds do not only comprise around half of the world's refugees, but they also make up a great proportion of a future generation that will have a great impact upon society.[452]

YoungMinds is a leading UK charity that helps those who come into contact with asylum-seeking and refugee children, such as foster carers, social workers, and school staff, by offering guidance on how best to manage their mental health. The charity previously constructed a "Foster Carers Toolkit".[453] This consisted of multiple sessions where carers could come together to learn from the experiences of one another and put forward ideas as to how young refugee and asylum-seeking people can be further supported.

The Children's Society is a charity that centres its attention on helping young people. They, too, acknowledge that far too many child refugees have experienced harrowing journeys and are often left to battle with the effects of trauma as a result. Alongside offering general guidance in the early stages of these individuals rebuilding their lives, The Children's Society has specially trained practitioners who can offer young people counselling and mental health support for the length of time it may take for them to overcome their health issues.[454]

---

[451] (Refugee Council n.d.)

[452] (The Separated Child Foundation 2020)

[453] (YoungMinds n.d.)

[454] (The Children's Society n.d.)

Such groups are few and far between, however. Efforts to provide medical assistance to migrants in Europe in response to a crisis, such as the European Migrant Crisis, only work towards a short-term fix.

Fundamentally, to create beneficial and long-lasting change, there must be structural changes to the EU healthcare systems and how they operate.

Now that we've discussed safer access, economic support and help with integration for refugees and migrants, what is the next thing governments can help with?

It's employment!

There are many different policies in each country with regards to supporting employment for refugees and migrants and a number of businesses, charities and non-profit organisations are helping to support refugee employment opportunities.

Sweden is a great example of a country with good systems in place to help newly arrived immigrants and refugees quickly find relevant work.

Their Fast Track model, for instance, involves the Swedish Public Employment Service in which a system has been put in place where newly arrived peoples are given the ability to learn new skills.[455]

Why would they want to teach people new skills?

---

[455] (Ministry of Employment 2019)

It's because they have labour shortages in many different sectors and by training up staff who are willing to work, they can solve two problems at once.

The Swedish Government is making it easier for newly arrived immigrants and refugees to establish themselves in the country's labour market. By searching for existing skills among arrivals, they can place individuals into jobs they have expertise and experience in. If this isn't the case, then they still have the opportunity to develop new skills and be placed in roles in which there are significant shortages. This is merely a steppingstone for the young first-time workers to help them find their feet when they arrive - they can still later pursue the careers they are striving to have in the future.

The fast-track system does not apply to a single sector or specific level, it has specifications for chefs, healthcare professionals, teachers, social workers, economists, lawyers and many others.

For example, the fast track for newly arrived social scientists means that work experience can be combined with lessons in Swedish for the workplace. To make use of the skills of university graduates educated abroad and to ensure that they find employment that's in line with their education and experience, the Swedish Government sees the need to establish a fast track for those with an academic background in different sectors.

Although it is true that in the case of Sweden, they are seeing employment shortages in certain areas and are looking to fix that, they have still been at the forefront of equal opportunities and fair employment for many years. And a nation who may be looking towards implementing the Swedish methods is the UK, which has only become more apparent through the UK's exit from the European Union.

The long-awaited trade deal that never came ended on December 31, 2020, and saw the UK suffer a no-deal Brexit, which most agreed would have been a catastrophic development for the agricultural sector (amongst others). This resulted in tariffs no longer being a threat but has meant the end to free movement of labour, ultimately leaving the food and farming sectors exposed to a potentially huge shortage of seasonal and casual workers which have traditionally been filled by EU nationals.

Workers who usually came to the UK from the EU to carry out jobs such as livestock slaughter and vegetable picking and packing have struggled to meet the criteria required under the Government's new points-based system. The Government has, however, relaxed the rules for vets, veterinary nurses, butchers, and agricultural engineers and announced a seasonal worker's pilot scheme set for 2021, but a shortfall of workers is still highly likely.

There are currently many UK farms who arrange volunteer schemes for asylum seekers. They do this because for asylum seekers, finding jobs is not yet an option, and providing them with an interesting day helping and learning about British farming traditions is seen as beneficial to their wellbeing. These volunteer days have been running for several years, and with the inevitable shortage of labour in many of these industries, it seems a perfect fit to transition displaced people into staple workers of the country.[456] If a system were to be put in place, like those in Sweden, it could go some way to closing the labour shortage gap the UK will inevitably face.

One such pilot scheme that has shown results in the UK is the Refugee Entrepreneur pilot, a business start-up training scheme. The pilot is funded by the Home Office and the National Lottery

---

[456] (J. Bulman 2019)

Community Fund and supports displaced people for a year, guiding them from the initial idea stage to their business launch. Since the start of the scheme in 2019, over 112 people have gone through the programme, and it is said that a further 585 will be helped through the scheme over the next 18 months (2021-2022). 25% of the people who have completed the course did so during the 2020 pandemic which would have been a major boost for people who were struggling financially. The pilot has been given an additional £1.7 million to expand its locations and according to the Asylum, Migration and Integration Fund, the scheme will be looking to have similar success in the future.[457]

The Centre for Entrepreneurs, who currently oversees the pilot scheme, says the "pilot proves that tailored business support for refugees works", and is now calling for it to go further. Matt Smith, policy director at the centre, added *"What we now need is commitment and collaboration at a national level from businesses, banks, local authorities and the third sector to ensure that every interested refugee can access this vital support and start to rebuild their lives through entrepreneurship".[458]*

The need for refugees in employment is not just in Europe, but all over the world.

Following Starbucks' announcement in 2018 to hire 10,000 refugees across European stores by 2022, many companies in the USA are looking to benefit also.[459]

A short study was completed in 2018 with the help of 26 employers in the USA. The report found that 73% of these

---

[457] (Centre for Entrepreneurs 2021)
[458] Ibid
[459] (CBS News 2017)

companies recorded higher retention rates for refugees than for the workforce as a whole. This even applied to industries in which high turnover is common, such as meatpacking, where refugees left the job in far smaller numbers.[460]

The executive director of the Tent Partnership for Refugees felt that *"refugees really crave stability, and I think they really feel a sense of loyalty to companies that might have taken a chance on them."*[461]

In the West, and in particular the USA, there is a stigma that refugees and immigrants are all looking for manual labour and are of no real benefit to industries outside of this area.

In the US, an investigation by think tank Migration Policy Institute found that nearly half (48%) of all immigrants that arrived between 2011 and 2015 had a university degree and the eagerness to learn and progress.[462] Once you learn this, it's quite shocking to realise how many talented individuals aren't being utilised or being given chances, even when compared to people who are less educated.

Companies are only recently becoming aware of the vast experience and education that many displaced people possess. This could mean that, finally, people will be hired based on their skill rather than their national background. You shouldn't be asking where somebody comes from, you should be asking what that person can do.

If the reasons above are still not enough for a business to invest in displaced peoples, there is another way to incentivise companies. That's to give them money. It may seem crude, but if that's what it takes to get the ball rolling, then so be it.

---

[460] (Roldan 2018)
[461] (Peters 2018)
[462] (Jeanne Batalova 2021)

Costa Rica has been using this method of hiring refugees. The United Nations High Commissioner for Refugees (UNHCR) and the Ministry of Labour and Social Security (MTSS) have established, through a programme called Employment Integration (Intégrate al Empleo), a scheme whereby companies who sign an agreement with these institutions will receive an economic bonus for every refugee they hire. This bonus is ₡500,000 Costa Rican Colón's (approximately £577) for each refugee they hire.[463]

This programme was in response to the increase in the flow of Nicaraguans to Costa Rica in 2018 when many had to leave their country due to the political situation in the neighbouring country. The program states that the company's payroll must increase with these hiring's, that is, there can be no substitutions of the company's current employees to grant work to the refugees.

Only full-time refugee hires are accepted. The economic incentive will be given to the company in a single instalment at the end of the three months following the hiring. If the refugees do not comply with the employment contract and must be dismissed before these three months, the company will not receive the money.

As explained above, this is a very blunt way to lure companies into hiring people who have been displaced, but hopefully this is just the way to open the door and that it will eventually lead to future hiring, hopefully without the need for cash incentives.

Ah, but I can already hear you grumbling.

---

[463] (Leandro 2018)

"But, that's all well and good and obviously would be lovely for them. But how on earth can we afford all that house building, income support, refugee training and hiring schemes? It's all too much! Surely these policies are all pie in the sky?"

Honestly, you're so predictable.

In fact, it's very much affordable to enact all these policies, particularly for Western countries.

All governments need to do is to raise taxes on the wealthiest 5% of the population, borrow some money and use these funds to enable the financing of house construction, income support, public healthcare and women's support centres.[464] Taxing the wealthiest and borrowing money to fund such social welfare projects are relentlessly criticised in right wing media because such things threaten the wealth of the billionaires who own these papers and TV stations and control their output.[465]

However, both are very achievable.

Firstly, a significant amount of money could be raised for social projects without the Government even having to increase the tax rate on the wealthy. This is because the wealthiest 5% of the population at present avoid significant amounts of tax that they are legally required to pay. They do this through funnelling money into tax havens and distributing profits made in countries like the UK into countries with lower tax rates. This causes our countries to lose trillions of pounds each year. For example, in 2019, the UK Government alone lost £35 billion that should have been paid in tax.[466]

---

[464] (Shaxson 2020)
[465] (Chivers 2021)
[466] (Turner 2019)

Western governments can clamp down on this activity in a variety of ways. For example, a global minimum corporation tax limit can be imposed, as was recently agreed upon by the G7.[467] This would prevent some countries from having significantly lower tax rates than others, which would remove the possibility and incentive for the wealthiest to funnel their money away from where it is earnt into tax havens.

Another, comprehensive solution would be to impose a 'unitary tax'. This would take a firm's total global profits, then allocate those profits to the countries where it does business, using a formula based on the size of sales, employee headcount, and capital deployed in each place, then each country taxes at its own rate – including excess profits taxes.

Secondly, governments can close tax havens. For example, the Cayman Islands is a tax haven, but it is technically legally controlled by the UK Government. Should the UK Government choose to exert its authority, it could fairly easily stop the wealthy funnelling its money there by forcing them to adopt the same tax rates as the UK.[468]

Finally, it is perfectly possible to raise the tax rate on the wealthiest above what they currently are in many Western countries and instead use this money to fund social welfare. This can be done by raising income taxes on the highest earners and corporate tax on large businesses.

Indeed, that this is possible is proven by countries like Denmark, Sweden and Finland who have higher tax rates on the wealthy and use it to fund social welfare. In all these countries, the tax rate for the top 5% of earners is from 55-60%, significantly higher than in

---

[467] (BBC 2021)
[468] (Shaxson 2020)

other countries in Europe like the UK where it is 40%.[469] Similarly, Austria, for example, has higher rates of corporate tax than countries like the UK, 25% to Britain's 19%.[470]

Crucially, they have used this taxed money to enable them to fund a far more comprehensive social housing, income support and job training schemes for those in need.[471]

Finland for example has essentially eradicated homelessness and extreme poverty through this.[472] Likewise in Vienna, social housing provision is some of the most generous anywhere in the world, enabling the capital to achieve very low rough sleeping rates.[473] Meanwhile in the UK, where social housing provision is significantly reduced, over 200,000 people are homeless and prior to the pandemic there were 10,000 sleeping rough in London alone.[474]

Neither Finland's nor Austria's systems are perfect, however. Both could do even more to support the poor, refugees and migrants by providing more government funding for these projects. But their example does prove that governments can do a lot to support them just through increasing social housing and income support.

What's more, history proves we can fund social welfare and public housing too! Across Western Europe, there used to be far higher tax rates for the wealthy and far more comprehensive social housing and income support for the poor. In the UK for example, the top rate of tax from 1945-1973 fluctuated from 70-90%.[475] This

[469] (Trading Economics 2021)
[470] (Trading Economics 2021)
[471] (Frank Martela 2020)
[472] (Henley, 'It's a miracle': Helsinki's Radical Solution to Homelessness 2019)
[473] (Ball 2019)
[474] (The Big Issue 2021)
[475] (Kenner 2020)

enabled the Government to consistently fund comprehensive social housing such that 40% of people lived in social housing and homelessness and rough sleeping was at significantly lower rates than today.[476] Yet this did not destroy the economy; from 1945-1973, Britain had the highest economic growth rates in its history.[477]

Finally, the experience of the pandemic has proven beyond all doubt that the Government can end rough sleeping and provide shelter for all if it so wishes. Indeed, in the UK the Government funded the "everybody in" scheme which, overnight, housed thousands of rough sleepers in order to prevent the spread of COVID-19 amongst its massive homeless population. This reduced the number of rough sleepers by 37%.[478]

We can afford it; we just need the political will.

Some might say this is immoral, that those top 5% of billionaires deserve to keep every penny they have.

However, this is simply not the case for three reasons.

Firstly, even if you believe inequality is fair, are you really telling me a business owner like Jeff Bezos deserves to earn in one minute what the average worker earns in a year?[479] Is it in any way humanly possible that he works that much harder or contributes that much more as an individual to the economy? Surely not.

---

[476] (E. Hobsbawm 1995)
[477] Ibid
[478] (Rough Sleeper Numbers Down 37% in England During Covid Pandemic 2021)
[479] (Warren 2020)

Indeed, as economist Joseph Stiglitz highlights, the idea that the billionaire class is made up of 'geniuses' who gained their wealth 'fairly' through their ground-breaking contributions to society and greater work ethic is a myth.[480] Bezos and the wealthiest 1% like him by and large didn't make their money by working longer hours or making new discoveries, technologies, products or having new ideas that contributed significantly to scientific human advancement. Rather, they have profited largely by taking existing technology, infrastructure and inventions financed and produced by the public at large and figured out ways of capitalising on them to produce marketable products.

Did Mark Zuckerberg invent the internet? Did Elon Musk invent the technology that goes into Tesla cars or SpaceX shuttles? Did Jeff Bezos build or finance the global transport infrastructure of bridges, roads and boats that enable his Amazon delivery service to function. Absolutely not. The vast majority of those were created by unnamed scientists, technicians and workers in labs, factories and construction sites funded by the public taxpayer.[481] In light of this, surely, it's not unreasonable to demand that the 1% pays back more in taxes to the public who enabled them to profit so ridiculously off other people's ideas.

Secondly, as it is, the taxation system actually takes more money from the poorest than the richest. Studies have found that these groups actually pay fewer taxes than their poorer counterparts, when, by all logic, it should be the other way round.[482] Therefore, it only seems fair to raise taxes on the wealthiest.

Thirdly, the COVID-19 pandemic has made raising taxes on the rich even more logical. Throughout the pandemic this wealthy elite has only increased its income through the stock market which

---

[480] (Stiglitz 2013)
[481] Ibid
[482] (Ingrahamm 2019)

has been artificially inflated by government spending, whilst the poorest have lost jobs and income. The result has seen the poorest lose £3.7 trillion in wages whilst the rich have gained that same amount in assets.[483] Surely, it's only fair that we redress this imbalance and use some of the billionaire elite's money (money they won't even notice is missing) to support the poorest and most vulnerable in our society.

Equally, countries are more than capable of borrowing massive amounts of money without causing significant economic damage.[484] If borrowing in and of itself was a significant threat to Western economies, then it would follow that all Western countries would be in serious trouble as they are all in huge amounts of debt. The US, for example, has an immense sovereign debt of 28 trillion dollars as of 2021, and yet remains the largest economy and most powerful country on earth.[485]

How is this possible? Because, at base, governments aren't like individuals, households, or businesses.

Creditors basically always trust big Western economies to pay back their debt because these states technically control the whole national economy of trillions of dollars of value. They therefore always have the capacity to raise the necessary funds through taxes should they need. Indeed, creditors trust states far more than they trust any other business or individual to pay back debt and so are very keen to lend money to states.

For example, US state debt, known as 'treasuries', are the most popular asset to buy on the financial market. This makes borrowing very favourable for states as they can effectively make

---

[483] (TRT World 2021)

[484] (Pettifor 2018)

[485] (Gidin 2013)

creditors compete to lend money to them. Creditors will thereby let states borrow money for far longer than individuals or businesses and at far lower interest rates. So long as the state's economy is growing and they are capable of paying back the interest on this debt, it's not a problem as creditors will trust that the state won't default and that their money is secure. In fact, creditors prefer it if they aren't paid off quickly as that means they can extract more interest.[486] The fact that interest rates are so low, the lowest in 30 years, also means it's actually the best time for states to borrow money.

All this is to say that, in essence, the amount of borrowed money necessary to provide social housing and income support to those who need it - like refugees and migrants - would be a drop in the ocean next to the already existing debt Western states comfortably manage.

Indeed, if it's possible for governments to bail out banks and businesses with borrowed money as they did in the 2008 financial crisis and the 2020 COVID-19 pandemic, then surely, it's possible to do the same to protect the victims of poverty, war and natural disasters.

More importantly, in the long run, spending money on social housing, income support and training schemes would likely *make* money and enrich our economies.

Sounds weird, I know, but bear with me. This happens for many reasons.

---

[486] (Ilzetzki 2020)

Firstly, giving housing and income support to people who need it, lowers the amount of money people have to spend on rent and food supplies. This leaves them with more money to spend on goods, services or investments that they might otherwise not have been able to afford, which in turn stimulates businesses to grow and so the economy to thrive.[487]

If that sounds confusing, then just imagine this scenario. Tomorrow morning you get a letter from the government in the post. Inside the letter is a £300 cheque. You now have 300 extra pounds to spend.

What do you do?

Well, you're hardly likely to bury it under your mattress, unless that's the kind of shady thing you like to do. You might put it in a bank account and save it or invest it in stocks. But, let's be honest, with your housing secure, the thing you're most likely to do is spend it. Maybe you'll buy yourself a meal at a restaurant or put it towards that computer or holiday you wanted but couldn't afford before. Either way though, extra money is now flowing into businesses and the economy, either from you directly buying products or from banks investing in them with your money.

Now imagine this on a larger scale. This is what would happen if we gave more economic support to refugees through housing and income support. Where they may have previously been driven into poverty and homelessness, spent little and contributed little to the economy, through giving them support they are now able to spend money in the economy or invest, which helps promote growth.

---

[487] (Koukoulas 2015)

Similarly, studies show that by giving people the safety and security of housing and income, public health is improved. This lowers the cost of public health and social care services, reduces the likelihood of theft and other crime, overall, thereby lowering the cost of policing and imprisonment.[488]

Furthermore, giving those in need economic support, training in employability skills and lessons in the local language, ensures that the poor, refugees and migrants are able to have a secure and stable platform from which they can learn new skills, get a job and contribute to the economy.

By contrast, if these very same groups are forced into poverty and homelessness and denied access to training and integration schemes, they are completely unable to learn new skills, get a job and contribute to the economy. In all these ways and more, spending money on social housing, income support, job training and integration schemes actually contributes to the growth and enrichment of national economies.

And if you're still concerned about the debt then never fear, this helps with that too! By increasing economic growth through spending, governments increase the amount of money they get back from taxes which enables them to pay back money they borrowed. In many ways then, borrowing and spending on these services pays for itself in the long run.

So no, it is not 'pie in the sky' for the government to fund these policies. In fact, it is practical and economically logical.

---

[488] (London City Hall 2019)

CONCLUSION

ARE REFUGEES HERE TO STAY?

Author: You've made it! I bet you're relieved.

Reader: Is there nothing else to learn about Fugees...I mean refugees!?

Author: My how you've grown. So, other than the difference between Fugees and refugees, what would you say are the main things you've learnt from this?

Reader: Wait! You want me to write the conclusion?

Author: Yeah, to be honest, I'm tired.

Reader: Ok, here goes nothing...

It all started about 11 chapters ago when I found out who refugees are. Although I was a little bit confused at first, I *was* actually aware there is a global refugee crisis from what I have seen on the news, but I didn't know the difference between refugees, asylum seekers, and migrants.

I have to admit, initially I had thought a refugee was just someone who didn't like where they were living so they chose to move to another country to maybe get a better job or something. But I now realise it's much more complicated than that! So, I think I remember this one; a refugee is someone who is unable or unwilling to return to their country of origin owing to a well-founded fear of being persecuted for reasons of race, religion, nationality, membership of a particular social group, or political opinion."

Author: Crikey! You've got the UN definition of a refugee word for word!

Reader: I know I didn't give off the best first impression, but I have been trying to take this all in.

Author: No no, I'm impressed, please continue.

Refugees are entitled to a certain amount of protection in their new location, but things are slightly different for asylum seekers. These people have left their place of origin and have applied to gain refugee status. If the government of the new country in which they have settled accepts their claim as to why they left, then they become refugees. However, up until this approval they are on their own and so often applications are turned down.

That brings us to migrants. I struggle a bit with this one. Migrants are essentially long-term tourists, right?

Author: Ah! You were doing so well!

Reader: Oh, come on, bear with me here, I just need my memory jogging.

Author: Ok, migrants leave their homeland but not because -

Reader: Stop! I've got it.

Migrants are similar to refugees in the sense that they leave their home countries, but not because they are persecuted politically. They may leave because of economic reasons such as facing poverty or an unstable and volatile economic landscape or for climate reasons such as floods, droughts, hurricanes. Or even more simply, because their family and community has moved, and they want to be with them.

Author: Nice work, you've nailed that.

Reader: Yeh I realised knowing these terms is pretty important in the context of the whole book and understanding the ongoing refugee situation across the world. Anyway, let me continue.

I thought that the refugee crisis was quite a recent occurrence, so I was shocked to find out people have been fleeing their homelands because of political unrest since 740 BCE. The 'Lost Ten Tribes' from ancient Israel were banished by the Assyrians when trying to take control of what is now Syria, Iraq, Iran, Turkey and Kuwait.

Also did you know that 39% of the world's 80 million displaced people are hosted in just five countries?

Author: Well yes, I did write this book.
Reader: True. Still pretty crazy though.

It means that over 30 million people who have left their homes are now in Turkey, Colombia, Pakistan, Uganda, and Germany. You'd think some other countries would be more welcoming in helping these individuals out, wouldn't you?

Anyway, chapter 2 taught me about what really causes there to be refugees. There are 4 main factors that cause displaced people: war, political and religious persecution, economic collapse, and climate change.

I was not surprised that war was one of the biggest contributors, but outside of Syria and Afghanistan I hadn't realised the impact other wars have had. The civil war in South Sudan has caused the worst humanitarian crisis in Africa, with over 4 million people becoming displaced, meaning that the country falls only just behind Syria and Afghanistan in terms of the number of people who have fled.

Religious persecution and its detrimental effects, I'll admit, was something I was less aware of, but after reading about it, I now realise just how devastating it is. Rohingya Muslims have faced institutional discrimination since the 1970s. More recently, over 600,000 Rohingya Muslims and a minority of Rohingya Christians have crossed the border into Bangladesh since violence erupted in Myanmar's Rakhine State in 2017.

Although this is just one example, I now know that religious differences can cause fierce disputes that leave minorities in desperate situations. Being denied access to an equal and fair life because of the beliefs you hold seems inhumane, but sadly, it is the case in many parts of the world and therefore causes so many refugees to feel they have to flee.

I was more aware of the difficulties that economic hardship can bring, but less so the extent of the devastation it can cause in terms of displacing people. However, the example relating to Venezuela helped me come to understand the issues better. The Government chose to capitalise greatly on their rich oil resources which had been beneficial when oil prices were high, however, when they burst, the entire country's economy was left in tatters. They relied so heavily on oil that they had few investments to see them through this period of trouble.

Excessive borrowing created further problems, and the economy continued to shrink alongside the impact of hyperinflation. I remember reading that 1 million dollars in Venezuelan currency in 2013 would now be worth just $3.40! As a result, and alongside further complications such as food and medicine shortages, over 3 million have been displaced from Venezuela since then.

Climate change is a cause that many people, like me, don't realise has such a big impact in causing whole communities to flee their homes. The increase in global temperatures can and will be catastrophic. Sea levels are rising at such a rate that many low-lying settlements are starting to be destroyed. Over 2 million Pacific Islanders have already had to flee and the same has started to happen in parts of Bangladesh. Deadly storms are also becoming more frequent. It seems like it might be too late to stop the impacts of climate change, but even now I realise that something must be done to try and limit the consequences it might have on the planet.

Author: Wow, I sense a bit of passion in your tone there!
Reader: Where did that come from!? I've become more invested in this than I realised.
Author: That's great, we really need to spread this information.

Having learnt the main causes in the previous chapter, chapter 3 was useful in giving me a better idea of some of the horrific situations people are facing. The civil war in Yemen has not only resulted in thousands of deaths but has also destroyed roads and hospitals. Seeing your family die around you and living in a constant state of fear is no way to live.

Civil unrest in Ethiopia generated by political differences has led to thousands leaving the country and heading, instead, for the neighbouring Sudan. The Ethiopian Government declared war on the regional government of Tigray and neighbouring Eritrea took advantage of this and *also* invaded Tigray to destroy its rivals in the region. Thousands died and over 60,000 people have fled to Sudan, leading to millions in need of support. So many wars go on for years and often the local people have no sight of them ending. It has made me realise that if facing the same scenario, so many of us - if not all of us - would flee in search of a better life for ourselves and our families.

Reader: I'm a bit embarrassed to admit I thought that once people had managed to leave the crises taking place where they live, they would now be in relative safety and could begin their new lives.
Author: I think that's the case for a lot of people, so don't be too hard on yourself.

From what I have learnt, I feel it could be argued that the journey is the most dangerous stage of a refugee's path to settling somewhere new. Creating the funds to pay illegal and unreliable people smugglers is hard enough, but these journeys on boats and in the back of lorries so often result in many horrific deaths. Desperation forces people to take these incredibly risky journeys, highlighting just how bad conditions must be in their homeland.

In 2016, 71 Iraqi, Syrian and Afghan refugees suffocated in a truck whilst trying to reach safety in Germany. In 2019, 39 Chinese refugees died in similar circumstances in a refrigerated container travelling to the UK. Since 2014, over 500 refugees have died trying to reach Europe in this way. The fact these are just some examples of hundreds of similar stories of many losing their lives in such horrendous ways is gut wrenching. Taking time to read these stories and fully digest them really puts things into perspective. I think too often we see it pop up in the media and dismiss it as another tragedy rather than really considering that these are real people in truly hopeless circumstances.

Author: Precisely. I guess that that is a big aim of this book, to create a more vivid picture of the ongoing situation and get people to think more about those behind the stories they hear. Sadly, even beyond this stage, refugees still face a tremendous uphill struggle.
Reader: Yeah, the struggle certainly continues even after arriving in a new country.

We all have mental health and are affected by it to some degree - whether that be more severely in the form of mental health disorders or less significantly in wavering mood. But I can't imagine going through such terrible ordeals as refugees experience and then at the end, still having to handle current (and resulting) mental health issues. I dread to think how I would cope if I had to survive on just over £5 a day until I was given asylum. I've learnt that there are so many tough individuals who are able to not only push themselves through these circumstances, but a lot of the time, also push for their families and children who are dependent on them.

This leads to the point made about homelessness among many asylum seekers and refugees. 'Housing is seen as a privilege; but everyone deserves a place to live'. We in the West don't question what it is to have a place to live. So why is it any different for people who are arriving in the country with nothing. If I was in that situation, I would've thought that a roof over my head would be the least of my worries, but I was severely wrong.

Author: You're right about mental health affecting all of us, you were definitely wearing on my mental state when I first met you.
Reader: Yeah, I got that from your condescending tone in the first few chapters.

I, like many, was aware that refugees were often used as forced labour for illegal activities, but only when the local news felt that it was a big enough story. I did not realise the extent of which illegal work was carried out. Whether that be working within the smuggling industry or just working a normal job without proper identification, both are only reported when it suits the story. These stories rarely touch on why people are forced to take illegal jobs or work under the radar. Sometimes there are debts back home, or it could be the only source of income family members are receiving in war-torn countries.

Reader: Another issue which is an obvious one is racism.

Everyone knows that racism exists, but it is rarely understood as to why it exists. The book breaks down how racial abuse is given a cloak to hide under with intentionally misleading ideas and concepts.

One common misconception, 'they are going to take our jobs', was touched on quite a lot throughout several chapters in the book. When it was broken down how false this is, I began to wonder why that notion became so popular in the first place.

I can't imagine having to get up and move to a new country only to have everyone seemingly hate you for no reason as soon as you arrive. Imagine finding out that you are the cause of many people's problems in life, just because you are from a different country and have no money or home. Despicable.

Author: I know, I know. It's a sad world we live in where people play the victim card to actual victims. You remember anything else from part 1?
Reader: Er...oh yeah! Did you know that refugees and asylum seekers aren't actually the same thing? Mad.
Author: I told you that?
Reader: ...
Author: *And* you've already said that bit...Do you remember anything else? Like about why we've got responsibility to help support refugees?
Reader: Oh yeah...You want me to do some West bashing don't you?
Author: If you could!
Reader: Anytime.

So basically, the main cause of the refugee crises is CHINA!

Author: No that's not -

Reader: Don't worry, mate I'm just playing with you, give me some credit... Also, could you please pipe down, thought this was supposed to be my chapter?
Author: Ok I'll back off...
Reader: Where was I?

So, in chapter 6, I learnt that the West has a significant responsibility for causing refugee crises in recent history - from Syria, to Iraq, Afghanistan, Cuba, Venezuela.

While they are evidently not the only cause of this crisis, Western countries such as the United States, the United Kingdom, and other EU countries have contributed, through their economic and foreign policy decisions, to the displacement of millions of people.

The West has undertaken or helped fund destructive invasions, wars, and drone strikes in recent years, particularly in Middle Eastern countries. From 2001-2003, they invaded Iraq and Afghanistan and occupied them for close to two decades, and in 2011, they carried out bombing campaigns on Libya and Syria. They also financed the bombing of Yemen by Saudi Arabia throughout the 2010s.

The United States, in particular, has imposed harsh economic sanctions on countries like Cuba and Venezuela for decades.

And perhaps worst of all, the West contributes significantly to the impending climate change-induced refugee crises that are likely to occur in the future. The West has consistently been the most significant source of greenhouse gas emissions in raw terms as well as per capita. In fact, they remain the main contributor of emissions today when you include 'consumption emissions'. The majority of these emissions are caused by western corporations, state-owned companies, and wealthy elites, meaning that the west will bear the brunt of the roughly 1.2 billion refugees that could be created by 2050 if we don't change course soon.

All these Western policies have contributed to global instability and have resulted in millions of people being displaced from their homes. Thousands of people are fleeing Afghanistan right now due to a botched western invasion and interference that has destabilised the country. Our governments must acknowledge the huge damage they have done and stop it immediately.

However, this is not to suggest that people in the West should self-flagellate or apologise profusely in a useless manner. We should be doing everything in our power to end our destructive wars, arm funding, economic blockades, and greenhouse gas emissions as soon as possible. This is the main point of the chapter.

Let's face it - we helped cause the displacement of refugees, and we are also best positioned economically to provide them with support. We should be welcoming rather than being hostile towards them.

Author: That was an excellent explanation of the matter, well done!
Reader: Thank you!
Author: What did you think of the second part of the book? Was it as enthralling as the first one?
Reader: I didn't find it as captivating, but I found it extremely informative and it offered me insight into success stories, financial reasons for refugees, and also the impact that refugees have had on many countries around the world.
Author: Well, that still sounds pretty good to me, and by the sounds of it, you gained some useful information from this section as well.
Reader: Thank you, I was expecting a condescending joke, but I guess I have finally impressed you.

The second part of the book discussed what refugees have already done for us and what they can do for us in the future. Chapter 8 discussed the economic benefits that refugees can bring.

Clearly, refugees have overcome the negative effects many believe they are responsible for. They also add to increasing national average wages, and the economy of Lebanon, where a large percentage of refugees have fled Syria, reached its maximum growth rate after the heavy influx of refugees.

Perhaps they aren't such a huge burden on the economy as I first thought. Next, the chapter discussed ageing and how many countries are experiencing a drop in birth-rates and an increase in the percentage of over 65-year-olds. I've never considered either of these problems before, let alone proposed a solution. As soon as I read this topic, I immediately began to see how refugees can be beneficial. In a country where only 0.6% of refugees are over 65, young refugees could be useful as a stopgap measure for decreasing birth rates.

Reader: I also found it interesting to learn that in Russia, you could win a refrigerator for conceiving a child.
Author: I was also amused by that.

The statistics about independent businesses were particularly interesting to me. 21% of refugees in Uganda own a business that employs more than one Ugandan citizen. There are also 13% refugees in the USA who are entrepreneurs, compared to just 9% of citizens born in the United States.

A short anecdote like that is very useful to illustrate just how beneficial refugees can be.

The second part of this section examined the cultures that refugees and migrants bring to their new homes. Even though this chapter may not seem as important as the one before, most of it is taken for granted.

Author: Wow, you're on a roll. Would you be interested in writing the next book to follow this one?
Reader: Nice gesture, but no thanks.

Chapter 9 looked at cultural exchange and how people's own cultures impact their host countries.

I am aware of different cultures within my own country, such as various faiths, clothing, and food, but I still didn't realise to what extent refugees and migrants influenced my own culture. As a Brit, I of course enjoy fish and chips, but I would never have thought it was invented by a refugee. Ultimately, Jewish refugees who fled persecution in Europe would create a dish that the entire world associates with British people. It's hard to imagine something more influential than that.

Even though most British foods are not British, who would have thought it, eh?

Reader: What an eye-opening discovery to find in a book about refugees.

In addition, I appreciated learning about some pop culture references that I enjoy. Queen is regarded as one of the greatest rock bands in history, yet many people are unaware that the energetic frontman, Freddie Mercury, was a refugee. For me, discovering that his family left Zanzibar during the violent revolution for England in the 1960s was eye-opening.

Countless famous poets, artists and athletes have found refuge in another country, and if it weren't for them, the world may never have experienced Salvador Dali, Victor Hugo, or Khaled

Hosseini's artistic expression. Imagine a world where some of the most iconic people are prevented from creating their great works or distributing them to a wide audience.

Author: It is always fun to learn about famous people and their history. Hopefully, future refugees will be able to share their stories of success.

Reader: That's a good point, and speaking of success stories, the last chapter of part 2 is about social and scientific impact.

Author: Again...I know, I wrote the book.

Reader: Sorry, I get lost in what I'm saying and forget that I'm talking to you.

Chapter 10 focused entirely on the impact that refugees and immigrants have had on science and society, and it begins with a brilliant opening statement.

Author: Thank you very much.

It's a wonderful chapter that looks at the impact that people have had on the world. It has been demonstrated in a variety of different contexts, from scientists to politicians. Although everyone is familiar with Albert Einstein, most of us do not actually know what he accomplished, or even how he came to develop his theories. According to the chapter, Einstein's theories allow us to use things like GPS on our phones, as well as make science-fiction films more enjoyable.

I also found it very rewarding to hear the story of Sergey Brin, who founded Google, something most of us use almost every day. His background tells the poignant story of leaving the USSR during the 1970s as a result of rife anti-Semitism.

My eyes were closed before reading this book when it came to what refugees could bring to my country, or even how they have

REFUGEES ARE HERE TO STAY

helped us in the past, but this chapter has really helped to put things into perspective.

Author: Yeah, it's nice to be able to see what refugees and immigrants have contributed to the world, but it's important to realise that this shouldn't be the only reason for welcoming them. We made it a chapter near the end so you could see all the traumatic events that lead to these amazing success stories.

Reader: You were right to leave it for later in the book, as it is more effective after hearing the previous chapters.

Author: Do you remember anything about the final section?

Reader: Yeah, I just read it, so...yeah, obviously I remember it.

Author: Go on then...what were chapter 11 and 12 about?

Reader: It was about... ref... ref... refereezzzz... zzzz

Author: Oi, wake up!

Reader: Sorry, I'm really tired. We've been talking about refugees for ages.

Author: Get over yourself. You want a prompt?

Reader: Yes please.

Author: This section is about taking action.

Reader: Oh yeah, the aim of this section is to discuss what can be done to improve the problems refugees face and to do something about the cruelty they are subjected to.

This section of the book outlines ways we can help protect refugees, make our countries more hospitable to them, and help us flourish together as a society.

Chapter 11 discussed what we can do individually to help refugees. We could join political parties and help support refugees by funding and volunteering for charities. There is also information about the types of direct action you can take, such as resisting deportations of asylum seekers and immigrants by governments, as well as unionising in the workplace to protect immigrants and refugees from abusive working conditions.

Secondly, it explains what sorts of government policies should be enacted in order to assist refugees. Governments can help provide refugee passage into the country, support them financially to make sure they aren't made homeless or pushed into poverty, and help them (and everyone) get decent jobs.

Author: And?
Reader: And...while I was a little worried that all that government spending would cost me lots of money, it turns out that if these policies are implemented correctly, they won't cost me a penny. As a result of spending money to give refugees a secure platform to thrive, get a job, spend money, and contribute to the economy, these activities generate more money over time.

Author: And??
Reader: Oh yeah, and because closing tax loopholes and increasing taxes on the wealthy would make it very easy to afford. What a surprise! It turns out that all those billionaires sitting on their hordes of wealth do nothing to help the economy.
Author: Excellent! You hit all the key points...eventually. Congratulations! You did a decent job there.
Reader: Ah thanks! Perhaps we should go for a drink sometime. You could buy me a pint to congratulate me properly?
Author: Erm...
Reader: Excellent! What's your number? We can arrange something.
Author: Hmm... It's... 116...123
Reader: Let me just call it now so you have mine too. Wait, who's Sam Harry-Tans? Is that your name? Wait, where did you go?
Reader: Guess I'll have to wrap this up on my own.

It is difficult to predict what the future holds for refugees. Political instability, climate change, natural disasters, and war all play a significant role in the refugee crisis and can be unpredictable.

As we enter winter 2021, Afghanistan is experiencing yet another refugee crisis after 40 years of conflict, natural disasters, and poverty. According to the UN, *"the vast majority of Afghans are not able to leave the country through regular channels"* and *"those who may be in danger have no clear way out".*[489]

As a result of the COVID-19 outbreak and multiple national lockdowns across the world, many of us thought that a better time would come. But crises continue to occur, and millions of people are forced into unknown journeys that become detrimental to their physical and mental wellbeing.

We must question the notion that refugees come to the West solely for economic reasons and understand the difficulties and trauma refugees have faced. Thus, refugees, wherever they come from, will hopefully be accepted universally in the future - both politically and socially.

As has been noted throughout the book, refugees face dangers before, during and after their journey. Would parents really put themselves and their children through journeys that involve dangerous terrain, dangerous sea crossings, putting their trust and life savings in the hands of criminal smugglers for economic gain?

As individuals, we are responsible for raising awareness of the refugee crisis by educating the public about what is causing it - and how we should not see refugees as a burden but rather as opportunities for growth - whether economically or culturally. Only then can we truly ensure that refugees are here to stay.

---

[489] (Euro News 2021)

THE END

APPENDIX

HOW CAN BUSINESSES HELP?

Reader: Ah... we're back!

Author: Yes, it seems like there's still some unfinished 'business'... get it?

Reader: Yup, even my dog got it. Ok, so now I can see the huge benefits for businesses in hiring refugees.

Author: Great!

Reader: But how would you actually go about hiring refugees? Wouldn't it be really difficult?

Author: Not at all! There are loads of ways you can help your company hire refugees or help refugees get hired.

As of 2020 (pre Covid-19 pandemic), the refugee unemployment rate was at 18%. That's more than four times that of the UK average, thus refugee recruitment remains a key social and economic issue for over 150,000 refugees living in the UK.[490]

In attempting to enter the labour market, refugees are faced with several barriers, both social and systemic, which hinder their ability to find jobs.

Recruitment decisions are often based on misconceptions. For example, many employers are unaware that once an asylum seeker

[490] (Grierson 2019)

obtains refugee status in the UK, they are legally entitled to full and
equal rights to work as British citizens.[491] Why such a large percentage of businesses are unaware of this fact is bewildering, basic research and a willingness to help would provide all the information necessary.

Another obstacle faced by refugees is that professional and educational qualifications obtained in their countries of origin, are not recognised by British employers who tend to favour domestic qualifications. In addition, relevant UK work experience is usually a prerequisite to getting a job, something refugees often don't have.

For these reasons as well as language and other cultural barriers, refugees are put at a huge disadvantage in obtaining jobs and employment opportunities which leads to further employment gaps in their CVs.

There are various organisations within the UK and Europe that help to bridge the refugee unemployment gap by connecting socially conscious employers with the skilled and dependable refugee workforce. These organisations also promote equality not just within the workplace but also during the employment process for refugees.

The UK, in particular, has faced a stagnating labour force since 2019 and with the arrival of the Covid-19 pandemic, this problem is only getting worse. There's also the issue of the UK's ageing population, a trend which is only projected to continue over the next twenty years.

---

[491] (Citizens Advice 2021)

The solution? An effective integration strategy which includes refugees into the labour workforce, thus creating a reservoir of untapped potential as well as providing an effective integration method for economic and cultural socialisation.

Numerous studies have found that the refugee workforce could greatly benefit the future success of world economies and the businesses within them.

Let us remind ourselves of some advantages that refugees bring to the workplace: cultural diversity, higher retention rates, a wide range of skills and talents, and an appeal to a growing socially conscious consumer base who care about diversity and inclusion.

A lot of refugees have great skills and job experience. But when in a new country, the expectations and cultural norms are different from what they are accustomed to. This applies to crafting a resume as well.

It is essential for refugees and immigrants alike to increase their chances of landing a job, and by learning to match hiring managers' expectations, those chances are likely to increase.

Here are some important tips for boosting the odds, not just for refugees, but for anyone.

1. Essential information should come first

While every resume or CV is unique, there is essential information that should always be included on any resume in the UK and much of Western Europe.

- Your complete name (make it bold and use a shortened version of your name for easy reading)
- Contact details (including email and phone number; home address is *optional*)

- Academic background
- Previous work experience and a short description of each

This information may seem obvious, but every country has a certain format they follow. Below are some examples of personal information that is *not* necessarily important.

- Country of origin or immigration status
- Birthday and age
- Marital status
- Religion
- Political affiliation
- Any personal ID (i.e., social insurance, driver's license)

This information is unlikely to be relevant for a job and could be viewed by a hiring manager as oversharing or unprofessional. Or, equally, they could use it to discriminate against you. Typically, personal information is required only during the interview or when you have already accepted a job offer.

2. Showcase your skills

This entirely depends on the type of job you are applying for. But if your work is more technical and you are tapping into multiple industries, it can be a great idea to list down your skills and proficiencies, including the tools/machinery and software you use.

Adding languages is also a great indicator of skill, and some applicants often overlook a second language because it may not seem relevant to the job. On the other hand, it may not be necessary to add a skills section for "soft" skills such as communication, leadership, etc., especially if they are not relevant to the job. The only exception to the rule would be if you are an entry-level applicant and you have limited experience to showcase.

If this is the case, a skills section can help add much-needed depth to your resume.

3. List your accomplishments

In many countries, a resume can be a simple list of your job experience, with very little added detail. In countries like the UK, US, and Canada, an applicant is expected to highlight their accomplishments and strengths. Basically, you are selling yourself on your resume and so simply listing down your daily duties might not cut it. Your future boss will expect to see the impact you have had in your previous job or projects, instead of just a boring list of responsibilities. For example, instead of writing "created mobile app for a client", consider "created a mobile app using [app development software] to create a responsive version of our biggest client's website, making it more accessible to customers". The underlying responsibilities appear the same, but the latter is more specific and more impressive.

The only time it may be okay to have a short list of duties is for extra-curricular activities. This is because you don't want them to take up a lot of space, and short sentences may invoke the reader's interest and prompt them to enquire further about the experience or accomplishment.

Writing down your accomplishments in reverse chronological format is the standard way of writing a resume in the US and UK, and it is good to get yourself familiar with it. It simply requires you to list down your latest work experience and achievements first, and your oldest last. Don't forget to include the date range for each accomplishment!

4. Get the help of a friend (or a professional)

If you're in doubt or feeling lost about what to write in your CV, it may be time to call a friend or hire a professional writer. There's nothing wrong with getting a little help to polish up your resume. A friend who's had previous experience crafting a resume can be a big help even if they are not particularly skilled at resume writing. If, however, this option isn't available for you, your next best bet would be to hire a resume writer for a relatively small fee. For many refugee jobseekers, this option quickly pays itself off and has helped them land a much-needed job. Of course, you should always be wary of scammers and fraudsters, which is why it's important to look into writing service reviews first before paying someone to work on your resume or CV.

If hiring a professional isn't an option either, know that there are plenty of non-profit organizations out there that help refugees and immigrants build fundamental skills like resume writing. You can start by looking for them in your community.

5. Talk about your volunteering experience(s)

A lot of refugees don't include the many ways they have volunteered and helped their own community. For instance, you may be well-versed in English or any other language, and you've translated for other members of your community. Unless the only people you've helped are your family, you can include this in your resume as part of your volunteer experience. Vast numbers of people don't think to include small voluntary acts such as helping with a weekly religious group and caring for children or the elderly.

Once you've learned to write a stellar resume that is tailor-made to your next job prospect, you're one step closer to getting a pay check! Be sure to put in as much time as you can when applying and make sure that the effort you've put in shows through your resume. This way you can spend less time applying and more time earning money.

In the UK, the Government provides a huge amount of funding and incentives for businesses to encourage them to hire apprentices. For larger businesses, this includes the apprenticeship levy scheme. There are many benefits to using this scheme for both the apprentice and the employer involved.

So, what are apprenticeships?

Apprenticeships are paid training roles within a company that provide practical, on-the-job training for a particular trade or career. They are provided by a host business and a training provider, such as a local college, where the apprentices also learn about the trade in a classroom setting. At least 20% of the apprentice's time will be spent with the training provider. An apprenticeship can take between one and six years to complete. Apprenticeships develop a dedicated and qualified talent pipeline, suited perfectly to most companies. It gives businesses the opportunity to train employees specifically for the roles they may have in the future.[492]

How do refugees fit into this?

In the UK, refugees (those granted settled refugee status) have open access to the job market and can legally take part in any apprenticeship. However, the rules are a little different for people seeking asylum (who have not had their claim accepted).

As of June 2021, if an asylum seeker has been in the UK for 6 months without their asylum claim receiving a response, they are eligible to apply for and start an apprenticeship. This is also the

---

[492] (Apprenticeships 2022)

case if you have appealed against a rejection of an application and, after 6 months, still have not received a reply to your repeal.[493]

As refugees are often young (and so hold less experience of the working world), arriving from a break from work, or simply not used to UK workplace culture, apprenticeships are an ideal way to help talented, positive and bright refugees integrate into the UK workforce. Apprenticeships teach tangible, hands-on skills that are designed to make you job ready as soon as you leave the programme. This means that you are more likely to be able to secure a steady income quickly and easily.

So, if you haven't had a job before, or do not have experience with skilled work, then hands-on training that allows you to earn while you learn might be a perfect solution. There are several organisations with the aim of helping more refugees and people seeking asylum in the UK access valuable training and employment, allowing them to integrate into their new lives in the UK.

Ok, so now I'm sure you can see the huge potential benefit for your company in hiring refugees as well as why it's so morally important to help protect refugees.

However, as a business owner or manager you may, in practice, still be struggling to find the money and support you need to actually hire a refugee.

Luckily enough there are plenty of ways you can get help!

---

493 (Allen, A Guide to Apprenticeships for Refugees and Asylum Seekers n.d.)

The National Government, local authorities and other bodies provide funding schemes and support that enable you to provide opportunities and economic security for refugees.

Let's have a look at some of them.

One of the best ways a business can get help to hire refugees is through an apprenticeship scheme in which they claim an apprenticeship levy or grant.

Apprenticeship schemes are an ideal way to hire refugees. These schemes can help you hire more refugees and people seeking asylum in the UK, providing them with valuable training and employment and supporting their integration in the UK. By hiring a refugee on an apprenticeship scheme, you are able to claim significant financial support from the national and local government.

If your company has a payroll over £3 million, you will be automatically entitled to the Government's apprenticeship levy. This scheme was introduced by the Government in 2017 to encourage large businesses to provide high-quality apprenticeships.

As a company with a payroll of over £3 million, you will already be paying 0.5% of the monthly payroll (minus a levy allowance of 15,000) into a fund that can then be used to fund apprenticeship training. In addition, the UK government will add an extra 10% into this fund.

You then have 24 months to spend your levy fund on apprenticeship schemes within your business, or with partners in your supply chain (up to 25% of your fund). If you have not spent

HOW CAN BUSINESSES HELP?

this money on apprentices after 24 months, it will be claimed by HMRC.[494]

In a nutshell, if you aren't investing the levy back into your business through training apprentices, you lose it. So not hiring a refugee as an apprentice will actually lose you money!

It's also worth remembering that apprentices do not have to be young, untrained, new recruits. The money can be spent on training current employees, people of any age, or on people who already have some training or higher education, including people with degrees. In essence, you can use the apprenticeship levy to help provide work for all types of refugees.

Ah but I can tell you're thinking, "but my company doesn't have a payroll over 3 million! I'm doomed!". Never fear, dry your eyes.

If your company has a payroll under £3 million, there is still a lot of support for you to hire refugees as apprentices. If you do not qualify for paying the apprenticeship levy, you are eligible for direct government funding of up to 95% of an apprentice's training and assessment with a training provider. You will pay just 5%. In some situations, you may also be eligible for extra funding, especially if the apprentice is from a disadvantaged background.[495]

In addition to this initiative, local authorities sometimes provide grants for growth and new recruitment, including apprentices. In many ways, then, you actually have more support to hire a refugee as an apprentice if you have a payroll under 3 million.

That make you feel better? Good.

---

[494] (HM Government 2021)
[495] Ibid

273

Apprenticeship schemes and grants aren't the only way to get help hiring refugees. There are many other types of business grants your company can take advantage of in lots of different sectors.

Here is a list of some of the most useful ones in the UK as of June 2021:

1. Grants for graduates

If you are looking to hire a refugee who is also a UK University graduate, there are several grants and funding opportunities to assist with this. For example, a Knowledge Transfer Partnership could work for you if you want to run a particular project.[496]

Alternatively, the Santander SME internships programme is a fantastic scheme that supports anyone to access an internship with a UK SME but gives priority and extra funding to undergraduates from disadvantaged backgrounds. You'll need to be in contact with a university near you who runs this programme to get involved.[497]

2. Grants for the creative sector

Some sectors may have their own authorities or charities that will provide grants to help you hire from disadvantaged or minority communities. One of these is the creative sector.

Creative Access provides some grants and support for your company to hire those from disadvantaged backgrounds,

---

[496] (Knowledge Transfer Partnership 2021)
[497] (Imperial College London 2021)

including refugees. You simply have to register to be an employer partner online or over the phone.[498]

3. Local Grants for creating new opportunities

Finally, there are also many local grants from charities and local governments that you can use to help hire a refugee. Many local charities and government authorities support SMEs to hire new recruits who qualify for diversifying businesses by hiring refugees. Most of these opportunities focus on growth for your business and specify the creation of new roles in your business within six or twelve months. These may be training roles, like interns or apprentices. These grants are available in local areas across the UK.

For example, Arun District Council provides a host of grants for all sorts of businesses in its local area to help them grow. These range from the Shopfront Enhancement Grants for retailers, to the Start Up Grant for small start-up businesses, to the Invest 4 grant for established businesses.[499] Therefore, any business, regardless of its needs and scale, can take advantage of these grants to hire refugees to help grow and improve your products or services.

Likewise, the New Anglia enterprise partnership provides grants via the Growing Business Fund which support businesses to grow and develop. Through this, your business can gain up to £250,000 to grow, which can be used to hire refugees. Usually they provide 20-30% of the costs of a new business growth project.[500]

---

[498] (Creative Access 2021)
[499] (Arun District Council 2022)
[500] (New Anglia 2022)

If you feel passionately about workplace equality and the social integration of refugees, addressing a lack of diversity in your own workspace is a great place to start. Workplace discrimination is a problem that must be tackled to ensure a better working environment, not just for refugees but for all employees.

Research has shown that racial discrimination is rife throughout UK workplaces, with people of colour being hired less often despite being well qualified. Not only do refugees often face racial stereotyping but also stigmas associated with the refugee status. But having these types of conversations with your employers can be difficult, which is why we have created a list of key points that you can use to convince your boss to hire refugees.

1. Consumers care about diversity and inclusion

If your employer is reluctant to hire refugees, it's good to point out that consumers are increasingly concerned with the ethical values of the businesses they support. For example, in 2017 the Cone Communications CSR study found that 78% of consumers say they want companies to address important social justice issues. Additionally, 87% said they would purchase a product because a company advocated for an issue they cared about.[501] With an increase in awareness of systemic racism and racial bias, thanks to the Black Lives Matter movement, this stance is likely to gain some traction. Therefore, hiring refugees may have the advantage of satisfying socially conscious customers.

2. Potential to attract other skilled labour

Additionally, research has shown that millennials specifically want to work for companies that are more diverse and inclusive, and this affects which jobs they apply to.

---

[501] (Cone Communications 2017)

A study by Deloitte also found that millennials are more engaged with their jobs when they perceive their workplaces to be more inclusive.[502]

3. Refugees have a variety of employable skills

One reason many companies are reluctant to employ refugees is out of a perception that they lack relevant experience. However, often refugees' valuable qualifications and overseas experience are not recognised by UK employers. Therefore, the refugee population could be a large skilled workforce with untapped potential. It is a good idea to encourage your employer to be more open-minded about the types of previous experience and qualifications that could be highly relevant to their business.

4. Practice what you preach

If your employer likes to pride themselves on being socially conscious or 'human centric', it is worth reminding them that hiring refugees and creating a more diverse workplace, is a great way to prove that they really are.

5. You could be nominated for a diversity award

In various employment sectors there are a growing number of awards for diversity and inclusion. Examples include the Engage Awards[503] and the Inclusive Company Awards[504]. Being awarded with recognition for workplace diversity is something on which a company can pride themselves and will illustrate to consumers that they are dedicated to inclusivity.

---

[502] (Deloitte 2021)

[503] (Engage Awards 2021)

[504] (Inspiring Workplaces 2021)

So, now you are aware of improving refugees' rights to work, and you and your employer want to integrate refugees into the workplace. Congratulations on making a great business (and humanitarian) decision! Here are some top tips for making your recruitment practices refugee friendly.

1. Review language requirements

Refugees may still be developing their English language skills, and therefore job descriptions specifying a high level of English may be off-putting. Of course, some jobs, such as content writing roles, will require a thorough knowledge of the English language, but many roles will not. Have a second think through your role requirements to see what level of language skills is absolutely necessary.

In addition, consider whether key instructions and documents could be translated to different languages to accommodate refugee candidates and employees.

To make your roles even more accessible to refugees, you can embed English language training into your workplace. Currently, refugees can access funding for English tuition whilst unemployed and looking for a job, why not support their development by continuing this training in the workplace.

2. Support refugees to transfer qualification

Many refugees have prior qualifications, attended university, or were previously employed in skilled employment; however, the majority end up working in manual or unskilled labour in the UK. It is important for employers to be open to helping refugees prove and verify their qualifications, by working with regulatory and industry bodies, or by consulting the NARIC (National Academic Recognition Information Centre).[505] This will allow refugees to access employment that fits their skills and interests which will be both more rewarding for refugees and also enable employers to benefit from the full knowledge and talents of their employees.

3. Support employee's mental health

The long hours and demands on employees in the workplace can be stressful for us all. More employers across the country are coming to realise the importance of supporting their employee's mental health. This requirement is even more critical when working with refugees who have often had to overcome traumatic experiences before arriving at their host countries.

Making sure your workplace prioritises the mental health of employees, such as by allowing mental health sick days and creating a supportive and open environment around mental health, will help refugees (and other employees!) feel much more comfortable and also perform better.

4. Offer internships and apprenticeships

Internships and apprenticeships, can help refugees ease more gradually into the UK workplace, gain new skills, improve existing ones, learn about the workplace culture and also gain confidence. As with job applications, try to ensure that entry requirements for internships and apprenticeships are accessible to refugees, for example by reviewing the language requirements.

---

[505] (ENIC-NARIC 2022)

5. Publicise inclusivity in your workplace

Being a socially conscious and inclusive organisation is something to be very proud of. Be sure to let the world know that your practices are aligned with your values. Your actions could inspire others to follow suit. As a thought leader in the marketplace, this is your responsibility.

Make it clear on your website, social media, PR campaigns and also on job adverts that you are a refugee-friendly, diverse and inclusive employer. Share the steps you are taking to make your workplace inclusive, such as by making space for religious holidays or setting up a Cultural Awareness Network.[506]

6. Combat unconscious bias by educating employees

To make your workplace even more inclusive, be sure you are promoting inclusion and diversity at all levels. This can include delivering unconscious bias, anti-discrimination and harassment training to all employees, rather than just for the hiring managers. Engage senior management in the refugee hiring programme and offer training to supervisors to help them support their refugee hires. This will all lead to the creation of a positive, diverse workplace environment, not only for refugees, but for all employees.

---

[506] (iCan 2022)

ABOUT THE AUTHOR

SEYE ONABOLU is a globally experienced banking professional, social entrepreneur, and an advocate for equality. He has worked in corporate and investment banking for over 15 years across Africa, Middle East and Europe, specialising in (conventional and Islamic) financing and investment solutions for projects focused on Africa and the Middle East.

Alongside his professional journey, Seye is also motivated by his personal experiences. He believes that everyone deserves to be treated with equal dignity and provided with meaningful socioeconomic opportunity.

In 2017, Seye founded a non-profit social enterprise, Sona Circle which connects refugees with local opportunities through internships, apprenticeships, and paid employment. Sona Circle also raise awareness for refugees, in order to break down negative stigmas.

Seye has been invited as a guest speaker at corporate events including Facebook Friday for Good Summit, and at academic institutions such as Copenhagen Business School, Aston Business School and Ruskin College Oxford.

He has been recognised for his impact, with several awards including the Social Entrepreneur Award by Cause4 and he was also a finalist for the AMBA Entrepreneur of the year 2022 Award and the 5th Global Entreps Award.

Seye has been featured in numerous articles and publications including Yahoo Finance, Business Because, ABC News, Poets & Quants and more.

He is a fully qualified Management Accountant, he holds a BSc in Economics and International Politics, an MSc in Accounting and Finance, an MBA, CFA (level 1 certification) and the Islamic Finance Qualification. Seye is fluent in English and Greek.

BIBLIOGRAPHY

2020. *10 Facts About the Syrian Refugee Crisis in Jordan.*
https://www.nrc.no/perspectives/2020/the-10-countries-that-receive-the-most-refugees/.

2019. *5 Amazing Entrepreneurs Who Went From Refugees to the Rich List.*
https://www.inc.com/jessica-stillman/5-amazing-entrepreneurs-who-went-from-refugees-to-the-rich-list.html.

2020. *5 Key Benefits to Hiring Refugees.* https://sonacircle.com/5-key-benefits-to-hiring-refugees/.

2014. *5 refugee entrepreneurs who have thrived in Britain.*
https://realbusiness.co.uk/5-refugee-entrepreneurs-who-have-thrived-in-britain.

2020. *5.4: Time Dilation.*
https://phys.libretexts.org/Bookshelves/University_Physics/Book%3A_University_Physics_(OpenStax)/Book%3A_University_Physics_III_-_Optics_and_Modern_Physics_(OpenStax)/05%3A__Relativity/5.04%3A_Time_Dilation.

2017. *8 ways you can see Einstein's theory of relativity in real life.*
https://www.livescience.com/58245-theory-of-relativity-in-real-life.html.

Abu-Jamal, M. 2020. "Frantz Fanon and His Influence on the Black Panther Party and the Black Revolution." *Frantz Fanon and Emancipatory Social Theory: A View from the Wretched.*

ACORN, Union for the Community. n.d. https://www.acorntheunion.org.uk/.

Affairs, Watson Institute for International and Public. 2021. *Costs of War.* Providence: Brown University.

2017. *Afghan Entrepreneur is Behind one of Maryland's Most Successful Technology Startups.*
https://www.newamericaneconomy.org/feature/afghani-entrepreneur-is-behind-one-of-marylands-most-successful-technology-startups/.

2008. *Africa: Conflicts and Mining-induced Displacement.* https://wri-irg.org/en/story/2008/africa-conflicts-and-mining-induced-displacement.

Akbar, Aneesa. 2020. "New LAbour's Islamophobia." *Tribune.* July 13. Accessed August 26, 2021. https://tribunemag.co.uk/2020/07/new-labours-islamophobia.

Akwaaba. 2021. https://akwaaba.org.uk/.

2019. *Albert Einsten's Life As A Refugee.* https://borgenproject.org/albert-einsteins-life-as-a-refugee/.

Ali, Taz. 2021. "Lebanon Power Crisis: Blackouts Leave Families with Bills of £500 a Month of Two Hours of Electricity a Day." *iNews,* October 12. https://inews.co.uk/news/world/lebanon-power-economic-crisis-cuts-blackout-electricity-families-bills-two-hours-day-1242645.

Aljazeera. 2021. "Children 25% of Civilian Casualties in Yemen: Relief Agency." *Aljazeera,* March 23. https://www.aljazeera.com/news/2021/3/23/children-25-of-civilian-casualties-in-yemen-relief-agency.

—. 2020. "Thousands of Refugees Without Shelter After Bosnia Camp Burns." *Aljazeera*, December 24. https://www.aljazeera.com/news/2020/12/24/thousands-of-refugees-without-shelter-after-bosnia-camp-burns.

Allen, Zoe. n.d. "A Guide to Apprenticeships for Refugees and Asylum Seekers." *Sona Circle*. Accessed 2021. https://sonacircle.com/apprenticeships-for-refugees/.

—. 2020. "Greece Illegally Turns Away Thousands of Vulnerable People Seeking Asylum: A Crisis of Accountability." *Sona Circle*. Accessed 2021. https://sonacircle.com/greece-illegally-turns-away-refugees/.

—. n.d. "How Can Refugees and Asylum Seekers Learn English in the UK?" *Sona Circle*. Accessed August 2021. https://sonacircle.com/how-can-refugees-and-asylum-seekers-learn-english-in-the-uk/.

Alliant International University . 2019. *re Freud and Psychoanalysis Still Relevant?* . https://www.alliant.edu/blog/are-freud-and-psychoanalysis-still-relevant.

Amer Bisat, Marcel Cassard, Ishac Diwan. 2021. "Lebanon's Economic Critis: A Tragdy in the Making." *Middle East Institute*. March 29. Accessed 2021. https://www.mei.edu/publications/lebanons-economic-crisis-tragedy-making.

Amnesty International. 2019. "Afghanistan's Refugees: Forty Years of Dispossession." *Amnesty International.* June 20. Accessed August 2021. https://www.amnesty.org/en/latest/news/2019/06/afghanistan-refugees-forty-years/.

Anderson, Stephanie. 2016. "Peter Dutton Suggests Fraser Government Made Mistake By Resettling Lebanese Refugees." *ABC News.* November 21. Accessed August 26, 2021. https://www.abc.net.au/news/2016-11-21/peter-dutton-fraser-made-mistake-resettling-lebanese-refugees/8043624.

Anti-Raids Network . n.d. *About / anti raids.* https://antiraids.net/about/ .

Antonio Chiarenza, Marie Dauvrin, Valentina Chiesa, Sonia Baatout & Hans Verrept. 2019. "Supporting Access to Healthcare for Refugees and Migrants in European Countries Under Particular Migratory Pressure." *BCM Health Services Research.* https://bmchealthservres.biomedcentral.com/articles/10.1186/s12913-019-4353-1.

Apprenticeships. 2022. "Becoming An Apprentice." *Apprenticeships.* Accessed 2021. https://www.apprenticeships.gov.uk/apprentices/becoming-apprentice#.

2020. *Are Refugees Good or Bad for the Economy?* https://www.icmc.net/2020/07/14/refugees-good-or-bad-for-economy/#.

Arun District Council. 2022. "Business Grants and Funding." *Arun District Council.* Accessed 2022. https://www.arun.gov.uk/leap/.

2020. *As a Lebanese refugee, cooking has become my lifeline and my community.* https://www.independent.co.uk/voices/refugee-home-office-persecution-cooking-community-teaching-migrateful-a9566656.html.

Asher-Schapiro, Avi. 2015. "Who Are the Yazidis, the Ancient, Persecuted Religious Minority Struggling to Survive in Iraq?" *National Geographic*. August 11. Accessed 2021.

https://www.nationalgeographic.com/history/article/140809-iraq-yazidis-minority-isil-religion-history.

2021. *Audre Lorde.* https://www.britannica.com/biography/Audre-Lorde.

Azhari, Timour. 2021. "'Refugees in their own country': Lebanon Backs Aid for 500,000 Families." *Reuters.* June 30. Accessed 2021. https://www.reuters.com/world/middle-east/refugees-their-own-country-lebanon-backs-aid-500000-families-2021-06-30/.

Ball, Jonny. 2019. "'Housing as a basic human right': The Vienna Model of Social Housing." *The New Statesman,* September 3. https://www.newstatesman.com/spotlight/2019/09/housing-basic-human-right-vienna-model-social-housing.

Bano, Nick. 2021. "The Solution to the Housing Crisis: More Council Houses." *Tribune.* https://tribunemag.co.uk/2021/01/the-solution-to-the-housing-crisis-public-good-not-private-profit.

—. 2021. "The Solution to the Housing Crisis: More Council Houses." *Tribune.* https://tribunemag.co.uk/2021/01/the-solution-to-the-housing-crisis-public-good-not-private-profit.

BBC. 2020. "Christchurch Shootings: Brenton Tarrant Pleads Guilty to 51 Murders." *BBC News.* March 26. Accessed February 17, 17. https://www.bbc.co.uk/news/world-asia-52044013.

—. 2018. "Darren Osborne Guilty of Finsbury Park Mosque Murder." *BBC News.* February 1. Accessed February 17, 2021. https://www.bbc.co.uk/news/uk-42910051.

—. 2015. "David Cameron: 'Swarm' of Migrants Crossing Mediterranean." *BBC News.* July 30. Accessed August 26, 2021. https://www.bbc.co.uk/news/av/uk-politics-33714282.

—. 2016. "Druge Dealers, Criminals, Rapists': What Trump Thinks of Mexicans." *BBC News.* August 31. Accessed August 26, 2021. https://www.bbc.co.uk/news/av/world-us-canada-37230916.

—. 2021. "Essex Lorry Deaths: Two Found Guilty of Killing 39 Migrants." *BBC News.* DEcember 21. Accessed 2021. https://www.bbc.co.uk/news/uk-england-55399004.

—. 2021. "G7: Rich Nation Back Deal to Tax Multinationals." *BBC News.* June 5. Accessed 2021. https://www.bbc.co.uk/news/world-57368247.

—. 2021. "Napier Barracks: Housing Migrants at Barracks Unlawful, Court Rules." *BBC Newa.* June 3. Accessed 2021. https://www.bbc.co.uk/news/uk-england-kent-57335499.

BBC News. 2020. "Ethiopia's Tigray Crisis: UN 'Alarmed' by Treatment of Eritrean Refugees." *BBC News,* December 11. https://www.bbc.co.uk/news/world-africa-55277843.

—. 2020. "Myanman Rohingya: What You Need to Know About the Crisis." *BBC News,* January 23. https://www.bbc.co.uk/news/world-asia-41566561.

—. 2020. *Ethiopia parliament dissolves Tigray leadership.* https://www.bbc.co.uk/news/world-africa-54853362.

BBC. 2019. "Rwanda Genocide: 100 Days of Slaughter." *BBC News*. April 4. Accessed August 20021. https://www.bbc.co.uk/news/world-africa-26875506.

—. 2013. "Theresa May: Health Tourism 'Not Fair'." *BBC News*. October 10. Accessed August 26, 2021. https://www.bbc.co.uk/news/av/uk-24471679.

Bellingreri, Lorenzo Tondo and Marta. 2020. "Brutal Deaths of Exploited Migrants Shine a Spotlight on Italy's Farms." *The Guardian*. July 13. Accessed August 26, 2021. https://www.theguardian.com/global-development/2020/jul/13/brutal-deaths-of-exploited-migrants-shine-a-spotlight-on-italys-farms.

Benanav, A. 2020. "Automation and the future of work."

Benanav, A. 2020. "Automation and the future of work."

Bennett, John T. 2020. "Trump Says Minnesota Will Be 'Overrun and Destroyed' by Refugees If Biden Wins." *The Independent*, September 19. https://www.independent.co.uk/news/world/americas/us-election/trump-refugees-minnesota-rally-joe-biden-ilhan-omar-us-election-2020-b489990.html.

2021. *Birth Rate by Country 2021*. https://worldpopulationreview.com/country-rankings/birth-rate-by-country.

Bland, Archie. 2021. "Julie Burchill Agrees to Pay Ask Sarkar 'substantial damages' in Libel Case." *The Guardian*, March 2021. https://www.theguardian.com/media/2021/mar/16/julie-burchill-agrees-to-pay-ash-sarkar-substantial-damages-in-libel-case.

—. 2015. "Sending Soldiers to Calais Would Show Contempt for Desperate Migrants." *The Guardian*, July 30. https://www.theguardian.com/commentisfree/2015/jul/30/soldiers-calais-migrants-swarm-army.

Boswell, Alan. 2021. "In South Sudan, War Still Looms Over Everything." *World Politics Review*. February 23. Accessed August 2021. https://www.worldpoliticsreview.com/articles/29442/in-south-sudan-war-still-looms-over-everything.

Bradley Jardine, Edward Lemon and Natalie Hall. 2021. "No Space Left to Run: China's Transnational Repression of Uyghurs." *Uyghur Human Rights Project* 48. https://oxussociety.org/wp-content/uploads/2021/06/transnational-repression_final_2021-06-23.pdf.

Breaking Barriers. 2020. *The Impact of Covid-19 on Refugees and Those From Refugee Background in London*. Policy Report, London: Breaking Barriers. https://breaking-barriers.co.uk/wp-content/uploads/2020/06/Breaking-Barriers-Client-Needs-Assessment-May-2020-1.pdf.

2021. *Britannica*. https://www.britannica.com/biography/Freddie-Mercury.

2021. *British arms sales prolonging Saudi war in Yemen*. https://www.theguardian.com/world/2021/feb/22/british-arms-sales-prolonging-saudi-war-in-yemen-says-oxfam.

British Red Cross. 2021. *Donate to help Yemen: a large humanitarian crisis*. https://donate.redcross.org.uk/appeal/yemen-crisis-

appeal?c_code=175151&c_source=google&c_name=Yemen%20Crisis%2
0Appeal&adg=red%20cross%20yemen&c_creative=brand&c_medium=cp
c&gclid=CjwKCAjwn6GGBhADEiwAruUcKq6vlXaLYx_m2peU_Vlu-
TSl1Ol3ZJUcW3h9zXThkM5nZgEW_b_Q.

Brooks, L. 2021. *Glasgow politicians call on Home Office to halt immigration raids.*
https://www.theguardian.com/uk-news/2021/may/21/glasgow-politicians-
call-on-home-office-to-halt-immigration-raids.

Bukhari, Allia. 2020. "'Discriminated, Dehumanised' - Denmark's Syrian Refugees."
EUobserver. June 25. Accessed August 26, 2021.
https://euobserver.com/opinion/152235.

Bulman, James. 2019. "Counting Sheep: Refugees Lighten UK Farmer's Load in
Lambing Season." *UNHCR.* August 21. Accessed 2021.
https://www.unhcr.org/uk/news/stories/2019/8/5d4d63714/counting-
sheep-refugees-lighten-uk-farmers-load-in-lambing-season.html.

Bulman, May. 2021. "Refugees Face Risk of Deportation Under Priti Patel's 'cruel'
Asylum Overhaul. Charities Warn." *The Independent*, March 25.
https://www.independent.co.uk/news/uk/home-news/asylum-plan-
refugees-priti-patel-b1821290.html.

Bunglawala, Inayat. 2012. "Islamaphobia and The Press." *The New Statesman*,
January 29. https://www.newstatesman.com/politics/2012/01/press-story-
group-muslims.

Burke, Jason. 2020. "Rise and Fall of Ethiopia's TPLF - from rebels to Rulers and
Back." *The Guardian*, November 2020.
https://www.theguardian.com/world/2020/nov/25/rise-and-fall-of-ethiopias-
tplf-tigray-peoples-liberation-front.

Business Standard. 2017. "Migrant Influx 'Ethnic Cleansing Against Italians' says
Salvini." *Business Standard.* May 15. Accessed August 26, 2021.
https://www.business-standard.com/article/news-ians/migrant-influx-ethnic-
cleansing-against-italians-says-salvini-117051501484_1.html.

C. Nicholas Cuneo, Richard Sollom and Chris Beyrer. 2017. "The Cholera Epidemic
in Zimbabwe, 2008–2009: A Review and Critique of the Evidence."
Health and Human Rights Journal. July 14. Accessed 2021.
https://www.hhrjournal.org/2017/07/the-cholera-epidemic-in-zimbabwe-
2008-2009-a-review-and-critique-of-the-evidence/.

CBS News. 2017. "Starbucks Vows to Hire 10,000 Refugees Over Next 5 Years."
CBS News. January 30. Accessed 2021.
https://www.cbsnews.com/news/starbucks-hire-refugees-trump-
immigration/.

2014. *Celebrating East London's Jewish Community on Passover.*
https://www.eatingeurope.com/blog/jewish-east-end-london/.

Center for Civilians in Conflict. 2021. *Civilian Protection in South Sudan.* Accessed
August 2021. https://civiliansinconflict.org/our-work/where-we-
work/south-sudan/.

Centre for Entrepreneurs. 2021. "Refugee Entreprenurship Pilot." *Centre for
Entrepreneurs.* Accessed 2021.
https://centreforentrepreneurs.org/releases/new-report-highlights-huge-

potential-of-refugee-entrepreneurs-and-calls-for-national-roll-out-of-tailored-business-support-programmes/.

Chalabi, Mona. 2013. "What Happened to History's Refugees?" *The Guardian,* July 25.
https://www.theguardian.com/news/datablog/interactive/2013/jul/25/what-happened-history-refugees#Israelites.

2021. *Challenges of an ageing population.*
https://www.parliament.uk/business/publications/research/key-issues-parliament-2015/social-change/ageing-population/.

Channel Rescue. 2021. https://channelrescue.wordpress.com/.

Chivers, Tom. 2021. "Britain's Media Monopoly Is a Threat to Democracy." *Tribune,* April 16. https://tribunemag.co.uk/2021/04/britains-media-monopoly-is-a-threat-to-democracy.

Choose Love. 2021. *Choose Love: Gifts with Heart.* https://choose.love/.

—. 2021. *Our Story.* https://choose.love/pages/about-choose-love?gclid=CjwKCAjwn6GGBhADEiwAruUcKm5qxlKorT3uYBj7pR39 xYkwyrcCR76w9GLgCoMHqRpBczs18_0YDxoCUhgQAvD_BwE.

2017. *Christians remain world's largest religious group.*
https://www.pewresearch.org/fact-tank/2017/04/05/christians-remain-worlds-largest-religious-group-but-they-are-declining-in-europe/.

Citizens Advice. 2021. "After You Get Refugee Status." *Citizens Advice.* Accessed 2021. https://www.citizensadvice.org.uk/immigration/after-you-get-refugee-status#:~:text=Once%20you've%20got%20refugee,can%20apply%20for%20benefits%20instead.

City of Sanctuary UK. 2021. "About." *City of Sanctuary UK.* Accessed 2021. https://cityofsanctuary.org/about/.

Clark, D. 2009. *West blamed for rapid increase in China's CO2.*
https://www.theguardian.com/environment/2009/feb/23/china-co2-emissions-climate.

Collard, Rebecca. 2021. "'Sometimes I feel like I betrayed my country': Lebanon's Doctors Are Leaving for Good." *Yaliban.* April 28. Accessed 2021. https://yalibnan.com/2021/04/28/sometimes-i-feel-like-i-betrayed-my-country-lebanons-doctors-are-leaving-in-droves/.

Cone Communications. 2017. "2017 Cone Communications CSR Study." *Cone.* Accessed 2021. https://www.conecomm.com/research-blog/2017-csr-study#download-the-research.

Conley, Julia. 2021. "Lawsuit Initiated Against Trump for 'Illegal' Deportations Resumes Against Biden." *Common Dreams.* August 2. Accessed August 26, 2021. https://www.commondreams.org/news/2021/08/02/lawsuit-initiated-against-trump-illegal-deportations-resumes-against-biden.

2020. *Consequences of population structure.*
https://www.bbc.co.uk/bitesize/guides/zy6mmp3/revision/3.

Cordaid. 2019. "Humanitarian Response to the Crisis in Venezuela." *Cordaid.* February 15. Accessed 2021.
https://www.cordaid.org/en/news/humanitarian-response-to-the-crisis-in-venezuela/.

289

Cottrell, Katy. n.d. "The Culture and Geritage That Refugees Leave Behind." *Sona Cicle.* Accessed 2021. https://sonacircle.com/culture-that-refugees-leave-behind/.

2020. *Could refugees help solve the problem of ageing populations?* https://sonacircle.com/solve-the-problem-of-ageing-populations/.

Council on Foreign Relations. 2021. *Civil War in South Sudan.* November 23. Accessed November 24, 2021. https://www.cfr.org/global-conflict-tracker/conflict/civil-war-south-sudan.

Creative Access. 2021. *Creative Access.* Accessed 2021. https://opportunities.creativeaccess.org.uk/.

2021. *Cuban Revolution.* https://www.britannica.com/event/Cuban-Revolution.

Daily Sabah. 2021. "Islamophobic Attacks in France Increase By 53% in 2020." *Daily Sabah,* January 29. https://www.dailysabah.com/world/europe/islamophobic-attacks-in-france-increase-by-53-in-2020.

Dalton, Jane. 2019. "Trump's Migrant Camps on US Border 'undignified and damaging', says UN Human Rights Chief." *The Independent,* July 8. https://www.independent.co.uk/news/world/americas/us-border-migrant-camp-mexico-trump-un-human-rights-children-a8994831.html.

Delahunty, S. 2021. *Kenmure Street: A "small victory" in a hostile environment.* . https://www.thirdsector.co.uk/kenmure-street-small-victory-hostile-environment/policy-and-politics/article/1722629.

Deloitte. 2021. "The Deloitte Global 2021 Millennial and Gen Z Survey." *Deloitte.* Accessed 2021. https://www2.deloitte.com/content/dam/Deloitte/global/Documents/2021-deloitte-global-millennial-survey-report.pdf.

Dempster, Sekou Keita and Helen. 2020. "Five Years Later, One Million Refugees Are Thriving in Germany." *Center for Global Development.* December 4. Accessed 2021. https://www.cgdev.org/blog/five-years-later-one-million-refugees-are-thriving-germany.

Deutsche Welle. 2020. "European Human Rights Court Condemns France for Treatment of Asylum-Seekers." *Deutsche Welle.* July 2. Accessed August 26, 2021. https://www.dw.com/en/european-human-rights-court-condemns-france-for-treatment-of-asylum-seekers/a-54026049.

Dickerson, Caitlin. 2019. ""There Is a Stench": Soiled Clothes and No Baths for Migrant Children at a Texas Center." *The New York Times,* June 21. https://www.nytimes.com/2019/06/21/us/migrant-children-border-soap.html.

Divers. 2016. "Refugee Women on the Move in Europe Are At Risk, says UN." *UNHCR.* January 20. Accessed August 24, 2021. https://www.unhcr.org/uk/news/latest/2016/1/569fb22b6/refugee-women-move-europe-risk-says-un.html.

2017. *Does migration undermine workers' rights?* https://www.rs21.org.uk/2017/07/30/does-migration-undermine-workers-rights-a-case-study-from-waste-management/.

Dowling, Owen. 2020. "The Political Economy of Super-Explotation in Congolese Mineral Mining." Thesis.

Doyle, I. 2018. *These Are the Charities Helping Refugees in Greece.* https://theculturetrip.com/europe/greece/articles/these-are-the-charities-helping-refugees-in-greece/.

Drabinski, J. 2019. *Frantz Fanon (Stanford Encyclopedia of Philosophy).* https://plato.stanford.edu/entries/frantz-fanon/.

—. 2019. *Frantz Fanon (Stanford Encyclopedia of Philosophy).* https://plato.stanford.edu/entries/frantz-fanon/.

Dunai, Marton. 2017. "Migrants Battle Freezing Temperatures and Cold Shoulder at Hungarian Border." *Reuters.* January 9. Accessed 2021. https://www.reuters.com/article/us-europe-migrants-serbia-hungary-idUSKBN14T1PV.

2007. "Economic Sanctions." *Agencies Face Competing Priorities in Enforcing the U.S. Embargo on Cuba.*

Edward Said. 2006. *Orientalism.*

2021. *Einstein's Theory of Special Relativity.* https://www.space.com/36273-theory-special-relativity.html.

2021. *Emmanuel Dongala.* https://writersfestival.org/authors/earlier/emmanuel-dongala.

Encyclopedia Britannica. 2016. "Rwanda Genocide of 1994." *Encyclopedia Britannica.* August 5. Accessed 2021. https://www.britannica.com/event/Rwanda-genocide-of-1994.

Engage Awards. 2021. *Engage Awards.* Accessed 2021. https://engageawards.co.uk/.

ENIC-NARIC. 2022. *NARIC.* Accessed 2021. https://www.enic-naric.net/.

Environmental Justice Foundation. n.d. "Climate Displacement in Bangladesh." *Environmental Justice Foundation.* Accessed 2021. https://ejfoundation.org/reports/climate-displacement-in-bangladesh.

EU Parliamentary Assembly. 2014. "Refugees and the Right to Work." *Parliamentary Assembly.* London: Council of Europe. https://assembly.coe.int/nw/xml/XRef/Xref-XML2HTML-en.asp?fileid=20569&lang=en.

Euro News. 2021. "Afghans At Risk 'have no clear way out' - UN Refugee Agency." *Euro News.* 08 21. Accessed 2021. https://www.euronews.com/2021/08/21/uk-afghanistan-conflict-un.

European Commission. 2020. "2050 Long-Term Strategy." *European Commission.* Accessed 2021. https://ec.europa.eu/clima/eu-action/climate-strategies-targets/2050-long-term-strategy_en.

European Parliament. 2020. "Exploring Migration Causes - Why People Migrate." *European Parliament.* October 30. Accessed 2021. https://www.europarl.europa.eu/news/en/headlines/world/20200624STO81906/exploring-migration-causes-why-people-migrate.

European Resettlement Network. 2014. "Afghan Refugees in Iran and Pakistan." *European Resettlement Network.* Accessed 2021. http://www.resettlement.eu/page/afghan-refugees-iran-pakistan-0.

2021. *Events of 1901*.
https://www.nationalarchives.gov.uk/pathways/census/events/britain4.htm.

2021. "Facts about refugees." *Refugee Action*. https://www.refugee-action.org.uk/about/facts-about-refugees/.

Ferhallad, Mélanie. 2016. "Vaucluse - Meurtre de M. El Makouli : L'irresponsabilité Pénale Requise." *La Provence*. June 16. Accessed August 26, 2021. https://www.laprovence.com/article/edition-vaucluse/3988643/meurtre-de-m-el-makouli-lirresponsabilite-penale-requise.html .

Fernández-Reino, Mariña. 2020. "Migrants and Discrimination in the UK." *The Migration Observatory*. January 20. Accessed 2021. https://migrationobservatory.ox.ac.uk/resources/briefings/migrants-and-discrimination-in-the-uk/.

2021. In *An Analysis on the US Economic Sanctions and the Cuban Embargo*, by Dr. Deborah Manoushka Paul Figaro. Bloomington: AuthorHouse Books.

2021. In *An Analysis on the US Economic Sanctions and the Cuban Embargo*, by Dr. Deborah Manoushka Paul Figaro. Bloomington: AuthorHouse Books.

2021. *Fish and chips, the quintessentially British dish*.
http://peartreelife.blogspot.com/2018/06/fish-and-chips-quintessentially-british.html.

Fisher, Max. 2015. "Nothing Captures Western Hypocrisy on Refugees Like These British Tabloid Front Pages." *Vox*. September 3. Accessed August 26, 2021. https://www.vox.com/2015/9/3/9252649/syrian-refugee-boy-british-tabloids.

Flanagan, C. 2018. *"Lolita" Continues to Seduce Readers*.
https://www.theatlantic.com/magazine/archive/2018/09/how-lolita-seduces-us-all/565751/.

Ford, Gabriel Salter & Felix. 2021. "Mother's Day in the Greek Refugee Camps." *Sona Circle*. Accessed 2021. https://sonacircle.com/mothers-day-in-the-greek-refugee-camps/.

France24. 2015. "French Far-Right Leader Marine Le Pen Goes On Trail For Inciting Racial Hatred." *France24*. October 21. Accessed August 26, 2021. https://www.france24.com/en/20151020-france-marine-le-pen-trial-court-racial-hatred-anti-muslim-hate-speech.

2021. *Francis Ngannou: From The Underdog To The Favourite*.
https://sonacircle.com/francis-ngannou-from-the-underdog-to-the-favourite/.

2021. *Francis Ngannou: From The Underdog To The Favourite*.
https://sonacircle.com/francis-ngannou-from-the-underdog-to-the-favourite/.

Frank Martela, Bent Greve, Bo Rothstein, Juho Saari. 2020. *The Nordic Exceptionalism: What Explains Why the Nordic Countries Are Constantly Among the Happiest in the World*. Scientific Research Report, World Happiness Report.

Fraser C. Lott, Nikolaos Christidis and Peter A. Stott. 2013. "Can the 2011 East African Drought Be Attributed to Human-Induced Climate Change?" *Geophysical Reseach Level* 1177-1181. https://agupubs.onlinelibrary.wiley.com/doi/full/10.1002/grl.50235.

Freedman, Jane. 2016. "Sexual and Gender-Based Violence Against Refugee Women: A Hidden Aspect of the "Refugee Crisis"." *Reproductive Health Matters* 24 (47): 18-26.

2021. *From Gaza to Mars.* https://www.timesofisrael.com/from-gaza-to-mars-palestinian-engineer-behind-drone-flight-on-red-planet/.

Gandhi, L. 2018. *With "First They Killed My Father," Cambodian activist wanted to honor her parents.* https://www.nbcnews.com/news/asian-america/first-they-killed-my-father-cambodian-activist-wanted-honor-her-n833316.

Gauthier, Philippe. 2018. "The Limits of Renewable Energy and the Case for Degrowth." *Resilience.* November 21. Accessed 2021. https://www.resilience.org/stories/2018-11-21/the-limits-of-renewable-energy-and-the-case-for-degrowth/.

2021. *Gaza refugee designs first NASA helicopter to fly on Mars.* https://spectrumnews1.com/ca/la-west/technology/2021/05/21/gaza-refugee-designs-first-nasa-helicopter-to-fly-on-mars.

2021. *Gaza refugee designs first NASA helicopter to fly on Mars.* https://spectrumnews1.com/ca/la-west/technology/2021/05/21/gaza-refugee-designs-first-nasa-helicopter-to-fly-on-mars.

2021. *George Radda Biography.* https://royalsociety.org/people/george-radda-12132/.

2019. *German dramatist. In: Encyclopædia Britannica.* https://www.britannica.com/biography/Bertolt-Brecht.

Gidin, Leon Panitch & Sam. 2013. *The Making of Global Capitalism: The Political Economy of American Empire.* New York: Verso.

2021. *Gifted Palestinian dreamers defy Israel's occupation nightmare.* https://www.middleeastmonitor.com/20210502-gifted-palestinian-dreamers-defy-israels-occupation-nightmare/.

Gleick, Peter H. 2014. "Water, Drought, Climate Change, and Conflict in Syria." *Weather, Climate amd Society* 331-340.

2020. *Global Figures.* https://www.nrc.no/shorthand/fr/a-few-countries-take-responsibility-for-most-of-the-worlds-refugees/index.html.

Global One. 2021. *Protect Mothers and Babies.* https://globalone.org.uk/cause/mothers-and-babies/.

Global Witness. 2015. "Conflict Minerals in Eastern Congo." *Global Witness.* March 2. Accessed 2021. https://www.globalwitness.org/en/campaigns/conflict-minerals/conflict-minerals-eastern-congo/.

2021. *Goodreads: Emmanuel Dongala.* https://www.goodreads.com/author/show/184659.Emmanuel_Dongala.

Gossard, J. 2013. *Les Misérables: A Historian's Review.* https://alcalde.texasexes.org/2013/01/les-miserables-a-historians-review/.

Grierson, Jamie. 2019. "Refugees Missing Out on Jobs in UK, Say Humanitarian Groups." *The Guardian,* May 2.

https://www.theguardian.com/world/2019/may/02/refugees-are-missing-out-on-jobs-in-uk-charities-warn.

Grimm, Matthew. 2014. "A Bried History of the Yazidis of Iraq." *Jstor Daily.*
    September 20. Accessed 2021. https://daily.jstor.org/history-of-yazidi/.

Gross, T. 2015. *Remembering Islamic Feminist Fatema Mernissi.*
    https://www.npr.org/2015/12/10/459223430/remembering-islamic-feminist-fatema-mernissi?t=1628871910171.

Gurman, Dr SJ. 2021. *Professor Sir George Radda.* https://www.le.ac.uk/ebulletin-archive/ebulletin/publications/2000-2009/2006/07/npfolder.2006-07-11.5678371783/raddaoration.html.

Gwynn, Robin. 1985. "England's First Refugees'." *History Today* 35 (5). Accessed
    2021. doi:https://www.historytoday.com/archive/englands-first-refugees.

Hadid, Zaha. 2016. *Zaha Hadid Architects.* https://www.zaha-hadid.com/people/zaha-hadid/.

Hanif, Faisal. 2019. *State of Media Reporting on Islam and Muslims.* Policy Report,
    London: Centre of MEdia Monitoring. https://cfmm.org.uk/wp-content/uploads/2019/07/CfMM-Quarterly-Report-Oct-Dec-2018.pdf.

Hardikar, Neha. 2018. "Venezuelan Refugee Crisis and How It Is Altering the
    Surrounding Regions." *The Kootneeti.* August 27. Accessed August 2021.
    https://thekootneeti.in/2018/08/27/venezuelan-refugee-crisis-and-how-it-is-altering-the-surrounding-regions/.

Hauslohner, Jenna Johnson and Abigail. 2017. "'I think Islam hates us': A Timeline
    of Trump's Comments About Islam and Muslims." *The Washington Post,*
    May 20. https://www.washingtonpost.com/news/post-politics/wp/2017/05/20/i-think-islam-hates-us-a-timeline-of-trumps-comments-about-islam-and-muslims/.

Henley, Jon. 2020. "Climate Crisis Could Displace 1.2bn People by 2050, Report
    Warns." *The Guardian,* September 9.
    https://www.theguardian.com/environment/2020/sep/09/climate-crisis-could-displace-12bn-people-by-2050-report-warns.

—. 2019. "'It's a miracle': Helsinki's Radical Solution to Homelessness." *The
    Guardian,* June 3. https://www.theguardian.com/cities/2019/jun/03/its-a-miracle-helsinkis-radical-solution-to-homelessness.

Heron, Kai. 2021. "Extinction Isn't the Worst That Can Happen." *Novara Media.*
    June 24. Accessed 2021. https://novaramedia.com/2021/06/24/extinction-isnt-the-worst-that-can-happen/.

HM Government. 2021. "Hate Crime." *HM Government .* Accessed August 26,
    2021. https://hatecrime.campaign.gov.uk/.

—. 2021. "Hire An Apprentice." *Apprenticeships.* Accessed 2021.
    https://www.apprenticeships.gov.uk/employers.

Hobsbawm, E. 1997. *The Age of Capital, 1848-1875.* London: Abacus.

Hobsbawm, E. 1995. *The Age of Extremes, 1914-1991. .* London: Abacus.

—. 1977. *The Age of Revolution, 1789-1848.* London: Abacus.

Hobsbawm, Eric. 1995. *The Age of Extremes.* London: Abacus.

Hobsbawn, E. 1997. *The Age of Capital, 1848-1875.* London: Abacus.

Hosseini, K. 2019. *Khaled Hosseini.* https://khaledhosseini.com/bio/.

2017. *How a Street Sweeper and His Wife Built Britain's Largest Indian Food Empire.* https://www.thebetterindia.com/80529/pataks-indian-food-britain-laxmishanker-pathak-shanta-gaury/.

2018. *How refugees can actually create jobs for locals in growing cities.* https://www.independent.co.uk/voices/refugees-cities-jobs-migration-gdp-economy-a8348816.html.

2015. *How Refugees can benefit the economy.* https://www.weforum.org/agenda/2015/10/how-refugees-can-benefit-the-economy/.

2021. *How to Go on Strike & Give Notice of Industrial Action.* https://www.safeworkers.co.uk/employee-relations/going-on-strike/.

Human Rights Watch. 2021. "Mexico: Abuses Against Asylum Seekers at US Border." *Human Rights Watch.* March 5. Accessed 2021. https://www.hrw.org/news/2021/03/05/mexico-abuses-against-asylum-seekers-us-border.

Hunter, Walt. 2018. "The Story Behind the Poem on the Statue of Liberty." *The Atlantic,* January 16. https://www.theatlantic.com/entertainment/archive/2018/01/the-story-behind-the-poem-on-the-statue-of-liberty/550553/.

Hussain, Shere. 2021. "The Yazidi Genocide - 6 Years Later." *Sona Circle.* Accessed August 24, 2021. https://sonacircle.com/the-yazidi-genocide-6-years-later/.

Ibrahim, Arwa. 2020. "A New Exodus From Lebanon After Deadly Beirut Blast." *Aljazeera.* August 22. Accessed 2021. https://www.aljazeera.com/news/2020/8/22/a-new-exodus-from-lebanon-after-deadly-beirut-blast.

iCan. 2022. *The Insurance Cultural Awareness Network.* Accessed 2021. https://www.I-can.me/.

Ilzetzki, Ethan. 2020. "How Worrying is Britain's Debt? Surprisingly, We Ecomomists Say: Not Very." *The Guardian,* June 12. https://www.theguardian.com/commentisfree/2020/jun/12/britain-public-debt-economists-coronavirus-deficit-austerity.

Imperial College London. 2021. "SME Graduate Internship Fund." *Imperial College London.* Accessed 2021. https://www.imperial.ac.uk/careers/employers/develop/sme-graduate-internship-fund/.

2021. *In Conversation with Lord Alf Dubs about Refugees in the UK.* https://sonacircle.com/lord-dubs-on-refugees/.

Ingrahamm, Christopher. 2019. "US Billionaires Pay Lower Tax Rate Than Working Class For First Time in History." *The Independent,* November 17. https://www.independent.co.uk/news/world/americas/us-billionaires-low-tax-rate-working-class-cost-a9148746.html.

Inspiring Workplaces. 2021. *Inspiring Workplaces Awards.* Accessed 2021. https://www.inspiring-workplaces.com/awards/.

Institute For Government. 2020. "UK Net Zero Target." *Institute For Government.* April 20. https://ec.europa.eu/clima/eu-action/climate-strategies-targets/2050-long-term-strategy_en.

International Organisation for Migration (IOM). 2021. "Migration Within The Mediterranean ." *International Organisation for Migration.* Accessed 2021. https://missingmigrants.iom.int/region/mediterranean.

—. 2021. "Missing Migrants: Tracking Deaths Along Migratory Routes." *Missing Migrants Project.* Accessed 2021. https://missingmigrants.iom.int/region/europe.

International Organisation for Migration. 2020. *World Migration Report 2020.* Geneva: International Organisation for Migration. Accessed 2021. https://www.un.org/sites/un2.un.org/files/wmr_2020.pdf.

2020. *Iraq War.* https://www.britannica.com/event/Iraq-War.

2010. *Iraqi Refugees: Is the UK doing the right thing?* https://blogs.lse.ac.uk/politicsandpolicy/iraqi-refugees-is-the-uk-doing-the-right-thing/.

2016. *Islam Daily.* http://islamdailypost.blogspot.com/2016/06/you-do-not-do-evil-to-those-who-do-evil.html.

Jalal, Ibrahim. 2020. *Continuity and change in British Foreign policy toward Yemen.* https://www.mei.edu/publications/continuity-and-change-british-foreign-policy-toward-yemen.

Jangiz, Holly Johnston and Khazan. 2021. "'We Need Help': Suicides Spike at Duhok's Camps for Yazidis." *Rudaw.* January 18. Accessed 2021. https://www.rudaw.net/english/kurdistan/180120211.

Jay, Martin Evan. 2018. *Sigmund Freud | Austrian psychoanalyst. In: Encyclopædia Britannica.* https://www.britannica.com/biography/Sigmund-Freud.

Jeanne Batalova, Mary Hanna, and Christopher Levesque. 2021. "Frequently Requested Statistics on Immigrants and Immigration in the United States." *Migration Policy Institute.* February 11. Accessed 2021 2021. https://www.migrationpolicy.org/article/frequently-requested-statistics-immigrants-and-immigration-united-states.

Katwala, Amit. 2018. "The Spiralling Environmental Cost of Our Lithium Battery Addiction." *Wired.* August 5. Accessed 2021. https://www.wired.co.uk/article/lithium-batteries-environment-impact.

Kenner, Dario. 2020. "Post-War Reconstruction Involved Taxing Richest - It Could Be a Model for Building a Low Carbon Economy." *The Conversation.* May 8. Accessed 2021. https://theconversation.com/post-war-reconstruction-involved-taxing-richest-it-could-be-a-model-for-building-a-low-carbon-economy-137717.

King, Esther. 2017. "Matteo Salvini: Islam Incompatible with European Values." *Politico.* January 3. Accessed August 26, 2021. https://www.politico.eu/article/matteo-salvini-islam-incompatible-with-european-values/ .

Kirchgaessner, Stephanie. 2016. "Beppe Grillo Provokes Outrage with Sadiq Khan 'bomb' Joke." *The Guardian,* May 15. https://www.theguardian.com/politics/2016/may/15/beppe-grillo-sparks-explosion-of-outrage-with-sadiq-khan-joke .

Kishi, Katayoun. 2017. "Assults Against Muslims in U.S. Surpass 2001 Level." *Pew Research Center.* November 15. Accessed August 26, 2021.

https://www.pewresearch.org/fact-tank/2017/11/15/assaults-against-muslims-in-u-s-surpass-2001-level/.

Knowledge Transfer Partnership. 2021. *Knowledge Transfer Partnership.* Accessed 2021. https://www.ktp-uk.org/.

Knudson, Sonja. 2021. *10 Eye-Opening Facts to Share on World Refugee Day.* June 1. Accessed September 2021. https://www.globalgiving.org/learn/world-refugee-day-facts/.

Koh, Lyndsey. 2018. "Venezuelans Are South America's Largest Refugee Crisis." *Teach Beyond.* November 19. Accessed August 26, 2021. https://teachbeyond.org/news/2018/11/venezuelans-south-americas-largest-refugee-crisis/.

Kopestinsky, Alex. 2021. "Electric Car Statistics in the US and Abroad." *Policy Advice.* August 12. Accessed 2021. https://policyadvice.net/insurance/insights/electric-car-statistics.

Koukoulas, Stephen. 2015. "Economic Growth More Likely When Wealth Distributed to Poor Instead of Rich." *The Guardian* , June 4. https://www.theguardian.com/business/2015/jun/04/better-economic-growth-when-wealth-distributed-to-poor-instead-of-rich .

Kumar, Ashok. 2021. *Monopsony capitalism power and production in the twilight of the sweatshop age.* Cambridge, UK: Cambridge University Press.

Lang, Cady. 2021. "Who Gets to Wear a Headscarf? The Complicated History Behind France's Latest Hijab Controversy." *Time,* March 19. https://time.com/6049226/france-hijab-ban/.

Leandro, Anna Jiménez and Gloria. 2018. "Incentives for Companies That Hire Refugees." *JD Supra.* August 28. Accessed 2021. https://www.jdsupra.com/legalnews/incentives-for-companies-that-hire-48083/.

2019. *Liberal Democrats Manifesto.* https://www.libdems.org.uk/plan.

2021. *Life as a Refugee trying to find Opportunities | Imad Alarnab | SonaTalks | Inspiring Story.* https://www.youtube.com/watch?v=mo-eglt0hZ8.

Lift the Ban. 2016. "Lift the Ban." *Refugee Action.* Accessed 2021. https://www.refugee-action.org.uk/lift-the-ban/.

Lift the Ban. 2020. *Lift the Ban: Why Giving People Seeking Asylum the Right to Work is Common Sense.* Policy Report, London: Lift the BAn.

2020. *Little known history of fish and chips.* https://www.rescue-uk.org/article/little-known-history-fish-and-chips.

Living Rent. n.d. *Living Rent.* https://www.livingrent.org/.

Lobstein, D. 2002. *Monet, Quintin: Editions Jean Paul Gisserot.*

London City Hall. 2019. "Revealed: Full Links Between Poverty and Violent Crime in London." *London City Hall.* July 15. Accessed August 27, 2021. https://www.london.gov.uk/press-releases/mayoral/full-links-between-poverty-and-violent-crime.

London Renters Union. 2021. *Homepage.* https://londonrentersunion.org/.

Lord, Victoria. n.d. "History of the Yezidis." *The Ultimate History Project.* Accessed 2021. http://ultimatehistoryproject.com/history-of-the-yezidi.html.

1922-2011. *Lucian Freud .* https://www.tate.org.uk/art/artists/lucian-freud-1120.

2021. *M&S Employee Welfare* .
    https://marksintime.marksandspencer.com/download?id=13174.
Macey, D. 1996. *Frantz Fanon 1925-1961. History of Psychiatry.*
Mackey, Robert. 2015. "Fox News Apologizes for False Claims of Muslim-Only
    Areas in England and France." *The New York Times,* January 18.
    https://www.nytimes.com/2015/01/19/world/europe/fox-news-apologizes-
    for-false-claims-of-muslim-only-areas-in-england-and-france.html.
Maizland, Eleanor Albert and Lindsay. 2020. "The Rohingya Crisis." *Council on
    Foreign Relations.* January 23. Accessed August 2021.
    https://www.cfr.org/backgrounder/rohingya-crisis.
Margolis, Hillary. 2020. "Greece Migrant Camps Unfit for Pregnant People." *Human
    Rights Watch.* May 27. Accessed August 2021.
    https://www.hrw.org/news/2020/05/27/greece-migrant-camps-unfit-
    pregnant-people.
Marshall, Aarian. 2019. "Why Electric Buses Haven't Taken Over the World—Yet."
    Wired. July 06. Accessed 2021. https://www.wired.com/story/electric-
    buses-havent-taken-over-world/.
Marx, K. 2021. *Eighteenth Brumaire Of Louis Bonaparte.* S.L: Hansebooks.
Marx, K., Fowkes, B. and Mandel, E. 1990. *Capital : a critique of political economy.*
    Harmondsworth: Penguin In Association With New Left Review.
Mason, Rowena. 2016. "NHS Loses £700m a Year On Treating EU Citizens, Brexit
    Campaign Claims." *The Guardian,* April 5.
    https://www.theguardian.com/politics/2016/apr/05/nhs-loses-700m-a-year-
    treating-eu-citizens-brexit-campaign-claims.
Matthew. 2:13-23. *The New Testament.*
Maughan, Tim. 2015. "The Dystopian Lake Filled by the World's Tech Lust." *BBC
    Future.* April 2. Accessed 2021.
    https://www.bbc.com/future/article/20150402-the-worst-place-on-earth.
McDonnell, Tim. 2019. "Climate Change Creates a New Migration Crisi for
    Bangladesh." *National Geographic.* January 24. Accessed 2021.
    https://www.nationalgeographic.com/environment/article/climate-change-
    drives-migration-crisis-in-bangladesh-from-dhaka-sundabans.
Medecins Sans Frontieres. 2021. *Tigray violence scatters people across two countries.*
    https://www.msf.org/ethiopia-tigray-crisis-update.
2021. *Meet Me at Fatma's: An Inspirational Story of Refugees in Entrepreneurship.*
    https://sonacircle.com/meet-me-at-fatmas/.
Mercy Corps. 2019. "The Facts: Afghanistan." *Mery Corps.* June 04. Accessed August
    2021. https://www.mercycorps.org/blog/quick-facts-afghanistan.
2018. *Migrants and refugees are good for economies.*
    https://www.nature.com/articles/d41586-018-05507-0.
2021. *Migration and Immigrants in Europe: A Historical and Demographic
    Perspective.* https://link.springer.com/chapter/10.1007%2F978-3-319-
    21674-4_3.
Migration Watch UK. 2013. "Asylum Seekers and the Right to Work in the
    European Economic Area." *Migration Watch UK.* Accessed 2021.
    https://www.migrationwatchuk.org/briefing-paper/4.24.

Mike Berry, Inaki Garcia-Blanco, Kerry Moore. 2015. *Press Coverage of the Refugee and Migrant Crisis in the EU: A Content Analysis of Five European Countries.* Policy Report, UNHCR, 39. https://www.unhcr.org/56bb369c9.pdf.

Milanovic, B. 2016. "Global Inequality: A New Approach for the Age of Globalization." 106-10.

Milanovic, B. 2016. "Global Inequality: A New Approach for the Age of Globalization."

2015. *Millenium Development Goals.* https://www.un.org/millenniumgoals/gender.shtml.

Miller, C. 2019. *Almost a quarter of those seeking shelter at key homeless agencies in Manchester, London and Leicester are refugees.* https://www.independent.co.uk/news/uk/home-news/homeless-crisis-rough-sleepers-asylum-shelter-london-manchester-leicester-a8965671.html.

Miller, Corazon. 2019. "'One in four' Seeking Shelter at Key Homeless Agencies in Manchester, London and Leicester Are Refugees." *The Independent,* June 20. https://www.independent.co.uk/news/uk/home-news/homeless-crisis-rough-sleepers-asylum-shelter-london-manchester-leicester-a8965671.html.

Miller, Nick. 2017. "Report of Mass Sexual Assault by Refugees in Frankfurt Was 'baseless', Police Say." *The Sydney Morning Herald,* February 16. https://www.smh.com.au/world/newspaper-report-of-mass-sexual-assault-by-refugees-in-frankfurt-was-baseless-police-say-20170216-gudybw.html.

Miller, Sarah Deardorff. 2018. "Assessing the Impacts of Hosting Refugees." *Centre for International Governance Innovation.* https://www.cigionline.org/sites/default/files/documents/WRC%20Research%20Paper%20no.4.pdf.

Ministry of Employment. 2019. "Fast Track - A Quicker Introduction of Newly Arrived Immigrants." *Government Offices of Sweden.* December 11. Accessed 2021. https://www.government.se/articles/2015/12/fast-track---a-quicker-introduction-of-newly-arrived-immigrants/.

Missing Migrants Project. 2021. *Mediterranean Missing Migrants.* November 11. Accessed September 2021. https://missingmigrants.iom.int/region/mediterranean.

2019. *Modern Slavery | Exposing Systemic Racism in the UK | Ake Achi | TEDx style SonaTalks.* https://www.youtube.com/watch?v=lHuDDGb0RBw.

Momodu, Sulaiman. 2018-2019. "Uganda Stands Out in Refugees Hospitality." *Africa Renewal.* Accessed 2021. https://www.un.org/africarenewal/magazine/december-2018-march-2019/uganda-stands-out-refugees-hospitality.

Moody, Oliver. 2020. "Tobias Rathjen: Hanau Shisha Bar Murderer Wanted to 'Cleanse' Germany." *The Times,* February 21. https://www.thetimes.co.uk/article/tobias-rathjen-shisha-bar-murderer-wanted-to-cleanse-germany-klc5nj9bc.

2010. *Muhammad completes Hegira.* https://www.history.com/this-day-in-history/muhammad-completes-hegira.

2019. *My Name Is Not 'Refugee' | Akoi Bazzie Shares Shocking Experience | TEDx style SonaTalks.* https://www.youtube.com/watch?v=8tHlxC0YE1I.

NACCOM. 2021. https://naccom.org.uk/.

New Anglia. 2022. "Growing Business Fund." *New Anglia.* Accessed 2022. https://newanglia.co.uk/grant/growing-business-fund/.

2004. *No Dirty Gold Campain Launch.* https://earthworks.org/media-releases/no_dirty_gold_campaign_launch/.

Norwich University Online. 2017. "Five Major African Wars and Conflicts of the Twentieth Century." *Norwich University Online.* September 4. Accessed 2021. https://online.norwich.edu/academic-programs/resources/five-major-african-wars-and-conflicts-of-the-twentieth-century.

Now_You_See_Me_Moria. 2021. "Now_You_See_Me_Moria." *Instagram.* March 4. Accessed August 24, 2021. https://www.instagram.com/p/CL_qkJ3lIai.

Office for National Statistics. 2020. "Coronavirus and the Social Impacts on Great Britain: 5 June 2020." *Office for National Statistics.* June 5. Accessed 2021. https://www.ons.gov.uk/peoplepopulationandcommunity/healthandsocialcare/healthandwellbeing/bulletins/coronavirusandthesocialimpactsongreatbritain/5june2020.

O'Halloran, K. 2019. *What Germany's renters union can teach its radical British counterparts.* https://citymonitor.ai/politics/what-germany-s-renters-union-can-teach-its-radical-british-counterparts-4504.

Oltermann, Philip. 2020. "How Angela Merkel's Great Migrant Gamble Paid Off." *The Guardian*, August 30. Accessed 2021. https://www.theguardian.com/world/2020/aug/30/angela-merkel-great-migrant-gamble-paid-off.

2004. *On the Origins of Google.* August 17. https://www.nsf.gov/discoveries/disc_summ.jsp?cntn_id=100660.

Oxfam. 2019. *Forced From Home: Climate-Fulled Displaced.* Media Briefing, London: Oxfam.

2020. *Oxfam International.* https://www.oxfam.org/en/press-releases/carbon-emissions-richest-1-percent-more-double-emissions-poorest-half-humanity.

Oxfam International. 2016. "Six Richest Countries Host Less Than 9% of Refugees." *Oxfam International.* Accessed 2021. https://www.oxfam.org/en/press-releases/six-richest-countries-host-less-9-refugees.

2012. "Palestinian Employment in Lebanon - Facts and Challenges ." https://www.ilo.org/wcmsp5/groups/public/---arabstates/---ro-beirut/documents/publication/wcms_236502.pdf.

Panitch, L. and Gindin, S. 2013. *The Making of Global Capitalism: The Political Economy of American Empire.* London; New York: Verso.

Panitch, L. and Gindin, S. 2013. "The Making of Global Capitalism: The Political Economy of American Empire." 171-77.

Partington, Richard. 2020. "UK Jobless Claims Soar by Nearly 70% in April." *The Guardian*, May 19.

https://www.theguardian.com/business/2020/may/19/uk-jobless-april-coronavirus-crisis-unemployment-benefits.

Parveen, Nazia. 2019. "Boris Johnson's Burqa Comments 'Led to Surge in Anti-Muslim Attacks'." *The Guardian*, September 2. https://www.theguardian.com/politics/2019/sep/02/boris-johnsons-burqa-comments-led-to-surge-in-anti-muslim-attacks.

Perrone, Alessio. 2019. "Refugee Rescuers to be Fined up to €1m Under New Italian Law Promoted by Far-Right Salvini." *The Independent*, August 6. https://www.independent.co.uk/news/world/europe/italy-refugee-rescue-boat-fine-law-salvini-senate-vote-a9040936.html.

Peters, Adele. 2018. "Here's Yet Another Busniess Benefit of Hiring Refugees." *Fast Company*. June 1. Accessed 2021. https://www.fastcompany.com/40579059/heres-yet-another-business-benefit-of-hiring-refugees?itm_source=parsely-api.

Pettifor, Ann. 2018. "Do Tax Revenues Finance Government Spending?" *Ann Pettifor*. February 7. Accessed August 7, 2021. https://www.annpettifor.com/2018/02/do-tax-revenues-finance-government-spending/.

Pictures, Journeyman. 1999. "Military Uprising in Guinea-Bissau." *YouTube*. Journeyman Pictures. Accessed 2021. https://www.youtube.com/watch?v=wsp3ZhXCfNI.

Pidd, Helen. 2018. "Attack on Refugee Family Highlights Rising Hate Crime in Bolton." *The Guardian*, December 16. https://www.theguardian.com/uk-news/2018/dec/16/attack-on-refugee-mother-in-bolton-stokes-local-tension.

1872-1944. *Piet Mondrian*. https://www.tate.org.uk/art/artists/piet-mondrian-1651.

2019. *Population by Country*. https://www.worldometers.info/world-population/population-by-country/.

2019. *Population By Country*. https://www.worldometers.info/world-population/population-by-country/. .

Powers, A. 2011. *Obituary: Peter Moro*. https://www.independent.co.uk/arts-entertainment/obituary-peter-moro-1179587.html .

Prtorić, Jelena. 2021. "Along the Balkan Route, Refugees and Volunteers Face Growing Hostility." *Equal Times*. February 2021. Accessed 2021. https://www.equaltimes.org/along-the-balkan-route-refugees?lang=en#.YVw-p2LMJPa.

2014. *Queen's Tragic Rhapsody*. https://www.rollingstone.com/music/music-news/queens-tragic-rhapsody-234996/.

Quinn, Ben. 2019. "Hate Crimes Double in Five Years in England and Wales." *The Guardian*, October 15. https://www.theguardian.com/society/2019/oct/15/hate-crimes-double-england-wales.

2021. *Quintessentially British brands*. https://fabrikbrands.com/marks-and-spencer-branding/.

Rapier, Robert. 2020. "Fossil Fuels Still Supply 84 Percent Of World Energy — And Other Eye Openers From BP's Annual Review." *Forbes*, June 20.

https://www.forbes.com/sites/rrapier/2020/06/20/bp-review-new-highs-in-global-energy-consumption-and-carbon-emissions-in-2019/?sh=687ae05b66a1.

2021. *Real UK House Prices since 1975.* https://www.allagents.co.uk/house-prices-adjusted/.

Refugee Action. 2021. "Facts About Refugees." *Refugee Action.* Accessed 2021. https://www.refugee-action.org.uk/about/facts-about-refugees/.

—. n.d. "Khaalid and Nuuriya." *Refugee Action.* Accessed August 26, 2021. https://www.refugee-action.org.uk/khaalid-and-nuuriya-2/.

Refugee Council. n.d. "Mental Health Services for Unaccompanied Children." *Refugee Council.* Accessed 2021. https://refugeecouncil.org.uk/our-work/mental-health-support-for-refugees-and-asylum-seekers/mental-health-services-for-unaccompanied-children/.

—. 2021. *Private Rented Scheme London.* https://www.refugeecouncil.org.uk/get-support/services/private-rented-scheme/.

—. 2021. *Supporting and empowering refugees.* https://www.refugeecouncil.org.uk/?gclid=CjwKCAjwsNiIBhBdEiwAJK4k hvb--ol9rLdNXGcGVbVEVG6EZO-QljM_M06lArWwoNJXoVrCtYkbkRoCGUIQAvD_BwE.

2020. *Refugee Data Finder.* https://www.unhcr.org/refugee-statistics/.

2021. *Refugee mum who fled to Yorkshire from Syria without a penny to her name becomes top cheesemaker.* https://metro.co.uk/2021/07/31/refugee-mum-who-fled-syria-without-a-penny-to-her-name-becomes-top-cheesemaker-15018128/.

2016. *Refugee Olympic Team .* https://olympics.com/ioc/news/refugee-olympic-team-to-shine-spotlight-on-worldwide-refugee-crisis.

2021. *Refugee Olympic Team.* https://sonacircle.com/refugees-in-sport/.

2021. *Refugee Olympic Team.* https://sonacircle.com/refugees-in-sport/.

2021. *Refugee Olympic Team.* https://sonacircle.com/refugees-in-sport/.

2020. *Refugee Statistics.* https://www.unhcr.org/refugee-statistics/.

2015. *Refugees are Australia's most entrepreneurial migrants.* https://www.theguardian.com/world/2015/sep/04/refugees-are-australias-most-entrepreneurial-migrants-says-research.

2019. *Refugees are the most entrepreneurial migrants in Australia.* https://www.refugeecouncil.org.au/refugees-are-entrepreneurial/.

Refugees at Home. 2021. *Homepage.* https://www.refugeesathome.org/.

2021. *Refugees in Entertainment .* https://sonacircle.com/refugees-in-entertainment/.

2017. *Refugees in the U.S. Had More Than $56 Billion in Spending Power in 2015.* https://www.newamericaneconomy.org/press-release/refugees-in-the-u-s-had-more-than-56-billion-in-spending-power-in-2015-new-study-shows/.

ReliefWeb. 2021. "Yemen: Famine Arounf the Corner, Says World Food Programme." *ReliefWeb.* March 01. Accessed 2021. https://reliefweb.int/report/yemen/yemen-famine-around-corner-says-world-food-programme.

2020. *Responsibility sharing.* http://www.nrcstories.no/responsibility-sharing-can-solve-the-refugee-crisis/.

2020. *Responsibility sharing.* http://www.nrcstories.no/responsibility-sharing-can-solve-the-refugee-crisis/.

REvive Greece. 2021. *Home.* https://revivegreece.org/en/.

Ritche, H and Roser, M. 2020. *CO2 and Greenhouse Gas Emissions.* https://ourworldindata.org/co2-emissions#citation.

Ritchie. 2020. *CO2 and Greenhouse Gas Emissions.* https://ourworldindata.org/co2-emissions#citation.

Ritchie, H and Roser, M. 2020. *CO2 and Greenhouse Gas Emissions.* https://ourworldindata.org/co2-emissions#citation.

Ritchie, Hannah. 2020. "Sector by Sector: Where Do Global Greenhouse Gas Emissions Come From?" *Our World in Data.* September 18. https://ourworldindata.org/ghg-emissions-by-sector.

2018. In *How Europe underdeveloped Africa,* by W Rodney. London; New York: Verso.

Rodney, Walter. 1973. *How Europe Underdeveloped Africa.* London: Bogle-L'Ouverture Publications.

2017. *Rojin's Story: We Lost Everything | A Young Syrian Refugee Films Her Life.* https://www.youtube.com/watch?v=LZtIq6HyHvU.

Roldan, David Dyssegaard Kallick and Cyierra. 2018. *Refugees As Employees: Good Retention, Strong Recruitment.* Research Report, New York: Tent Partnership For Refugees & Fiscal Policy Institute.

Roser, Hannah Ritchie and Max. 2020. "Renewable Energy." *Our World in Data.* Accessed 2021. https://ourworldindata.org/renewable-energy.

Rousseau, J.-J. 2019. *On the Social Contract.* Indianapolis: Hackett Publishing Company, Inc.

2014. *Russell Brand & Nigel Farage clash over immigration.* https://www.youtube.com/watch?v=o7idh5BmsWk.

2007. *Russians given day off to make babies.* https://www.theguardian.com/world/2007/sep/12/russia.matthewweaver.

SACAP . 2019. *How Freud's psychoanalysis theories shaped modern-day psychology.* https://www.sacap.edu.za/blog/applied-psychology/psychoanalysis/.

Salem Media. n.d. "Mayans at War." *History on the Net.* Accessed 2021. https://www.historyonthenet.com/mayans-at-war.

Salter, G. 2021. *Refugee Homelessness: A National Crisis.* https://sonacircle.com/refugee-homelessness-a-national-crisis/ .

Salter, Gabriel. 2021. "5 Reasons Why Refugee Women Are Particularly Vulnerable to Violence." *Sona Circle.* Accessed August 24, 2021. https://sonacircle.com/5-reasons-why-refugee-women-are-particularly-vulnerable-to-violence/.

—. 2021. "5 Reasons Why Refugee Women Are Particularly Vulnerable to Violence." *Sona Circle.* Accessed August 24, 2021. https://sonacircle.com/5-reasons-why-refugee-women-are-particularly-vulnerable-to-violence/.

—. n.d. "5 Reasons Why Refugee Women Are Particularly Vulnerable To Violence." *Sona Circle.* Accessed 2021. https://sonacircle.com/5-reasons-why-refugee-women-are-particularly-vulnerable-to-violence/.

—. 2021. "Refugee Homelessness: A National Crisis." *Sona Circle*. Accessed 2021. https://sonacircle.com/refugee-homelessness-a-national-crisis/.

—. n.d. "Refugee Homelessness: A National Crisis." *Sona Circle*. Accessed 2021. https://sonacircle.com/refugee-homelessness-a-national-crisis.

—. 2021. "Stop The Government's Harsh New Refugee Policy." *Sona Circle*. Accessed 2021. https://sonacircle.com/stop-the-governments-harsh-new-refugee-policy/.

2014. *Salvador Dali - Salvador Dali Museum.* https://thedali.org/about-the-museum/timeline/.

Samphire. 2021. https://www.samphireproject.org.uk/.

Scherrer, Christian P. 2003. *Iraq: Genocide by Sanctions.*

Shaikh, Anwar. 2018. "Capitalism: Competition, Conflict, Crises."

Sharp, Jeremy M. 2021. "Yemen: Civil War and Regional Intervention." *Congressional Research Service.*

Shaxson, Nick. 2020. "It's Time to Make the Richest Pay More Tax." *Tribune*, May 12. https://tribunemag.co.uk/2020/05/corporations-and-the-wealthy-must-pay-more-for-the-coronavirus-crisis.

2021. *Shortfall threatens critical aid for nearly one million displaced Yemenis and refugees.* https://www.unhcr.org/uk/news/briefing/2020/4/5ea7ecd84/unhcr-shortfall-threatens-critical-aid-nearly-million-displaced-yemenis.html.

2012. *Singapore uses rap to try to boost birthrate.* https://www.bbc.co.uk/news/business-20542156.

Sly, Eleanor. 2021. "Denmark to Send Almost 100 Syrian Refugees Homes As Damascus Is 'safe'." *The Independent*, March 3. https://www.independent.co.uk/news/world/europe/denmark-syrian-refugees-residency-permits-b1811466.html.

Smith, Helena. 2017. "Welcome to Prison': Winter Hits in One of Greece's Worst Refugee Camps." *The Guardian*, December 22. https://www.theguardian.com/world/2017/dec/22/this-isnt-europe-life-greece-worst-refugee-camps.

Sona Circle. 2021. *4 Ways to Support Refugees in your Community.* https://sonacircle.com/4-ways-to-support-refugees-in-your-community/.

—. 2021. "An Insight to the Italian Migration and Asylum System." *Sona Circle*. Accessed August 26, 2021. https://sonacircle.com/the-italian-migration-and-asylum-system/.

—. 2021. "Stop The Government's Harsh New Refugee Policy." *Sona Circle*. Accessed August 26, 2021. https://sonacircle.com/stop-the-governments-harsh-new-refugee-policy/.

Soper, Kate. 2020. *Post-Growth Living: For an Alternative Hedonism.* Verso Books.

—. 2020. *Post-Growth Living: For an Alternative Hedonism.* Verso Books.

Statista Research Department. 2021. "Syrian Refugee Arrivals in the United States from FY 2011 to July 31 2021 ." *Statista*. Accessed 2021. https://www.statista.com/statistics/742553/syrian-refugee-arrivals-us/#statisticContainer.

Staunton, B. 2021. *"A worker is a worker": the trade unions organising migrants.*
https://www.etui.org/topics/health-safety-working-
conditions/hesamag/migrant-workers-in-fortress-europe/a-worker-is-a-
worker-the-trade-unions-organising-migrants.

Stead, D.R. n.d. *David Ricardo.* https://eh.net/encyclopedia/david-ricardo/.

Stiglitz, Joseph E. 2013. *The Price of Inequality.* London: Penguin.

stopthemaangamizi.com. 2021. *STOP THE MAANGAMIZI PETITION.*
https://stopthemaangamizi.com/category/stop-the-maangamizi-petition/.

2019. *Story of Resilience, Courage & Determination | Refugee | Gulwali Passarlay |
TEDx style SonaTalks.*
https://www.youtube.com/watch?v=WpZpWC4dmC8.

Stringer, J. 2019. *When European tenants' unions meet.*
https://radicalhousingjournal.org/wp-content/uploads/2019/09/RHJ_Issue-
1.2_15_Update_Stringer_201-205.pdf.

2019. *Success is an Attitude | Wizme CEO | Nour Mouakke | Refugee | TEDx
style SonaTalks.* https://www.youtube.com/watch?v=qmqc00kz1RE.

2020. *Sweden's support for parents with children is comprehensive and effective but
expensive.*
https://www.oecd.org/els/family/swedenssupportforparentswithchildrenisc
omprehensiveandeffectivebutexpensive.htm.

2016. *Syrian refugee Mardini.* https://olympics.com/ioc/news/syrian-refugee-mardini-
rot-swims-for-joy-after-swimming-for-her-life.

Taylor, Diane. 2021. "Asylum Seeker Cannot Remain at Kent Army Barracks, Court
Says." *The Guardian,* February 3. https://www.theguardian.com/uk-
news/2021/feb/03/asylum-seeker-cannot-remain-at-kent-army-barracks-
court-says.

—. 2020. "Shukri Abdi: Burnham Calls for Answers Over Drowning of 12-Year-Old
Refugee." *The Guardian,* June 10. https://www.theguardian.com/uk-
news/2020/jun/10/shukri-abdi-burnham-calls-for-wider-investigation-over-
drowning-of-12-year-old-refugee.

—. 2018. "Worse Than Prison: Life Inside Britain's 10 Deportation Centres." *The
Guardian,* October 11. https://www.theguardian.com/uk-
news/2018/oct/11/life-in-a-uk-immigration-removal-centre-worse-than-
prison-as-criminal-sentence.

Taylor, Rochelle Davis & Abbie. 2013. "What Do You Miss Most? Syrian Refugees
Respond." *Jadaliyya.* December 12. Accessed 2021.
https://www.jadaliyya.com/Details/29933.

The Big Issue. 2021. "How Many People are Homeless in the UK? And What Can
You Do About it?" *The Big Issue,* December 24.
https://www.bigissue.com/news/housing/how-many-people-are-homeless-
in-the-uk-and-what-can-you-do-about-it/.

2005. *The Birth of Google.*
https://www.wired.com/2005/08/battelle/?tw=wn_tophead_4.

The Children's Society. n.d. "About Us." *The Children's Society.* Accessed 2021.
https://www.childrenssociety.org.uk/about-us.

2019. *The Editors of Encyclopædia Britannica* .
    https://www.britannica.com/biography/Victor-Hugo/Exile-1851-70.
2019. *The Green Party Manifesto.* https://campaigns.greenparty.org.uk/manifesto/.
The Guardian. 2021. "Asylum Seeker Cannot Remain at Kent Army Barracks, Court
    Say." 3 f.
The Guardian. 2021. "Rough Sleeper Numbers Down 37% in England During Covid
    Pandemic." February 25.
    https://www.theguardian.com/society/2021/feb/25/rough-sleepers-england-
    covid-pandemic-homelessness.
The Guardian. 2017. "Calais: Hundreds of Migrants Remain a Year After Razing of
    Camp." *The Guardian*, October 23.
    https://www.theguardian.com/world/2017/oct/23/calais-refugees-year-after-
    razing-of-camp.
—. 2020. "Four Iranians Who Died Crossing Channel Were Part of Same Family."
    The Guardian, October 28.
    https://www.theguardian.com/world/2020/oct/28/four-migrants-died-
    channel-part-same-iranian-family.
2021. *The Korean War.* https://www.bbc.co.uk/bitesize/guides/zqqd6yc/revision/2.
2021. *The Korean War.* https://www.bbc.co.uk/bitesize/guides/zqqd6yc/revision/2.
2019. *The Labour Party Manifesto.* https://labour.org.uk/wp-
    content/uploads/2019/11/Real-Change-Labour-Manifesto-2019.pdf.
The School of Life. 2014. *Anna Freud - The Book of Life.*
    https://www.theschooloflife.com/thebookoflife/the-great-psychoanalysts-
    anna-freud/.
The Separated Child Foundation. 2020. "Refugee Facts." *The Separated Child
    Foundation.* Accessed 2021. https://separatedchild.org/our-work/refugee-
    facts/?gclid=CjwKCAjwt8uGBhBAEiwAayu_9YrAvDgdpQYOBQsbOtty
    waY9Y6Tv3pweVLPe5koBya8uJNf8R31kkBoCYuAQAvD_BwE.
2017. *The Story of Montague Burton – the Tailor of Taste.*
    https://buildingourpast.com/2017/01/28/the-story-of-montague-burton-the-
    tailor-of-taste/.
2021. *The Story Of Pnina Tamano-Shata.* https://sonacircle.com/from-desert-plight-
    to-the-blue-and-white-the-story-of-pnina-tamano-shata/.
2007-8. *The Story of Sergey Brin.* https://momentmag.com/the-story-of-sergey-brin/.
2010. *The Story of Sergey Brin.* May 20.
    https://www.patheos.com/resources/additional-resources/2010/05/story-of-
    sergey-brin?p=5.
2007. *The Story of Sergey Brin.* https://momentmag.com/the-story-of-sergey-brin/.
The World Bank. 2021. "10 Years On, Turkey Continues Its Support for an Ever-
    Growing Number of Syrian Refugees." *The World Bank.* June 22.
    Accessed 2021.
    https://www.worldbank.org/en/news/feature/2021/06/22/10-years-on-
    turkey-continues-its-support-for-an-ever-growing-number-of-syrian-
    refugees.

—. 2020. "Lebanon." *The World Bank.* Accessed 2021.
https://thedocs.worldbank.org/en/doc/a3d1489dafa646ee90f5a19abd950c
ab-0280012021/original/9-mpo-sm21-lebanon-lbn-kcm.pdf.

2020. *These 10 countries recieve the most refugees.*
https://www.nrc.no/perspectives/2020/the-10-countries-that-receive-the-
most-refugees/.

2020. *These 10 countries recieve the most refugees.*
https://www.nrc.no/perspectives/2020/the-10-countries-that-receive-the-
most-refugees/.

Thorpe, Bethany Bell & Nick. 2016. "Austria's Migrant Disaster: Why Did 71 Die? ."
BBC News. August 25. Accessed 2021.
https://www.bbc.co.uk/news/world-europe-37163217.

Tih, Felix. 2021. "Over 60,000 Ethiopian Refugeea Flee into Sudan." *AA.* January 07.
Accessed 2021. https://www.aa.com.tr/en/africa/over-60-000-ethiopian-
refugees-flee-into-sudan/2101344#.

Timberlake, Frances. 2021. *The UK's Policy Response to Small Boat Crossings in
The Channel.* Policy Response Report, Refugee Rights Europe.
https://refugee-rights.eu/wp-
content/uploads/2021/02/RRE_BoatCrossingsInTheChannel-
Timeline.pdf.

TNT World. 2021. "Denmark: Non-Whites Shouldn't Exceed 30% of Any
Neighbourhood." *TRT World.* March 18. Accessed August 26, 2021.
https://www.trtworld.com/magazine/denmark-non-whites-shouldn-t-
exceed-30-of-any-neighbourhood-45125.

2021. *Today's Winners and Losers.* https://www.forbes.com/real-time-
billionaires/#5696bcff3d78.

Trading Economics. 2021. "List of Countries by Corporate Tax Rate - Europe."
Trading Economics. Accessed 2021.
https://tradingeconomics.com/country-list/corporate-tax-
rate?continent=europe.

—. 2021. "List of Countries by Personal Income Tax Rate - Europe." *Trading
Economics.* Accessed 2021. https://taxfoundation.org/scandinavian-
countries-taxes-
2021/#:~:text=Top%20personal%20income%20tax%20rates.

2021. *Triumph in Adversity: Ilhan Omar.* https://sonacircle.medium.com/triumph-
in-adversity-ilhan-omar-9a4fe89630d3.

2021. *Triumph In Adversity: Ilhan Omar.* https://sonacircle.medium.com/triumph-
in-adversity-ilhan-omar-9a4fe89630d3.

TRT World. 2021. "Viral Inequality: Billionaires Gained $3.9tn, workers lost $3.7tn
in 2020." *TRT World.* January 28. Accessed August 27, 2021.
https://www.trtworld.com/magazine/viral-inequality-billionaires-gained-3-
9tn-workers-lost-3-7tn-in-2020-43674.

TUC. n.d. *Union Listing.* https://www.tuc.org.uk/unions.

Turner, George. 2019. "Billions Are Being Lost Due to Tax Avoidance - Yet a Weak
HMCR is Trying to Pretend Everything's Fine." *The Independent,* June

21. https://www.independent.co.uk/voices/hmrc-tax-gap-avoidance-billions-pounds-a8968591.html.

2020. *UK arms used in Yemen.* https://caat.org.uk/homepage/stop-arming-saudi-arabia/uk-arms-used-in-the-war-on-yemen/.

UK, The IRC in the. 2021. *Refugees in Limbo - Greece.* https://www.rescue-uk.org/country/greece#:~:text=Refugee%20population%20in%20Greece%3A%20About,and%20100%2C000%20on%20the%20mainland.

Umraw, Amil. 2017. "This Is How Mugabe Broke Zimbabwe's Economy." *Huffington Post.* November 21. Accessed 2021. https://www.huffingtonpost.co.uk/2017/11/21/this-is-how-mugabe-broke-zimbabwes-economy_a_23284108/.

UNCHR. 2021. *Ethiopia emergency.* https://donate.unhcr.org/int/en/ethiopia-emergency#.

2020. *UNHCR.* https://www.unhcr.org/cy/wp-content/uploads/sites/41/2018/05/UNHCR_Brochure_EN.pdf .

UNHCR. 2021. *Donate to Help Refugees Survive This Winter.* Accessed September 2021. https://donate.unhcr.org/int/en/winter-2021.

—. 2021. "Ethiopia's Tigray Refugee Crisis Explained." *UNHCR.* Accessed 2021. https://www.unrefugees.org/news/ethiopia-s-tigray-refugee-crisis-explained/.

—. 2020. "Internally Displaced People." *UNHCR.* Accessed 2021. https://www.unhcr.org/uk/internally-displaced-people.html?query=internally%20displaced.

—. 2019. "Rohingya Emergency." *UNHCR.* July 21. Accessed 2021. https://www.unhcr.org/uk/rohingya-emergency.html.

—. 2019. *South Sudan Refugee Crisis Explained.* May 1. Accessed August 2021. https://www.unrefugees.org/news/south-sudan-refugee-crisis-explained/.

—. 2019. *South Sudan Refugee Crisis Explained.* May 1. Accessed August 2021. https://www.unrefugees.org/news/south-sudan-refugee-crisis-explained/.

—. 2011. "The 1951 Refugee Convention." *UNHCR.* Accessed 2021. https://www.unhcr.org/1951-refugee-convention.html.

UNHCR. 2000. "The Rwandan Genocide and Its Aftermath." In *The State of the World's Refugees 2000: Fifty Years of Humanitarian Action*, by UNHCR, 245-273. Oxford: Oxford University Press. https://www.unhcr.org/3ebf9bb60.html.

UNHCR Turkey. n.d. "Refugees and Asylum Seekers in Turkey." *UNHCR Turkey.* Accessed 2021. https://www.unhcr.org/tr/en/refugees-and-asylum-seekers-in-turkey.

UNHCR. 2020. *UNHCR Global Trends - Forced Displcement in 2020.* December. Accessed August 2021. https://www.unhcr.org/flagship-reports/globaltrends/.

—. 2016. *UNHCR Redefines Role in Greece as EU-Turkey Deal Comes into Effect.* March 22. Accessed September 2021. https://www.unhcr.org/news/briefing/2016/3/56f10d049/unhcr-redefines-role-greece-eu-turkey-deal-comes-effect.html.

—. 2017. "What is a Refugee? ." *UNHCR.* Accessed 2021.
https://www.unhcr.org/uk/what-is-a-refugee.html.

—. 2021. "Yemen Humanitarian Crisis." *UNHCR.* Accessed 2021.
https://www.unrefugees.org/emergencies/yemen/.

2021. *United States Invades Grenada.* November 22. https://www.history.com/this-
day-in-history/united-states-invades-grenada.

2019. *Using Art, Music & Dance to Help Refugees | Jess Miller | Bike Project |
TEDx style SonaTalks.*
https://www.youtube.com/watch?v=Fy6LBp4GI9c&t=76s.

Veen, Erik Bleich and A. Maurits van de. 2018. "Newspaper Coverage of Muslims Is
Negative. And It's Not Because of Terrorism." *Washington Post,*
December 20. https://www.washingtonpost.com/news/monkey-
cage/wp/2018/12/20/newspaper-coverage-of-muslims-is-negative-and-its-
not-because-of-terrorism/.

2019. *Victor Hugo - Exile (1851-1870).* https://www.britannica.com/biography/Victor-
Hugo/Exile-1851-70.

2019. *Vladimir Nabokov, Biography, Books, & Facts. In: Encyclopædia Britannica.*
https://www.britannica.com/biography/Vladimir-Nabokov.

VOA News. 2021. *Hundreds of Schools in Yemen Attacked by Warring Parties.*
https://www.voanews.com/a/middle-east_hundreds-schools-yemen-
attacked-warring-parties/6195718.html.

2009. *Von Bechtolsheim.* https://www.dw.com/en/von-bechtolsheim-i-invested-in-
google-to-solve-my-own-problem/a-4557608.

Warren, Katie. 2020. "Jeff Bezos Is the First Person Ever to Be Worth $200 Billion.
This Is How the Amazon CEO's Immense Wealth Stacks Up To the
Average US Worker, the British Monarchy, and Entire Countries' GDP."
Business Insider. October 21. Accessed August 27, 2021.
https://www.businessinsider.com/how-rich-is-jeff-bezos-mind-blowing-facts-
net-worth-2019-
4?r=US&IR=T#:~:text=Based%20on%20the%20year%2Dover.

Warrick, John Campbell and Olivia. 2014. *Climate Change and Migration Issues in
the Pacific.* Policy Report, United Nations Economic and Social
Commission for Asia and the Pacific.
https://www.ilo.org/dyn/migpractice/docs/261/Pacific.pdf.

2021. *What Is Purchasing Power Parity (PPP)?*
https://www.investopedia.com/updates/purchasing-power-parity-ppp/.

2021. *What is secondary (or sympathy) industrial action and is it unlawful?*
https://my.ucu.org.uk/app/answers/detail/a_id/51/~/what-is-secondary-
%28or-sympathy%29-industrial-action-and-is-it-unlawful%3F.

Wheen, Francis. 2001. *Karl Marx.* London: Fourth Estate.

Whelan, Nathaniel. 2020. "The World's Oldest Civalisations." *World Atlas.* July
2020. Accessed 2021. https://www.worldatlas.com/articles/10-of-the-world-
s-oldest-civilizations.html.

Whitehead, Harriet. 2021. "One in Five Refuge Services Get No Local Authority
Funding. Research Finds." *Civil Society.* February 16. Accessed August

2021. https://www.civilsociety.co.uk/news/one-in-five-refuge-services-not-commissioned-by-a-local-authority.html.

2021. *Who is Mila Kunis?* https://www.xyz.ng/en/people/who-is-mila-kunis-see-net-worth-quote-awards-fact-wiki-1282156.

2016. *Who is Mona Hatoum?* https://www.tate.org.uk/art/artists/mona-hatoum-2365/who-is-mona-hatoum.

2017. *Why the South Korean Government Is Paying Families To Have More Babies.* https://nextshark.com/south-korean-government-paying-families-babies/.

Willner-Reid, Matthew. 2017. "Afghanistan: Displacement Challenges in a Country On the Move." *Migration Policy Institute.* November 16. Accessed August 2021. https://www.migrationpolicy.org/article/afghanistan-displacement-challenges-country-move.

Willsher, Kim. 2020. "Macron Outlines New Law to Prevent 'Islamist Separatism' in France." *The Guardian*, October 2. https://www.theguardian.com/world/2020/oct/02/emmanuel-macron-outlines-law-islamic-separatism-france.

Winter, Joseph. 2019. "Robert Mugabe: From Liberator to Tyrant." *BBC News.* September 6. Accessed 2021. https://www.bbc.co.uk/news/world-africa-27519044.

World Health Organisation. 2008. "Zimbabwe." *World Health Organisation.* December. Accessed 2021. https://www.who.int/hac/crises/zwe/zimbabwe_profile_dec2008.pdf.

World Vision. 2021. "Rohingya Refugee Crisis: Facts, FAQs and How to Help." *World Vision.* Accessed August 2021. https://www.worldvision.org/refugees-news-stories/rohingya-refugees-bangladesh-facts.

2019. *Worldometer.* https://www.worldometers.info/world-population/population-by-country/.

Worley, Will. 2016. "Sun Forced to Admit '1 in 5 British Muslims' Story Was 'significantly misleading'." *The Independent*, Marxh 26. https://www.independent.co.uk/news/media/ipso-sun-british-muslims-story-headline-significantly-misleading-a6953771.html.

2021. *Years of seclusion and exile of Jean-Jacques Rousseau.* https://www.britannica.com/biography/Jean-Jacques-Rousseau/Years-of-seclusion-and-exile.

2020. *Yemen Crisis.* https://www.unicef.org/emergencies/yemen-crisis.

2021. *Yemen Humanitarian Crisis.* https://www.unrefugees.org/emergencies/yemen/.

YoungMinds. n.d. "Foster Carers Toolkit." *YoungMinds.* Accessed 2021. https://www.youngminds.org.uk/media/w05j0nnm/youngminds-welcome-foster-carers-toolkit.pdf.

YouTube. 2019. *My Name Is Not 'Refugee' | Akoi Bazzie Shares Shocking Experience | TEDx style SonaTalks.* https://www.youtube.com/watch?v=8tHlxC0YE1I.

Zambrana, Marga. 2020. "Uyghur Refugees Speak Out Against Genocide and Crimes Against Humanity." *Equal Times.* November 18. Accessed August 2021.

https://www.equaltimes.org/uyghur-refugees-speak-out-against#.YapE4dDP1PY.

www.ingramcontent.com/pod-product-compliance
Lightning Source LLC
Chambersburg PA
CBHW032101040426
42336CB00040B/631